D0573686

Losing Legitimacy

CRIME & SOCIETY

Series Editor John Hagan
University of Toronto

EDITORIAL ADVISORY BOARD

John Braithwaite, Robert J. Bursik, Kathleen Daly, Malcolm M. Feeley, Jack Katz, Martha A. Myers, Robert J. Sampson, and Wesley G. Skogan

Losing Legitimacy: Street Crime and the Decline of Social Institutions in America, Gary LaFree

Casualties of Community Disorder: Women's Careers in Violent Crime, Deborah R. Baskin and Ira B. Sommers

Public Opinion, Crime, and Criminal Justice, Julian V. Roberts and Loretta Stalans

Poverty, Ethnicity, and Violent Crime, James F. Short

Great Pretenders: Pursuits and Careers of Persistent Thieves, Neal Shover

Crime and Public Policy: Putting Theory to Work, edited by Hugh D. Barlow

Control Balance: Toward a General Theory of Deviance, Charles R. Tittle

Rape and Society: Readings on the Problems of Sexual Assault, edited by Patricia Searles and Ronald J. Berger

Losing Legitimacy

Street Crime and the Decline of Social Institutions in America

Gary LaFree

Westview Press
A Member of Perseus Books, L.L.C.

All rights reserved. Printed in the United States of America. No part of this publication may be reproduced or transmitted in any form or by any means, electronic or mechanical, including photocopy, recording, or any information storage and retrieval system, without permission in writing from the publisher.

Copyright © 1998 by Westview Press, A Member of Perseus Books, L.L.C.

Published in 1998 in the United States of America by Westview Press, 5500 Central Avenue, Boulder, Colorado 80301–2877, and in the United Kingdom by Westview Press, 12 Hid's Copse Road, Cumnor Hill, Oxford OX2 9JJ

Library of Congress Cataloging-in-Publication Data
LaFree, Gary D.
  Losing legitimacy : street crime and the decline of social
institutions in America / Gary LaFree
     p.   cm. — (Crime & Society)
  Includes index.
  ISBN 0-8133-3450-0 (hardcover)
  1. Crime—United States.   2. United States—Social
conditions—1980–   3. Crime prevention—United States.   4. Social
control.   I. Title   II. Series: Crime & society (Boulder, Colo.)
HV6789.L34   1998
364.973—dc21   98-13957
                                                                                              CIP

The paper used in this publication meets the requirements of the American National Standard for Permanence of Paper for Printed Library Materials Z39.48–1984.

10   9   8   7   6   5   4   3   2   1

To Vicki, Andy, Kati, and Alix

Contents

List of Tables and Figures   xi
Preface   xiii
Acknowledgments   xv

1 Understanding Postwar Crime Trends   1

Interpreting American Crime Trends, 3
What the Crime Trends Tell Us, 5
Crime and Social Institutions, 6
Institutional Responses to Crime, 9

**2 Riding the Wave:
   Street Crime Trends in Postwar America**   12

Official Crime Data, 13
The Rise of the Self-Report Crime Survey, 14
The National Crime Victimization Survey, 15
Comparing Crime Data Sources, 17
Street Crime Trends in Postwar America, 19
Some Immediate Implications of Postwar Crime Trends, 25
Putting the Trends into Context, 27
Toward an Explanation of Postwar U.S. Crime Trends, 32

**3 Offender Characteristics and Crime Trends
   in Postwar America**   35

Data on Offender Characteristics, 36
Race and Crime in Postwar America, 47
Arrest Trends by Race and Ethnicity, 48
Cross-Sectional Arrest Rates by Race, 49
Postwar Trends in African American and White Crime, 51
Offender Characteristics and Postwar Crime Trends, 52

4 Evaluating Common Explanations of Crime   **56**

Common Theories of Crime, 56
Toward an Explanation of Postwar American Crime Trends, 68

5 Crime and Social Institutions   **70**

Institutional Legitimacy, Change, and Crime, 72
Crime and Social Institutions, 78
The Timing of Postwar Institutional Changes, 88

6 Crime and American Political Institutions   **91**

Political Institutions and Crime, 92
Entering the Age of Distrust, 97
Declining Political Legitimacy in Postwar America, 100
Crime Trends and Civil Rights–Related Actions, 108
Summary and Conclusions, 111

7 Crime and American Economic Institutions   **114**

Crime and Economic Institutions, 115
Economic Legitimacy and Crime in Postwar America, 121
Conclusions: Crime and the Postwar Economy, 133

8 Crime and Changes in the American Family   **135**

Family Organization and Legitimacy, 136
Family Change and Crime Trends, 140
Connections Between the Family and Other Institutions, 149
Conclusions and Implications, 150

**9 Institutional Responses to the Legitimacy Crisis:
  Criminal Justice, Education, and Welfare**   **152**

Postwar Trends in Criminal Justice, Education, and Welfare, 154
The Shifting Impact of New Institutional Responses, 157
Education, Welfare, and Crime, 159
Crime and the Criminal Justice System in Postwar America, 164
Summary and Conclusions, 171

10 Crime and Institutional Legitimacy in Postwar America   **173**

Connections Among the Three Institutions, 176

What Can Be Done to Reduce Crime? 178
Implications for Research, Theory, and Social Policy, 188
Institutions, Crime, and Social Change, 191

Notes 195
Index 233

Tables and Figures

Tables

2.1 Murder Rates (per 100,000 population) for United States
    and 17 Industrialized Nations, 1960 and 1991   29

3.1 UCR Arrest Rates by Race, United States, 1990   50
3.2 Estimated Annual Rates of Robberies per 100,000
    Potential Offenders in Each Population Subgroup,
    NCVS National Data, 1973–1977   53

Figures

2.1 Total Street Crimes, 1946–1996   20
2.2 Murder Rates, 1946–1996   22
2.3 Robbery Rates, 1946–1996   23
2.4 Burglary Rates, 1946–1996   24
2.5 Annual Percentage of Burglary Victims in 17 Nations   30

3.1 Ratio of Adult Female to Adult Male Robbery and
    Burglary Arrests, 1965–1992   41
3.2 Proportion of Young People and Robbery Rates,
    1946–1995   44
3.3 Ratio of Juvenile (Less Than 18) to Adult Arrest Rates
    for Murder, 1965–1992   45
3.4 Robbery Arrest Rates by Race, 1946–1996   51

5.1 Institutional Change, Legitimacy, and Postwar Street
    Crime Rates   87
5.2 Longitudinal Relationships Between Institutional
    Legitimacy and Street Crime in Postwar America   89

6.1 Percent of Americans Who Trust Their Government,
    1958–1996   102
6.2 Percent of Americans Who Believe Government Officials
    Are Crooked, 1958–1996   103

6.3   Total Civil Cases Filed in U.S. District Courts and
      Robbery Rates, 1946–1995   107
6.4   Collective Action Events and Robbery Rates, 1955–1991   109

7.1   Trends in Median Income of Males and Robbery Rates,
      1947–1995 (in 1995 Dollars)   123
7.2   Trends in Family Income Inequality and Robbery Rates,
      1957–1990 (in 1990 Dollars)   124
7.3   Annual Percentage Increase in Inflation and Robbery Rates,
      1948–1995   125
7.4   Trends in Median Income of African American and
      White Males, 1948–1995 (in 1995 Dollars)   129
7.5   Race and Family Income Inequality, 1957–1990
      (in 1990 Dollars)   130

8.1   Divorce and Robbery Rates, 1946–1994   144
8.2   Proportion of Female-Headed Households by Race,
      1957–1995   148

9.1   School Attendance of Three- and Four-Year-Olds and
      Robbery Rates, 1965–1993   160
9.2   Median Years of Schooling for African American Males
      and White Males, 1957–1990   161
9.3   Government Spending on Welfare and Robbery Rates,
      1948–1992 (in 1995 Dollars)   163
9.4   Imprisonment and Robbery Rates, 1946–1994   166

Preface

This book offers an explanation for the dramatic changes in street crime rates that have occurred in America since World War II. Although I didn't know it at the time, the book began in the summer of 1982 when I happened to run across a table showing trends in U.S. murder rates for the postwar years. The table fascinated me. It resembled an alpine range above a broad plain with a rapidly rising slope ending in two craggy peaks and then a series of high serrations. The period immediately following World War II was represented by the broad plain; the 1960s were shown by the rapid and steep ascent; and the late 1970s corresponded to the high, jagged peaks.

In fact, I later found out that in the fifty years following World War II street crime rates in America increased about eightfold. These increases were historically patterned; were often quite rapid; and were disproportionately driven by young, African American men. Much of the crime explosion took place in a space of just ten years beginning in the early 1960s. I gradually became convinced that common explanations of crime based on biological impulses, psychological drives, or slow-moving social developments could not account for the speed or the timing of these changes or their disproportionate impact on racial minorities.

To try to understand what had produced these crime trends, I began to collect information on a wide variety of potential explanations. This proved to be challenging. Although efforts to develop data sets on changes over time are beginning to increase in number, criminology is still overwhelmingly dominated by research that examines relationships at just one time point. Nevertheless, as data began to accumulate and analyses of these data continued, I became increasingly convinced that changing social institutions provided the most plausible explanation for the crime trends observed in postwar America.

Institutions are arguably the most important of all human creations. They are the major mechanisms for regulating human behavior, they are central to our moral values, and they are capable of rapid change. The research presented in this book shows that postwar crime rates were linked especially to changes in political, economic, and family institutions. In particular, crime increased along with growing political distrust, economic inequality, and family disintegration. These changes were especially pronounced for African Americans. American society responded to the crisis in traditional institutions by investing more in other social institutions, especially criminal justice, education, and welfare. As traditional institutions stabilized in the 1990s and as spending on new institutions continued to increase, crime rates finally began to decline in the last few years of the twentieth century. The trends in crime and institutional legitimacy reviewed in this book tell a story of transformation as the comparative stability of the 1940s and 1950s gave way to the tumultuous changes of the 1960s and 1970s and, finally, to the uneasy balance of the 1980s and 1990s.

Gary LaFree

Acknowledgments

It seems to take a village not only to raise a child but also to write a book. The final content of this book owes a great deal to the contributions of Kriss Drass, who has been my collaborator on several related research articles. In particular, Kriss was responsible for sophisticated quantitative analysis that although not directly included in this book was nevertheless critical in developing many of the conclusions on which the book is based.

I have also been fortunate to have a great many colleagues with sufficient interest and stamina to provide helpful advice and criticisms. Their number begins with a group of graduate student colleagues, especially Michelle Hussong, Pat O'Day, Chris Rack, and Aki Takeuchi, who helped in various stages of data collection and stimulated my thinking about many of the topics included. Chris Birkbeck, Malcolm Feeley, Bob Fiala, Bob O'Brien, Lynn Pickard, Larry Ross, Bert Useem, and Richard Wood read earlier drafts and provided helpful comments. I want to thank John Hagan, the series editor, not only for his comments but also for his unflagging support. Likewise, Marcus Boggs, Adina Popescu, and Lisa Wigutoff at Westview have been consistently supportive and helpful.

I spent a good deal of time working out the details of the arguments made here in shorter works before feeling comfortable enough to tackle a book-length project. Part of Chapter 3 is a revision of an article that first appeared in *Ethnicity, Race, and Crime*, edited by Darnell Hawkins and published by the State University of New York Press (1995); part of Chapter 6 is a revision of an article I wrote with Kriss Drass that originally appeared in *Social Forces* (volume 75, 1997); and parts of Chapters 7 and 9 are revisions of an article I wrote with Kriss Drass that originally appeared in the *American Sociological Review* (volume 61, 1996). These revisions are all included here with the permission of the press and journals.

Institutional support along the way has also been a big help. In particular, part of the research reported in the book was supported by a grant from the Harry Frank Guggenheim Foundation. I also received a paid semester from the University of New Mexico to help finish the project. Jeff Mix, Chris Pawley, and Brock Perkins at the university's Institute for Social Research and Rose Muller and Karen Majors from the Department of Sociology helped greatly with library sources, graphics, and the preparation of the manuscript.

I of course take full responsibility for interpretations and any technical errors. Nonetheless, without the help of these people and institutions, the mistakes would have been far more numerous.

G. L.

one

Understanding Postwar Crime Trends

History is as light as individual human life, unbearably light, as dust swirling in the air, as whatever will no longer exist tomorrow.
—**Milan Kundera,** *The Unbearable Lightness of Being,* **1984**[1]

[History:] that sinister mulch of facts our little lives grow out of before joining the mulch themselves, the fragile brown rotting layers of previous deaths, layers that if deep enough and squeezed hard enough make coal as in Pennsylvania.
—**John Updike,** *Rabbit at Rest,* **1990**[2]

From the end of World War II until the early 1990s, the number of crimes committed in the streets of America skyrocketed. Murder rates doubled; rape rates quadrupled; robbery and burglary rates quintupled. By the early 1990s, nearly 25,000 Americans were being murdered each year. In just two years, more Americans were murdered than were killed in the Vietnam War; in twelve years more were murdered than died during World War II. In 1994, an estimated 620,000 Americans were robbed, 102,000 were raped, and 1.1 million were assaulted.[3] Taken together, there was an eightfold increase in rates of murder, robbery, rape, aggravated assault, burglary, and theft reported to police between the end of World War II and the early 1990s.

It is difficult to gauge how important these trends have been for the social and political landscape of postwar America. Many Americans either remember or have heard stories about a time when people in their communities felt safe leaving the front doors of their homes unlocked at night or leaving keys in the ignitions of their cars while they ran off to do errands. Although some of these accounts are no doubt exaggerated, it is clear that increases in street crime since World War II have had major effects on virtually every aspect of daily life in America. As a nation, Amer-

1

icans now spend billions of dollars each year for protection against street crime: police, judges, lawyers, correctional officers, security systems, and private guards. Americans buy special antitheft devices for their cars; install elaborate alarm systems in their homes; and, more than people in any other developed nation, rely on firearms for protection against would-be criminals. Moreover, the price Americans pay for almost anything they buy is substantially increased by crime-related security and insurance costs.

Crime has also played an increasingly important role in shaping public policy and national politics in the postwar period. Because the United States began as a loose federation of local governments, criminal justice issues were historically viewed as state and local issues. In particular, there was long-standing opposition to anything resembling a national police force. The situation is quite different today. Law and order have become major issues in national politics. Every presidential election campaign since the early 1960s has prominently featured crime and law-and-order issues. The federal government now supports huge national bureaucracies the main official task of which is to help control crime. Crime prevention provided a major justification for the massive social programs of the 1960s. Fear of crime has been instrumental in the huge national increase in prison population beginning in the late 1970s. Concern about crime has now become an important political issue at all levels of government. And because of the influence of the United States on the rest of the world, understanding the dynamics of crime in the United States may also have important implications for other nations.

But beyond the monetary importance of crime, its impact on social policy in the United States, and its implications for other nations, there are a host of less tangible effects of crime that are more difficult to gauge but perhaps also more disturbing. Some Americans have become virtual prisoners in their own neighborhoods.[4] A great many others routinely avoid certain neighborhoods at night or change the direction they drive or walk home because of their fear of crime. Fear of crime has become an important issue for people in choosing a place to live and in selecting schools for their children. As confidence in the ability of police to offer adequate protection from crime has declined, an increasing number of people and businesses have begun to rely more on their own privately purchased security systems and guards. Walled perimeters, security gates, and armed patrols have become important selling points for housing subdivisions and apartment complexes throughout the nation.

In fact, it is probably impossible to put a value on the many ways in which street crime has affected American society. It is difficult to estimate the social costs of urban environments that, at their worst, have become so violent that many children grow up personally knowing another child who has been murdered. It is equally difficult to estimate the social costs to citizens of living in neighborhoods where they are afraid to walk, even in broad daylight, or the costs to society of diverting public resources away from new schools, parks, and community centers in favor of prisons, police substations, and detention facilities.

The purpose of this book is to describe and explain street crime trends in America following World War II; especially the crime "wave" of the 1960s and 1970s.[5] Although the term *street crime* is imprecise, it has generally come to include the familiar crimes of murder, robbery, rape, aggravated assault, burglary, and theft. The sociologist Daniel Glaser calls these crimes "predatory" because they all involve offenders who "prey" on other persons or their property.[6] He contrasts these offenses with "nonpredatory" crimes such as prostitution and gambling. I am especially interested in predatory crimes here because they evoke the greatest popular fear and concern. They also draw the most universal condemnation from society. Probably as a consequence of these characteristics, we also have more complete information on predatory crimes than on any other crime types.

Interpreting American Crime Trends

The approach I follow in this book is unique in three ways. First, I concentrate almost entirely on national rather than state, city, or individual-level crime data. These other data sources can tell us a great deal about how the characteristics of cities or states are related to crime rates or about the likelihood that individuals with particular characteristics will be involved in crime. Here, however, I am interested in developing a much broader understanding of crime trends during the second half of the twentieth century. My focus throughout is on how changes in the United States as a whole have been related to crime rates during the postwar years.

Second, much of the research on crime to date has been based on cross-sectional "snapshots," comparing individuals or geographical units (e.g., cities, counties, states) at one point in time. These snapshots provide useful comparative information on why certain types of individuals are more likely to commit crime or why certain areas or regions are characterized by high or low crime rates. But they provide few insights into how changes over time have been related to crime trends. As a result of this cross-sectional emphasis, much thinking about crime is trapped in what the historian Eric Hobsbawm has called "the permanent present."[7] For example, it has become common for researchers and policymakers these days to examine the current high crime rates in the United States and conclude that the United States has always been a violent or "criminogenic" culture.[8] But as we shall see, the allegedly criminogenic U.S. culture had relatively low crime rates in the 1940s and 1950s.[9]

Moreover, U.S. crime rates have undergone major changes in the past century that are lost in cross-sectional analysis. Crime rates did not rise uniformly in the postwar period: Some years were characterized by stable or declining rates whereas others witnessed rapid growth. By examining how crime rates have changed over time and by looking at the correlates of these changes, I hope to provide insights into how crime trends in postwar America are related to major social, economic, and political developments.

Finally, although certainly understandable, our unwillingness to deal directly with connections between race and crime in the postwar United States has probably hampered our ability to accurately describe crime problems and deal effectively with them. Like roadways circling a large city, discussions of crime and justice in the United States seem inevitably to lead to issues of race. This connection is not unprecedented. It resembles earlier connections between ethnicity and crime for other groups of Americans. Thus, research shows that in the nineteenth century Irish and German immigrants were disproportionately involved in street crimes in New York City[10] and during the first two decades of the twentieth century Italian immigrants were far more likely than other groups to be imprisoned for murders in Philadelphia.[11]

Although African Americans in the mid-1990s constituted only 12 percent of the U.S. population,[12] they accounted for 59 percent of all robbery arrests, 54 percent of all murder arrests, and 42 percent of all rape arrests.[13] This means that African American arrest rates for robbery were more than ten times higher than rates for all other groups combined. Late-twentieth-century estimates are that more than half of all African American men in the nation's largest cities will be arrested at least once during their lifetime for a serious crime.[14]

These same grim statistics are reproduced in the nation's prisons, jails, probation departments, and county morgues. In the mid-1990s, nearly 25 percent of all black men age 20 to 29 were in prison or jail or on probation or parole in the United States.[15] In fact, the United States in the 1990s had substantially more black men in the correctional system (609,690) than in colleges and universities (436,000).[16] For young black men in urban areas, murder has become the leading cause of death.[17] If these trends continue into the twenty-first century, one out of every twenty-one black men will be a murder victim.[18]

Because of the negative implications of these statistics, there has been a general unwillingness in the postwar United States to directly confront connections between race and crime. In fact, the sociologist William Julius Wilson[19] claims that many researchers have avoided race-related research on crime because of the sharp criticisms aimed at earlier scholars who examined these issues.[20] Nevertheless, it seems that any credible explanation of postwar crime trends is going to have to account for the disproportionate number of young, African American men enmeshed in the criminal justice system.

What the Crime Trends Tell Us

My review of postwar street crime trends in America permits three main conclusions. First, changes in crime rates were sometimes extremely rapid—especially from the early 1960s to the late 1970s. Second, the crimes reviewed here exhibited fairly consistent historical patterns. In general, we can identify three main postwar crime periods: an early period (1946–1960) with stable, low crime rates; a middle period (1961–1973) with rapidly accelerating crime rates; and a late period (after 1973) with stable, high crime rates. Finally, the data consistently show that African Americans, and in particular young, male African Americans, were disproportionately involved in producing the crime patterns observed. These three conclusions have important implications for understanding crime in postwar America.

The simple rapidity of crime change has far-reaching significance. In some ways, a crime wave is a more puzzling phenomenon than more highly organized social events such as the rise of a political party or a social movement. Crime waves occur through the actions of diverse individuals, largely working alone or in small groups, with little communication, with no organization and no special resources, and lacking a commonly shared ideology or worldview. Nevertheless, these diverse individuals, most often acting independently, have the ability to greatly increase criminal behavior, such as robberies, that is very similar in form from one region to another.

The rapidity of change in postwar crime rates clearly favors some explanations of crime and makes other explanations less convincing. Many popular explanations of criminal behavior are based on biological, psychological, or social characteristics that change only slowly. But if crime is produced by deep-seated biological drives, slowly evolving psychological characteristics, or widely held cultural values passed between generations, it is difficult to explain a doubling or tripling of crime rates in a short time. The rapidity of postwar crime change suggests that under the right circumstances the variables that regulate crime must be capable of equally rapid transformation. A major focus of this book is on identifying the changes in postwar America that were rapid enough to account for the explosive growth of crime during the middle postwar years.

The specific timing of postwar crime trends provides further insights. For example, if crime rates surged in the early 1960s, then variables explaining crime should have undergone commensurate changes at about the same time. Similarly, if crime rates were relatively low and steady during the 1950s, then variables explaining crime should exhibit similar temporal characteristics. In fact, the timing of the crime wave of the 1960s and 1970s wreaked havoc on several popular explanations of crime. Here was an explosion in crime that seemed to be occurring at a time when many economic variables looked favorable; educational opportunities were expanding as never before; and unprecedented gains were being made in extending equal rights to disadvantaged groups, especially members of racial minority groups.

Finally, the crime-related behavior of African Americans during the postwar period poses serious problems for both liberal and conservative views of crime. Liberals have a difficult time explaining why African American crime rates were lowest during the overtly discriminatory 1940s and 1950s and highest during the presumably less discriminatory 1970s and 1980s. Conservatives have problems explaining why crime rates for African Americans in the 1980s and 1990s remain at extremely high levels in the face of what is probably the most extensive regimen of punishment ever experienced by a particular societal subgroup in a modern democratic nation.

Based on what I now know about postwar street crime trends and the research of those who have studied these issues before me, I conclude that the most plausible explanation for the crime patterns observed in the postwar United States is the strength of American social institutions. I present this argument in detail later but provide a brief overview here by way of introduction.

Crime and Social Institutions

The main thesis of this book is that historical and social changes in America created a crisis in institutional legitimacy that produced the postwar crime wave. At the most basic level, institutions are the patterned, mutually shared ways that people develop for living together.[21] They include the rules, laws, norms, values, roles, and organizations that define and regulate human conduct. As used here, *legitimacy* refers to the ease or difficulty with which institutions are able to get societal members to follow these rules, laws, and norms.[22]

The sociologist Peter Berger points out that institutions channel human behavior into preestablished "grooves."[23] If we look at institutions in this way, we see that societies with tremendous conformity have deep and narrow grooves whereas less conformist societies have broader and wider grooves. I argue in this book that the grooves that contained human conduct in the postwar United States started to become broader and wider in the early 1960s. This process continued throughout the 1960s and most of the 1970s. It stabilized and even reversed a bit in the 1990s.

Given the potential threat that crime poses for societies, it would be logical to suppose that a great many social institutions play some role in controlling it. Some institutions are clearly more central for crime control than others, however. The three institutions that have probably been most often linked to crime and its control by researchers and policymakers are political, economic, and familial.

Political institutions include the entire governmental apparatus: courts, legislative bodies, the military, and the administrative agencies that implement political decisions. Because criminal laws are formulated by governments, political institutions are especially important for crime control. Political institutions can reduce crime by providing fair and just transactions that motivate individuals to follow social rules themselves and also help make sure that others adhere to these rules.

Economic institutions provide for basic physical and social needs and should satisfy at least rudimentary levels of material comfort. They help hold crime in check by reducing the motivation of individuals to offend and by making it easier for families, communities, and legal systems to keep members from committing crime and to apprehend, punish, and correct them if they nevertheless do offend. Economic institutions may increase crime by making it relatively more attractive than lawful behavior and by undermining the effectiveness of both formal and informal social control mechanisms in stopping crime.

Family institutions reduce crime by first socializing their members to be law abiding and then ensuring their members' conformity to social rules through constant feedback and monitoring. Thus, families are critical in controlling crime as agents both of socialization and of social control. Families are also important in directly protecting their members from the criminal behavior of others.

I assume that, at a minimum, a plausible explanation of postwar street crime trends in America must explain the known characteristics of these trends. If institutions are responsible for postwar crime trends, then they must have changed rapidly during the postwar period; these changes had to be patterned in ways that parallel what we know about crime trends; and institutional changes should have affected different racial, gender, and age subgroups (especially African Americans) in ways that resemble group-level crime rates.

Changing Social Institutions in Postwar America

Again, although I spend a good share of this book describing the specific relationships between major social institutions and crime patterns during the postwar period, by way of introduction I briefly present the general contours of changes in political, economic, and family institutions. For most people, the idea that social institutions are capable of rapid change is not commonsensical and may even be counterintuitive. Indeed, institutions generally function most efficiently when they successfully convince societal members of their solidity, permanence, and unchanging nature.[24] But even a brief consideration of trends in major American institutions during the past half century provides impressive evidence of just how fast these institutions have in fact changed.

Institutions and Historical Crime Patterns

It seems unassailable that most Americans entered the postwar period with historically high levels of trust in their political institutions. When judged from the somewhat jaundiced perspective of the 1990s, the amount of faith Americans had in their government and its laws in the 1940s now seems positively naive. If I were to pick one specific historical event that more than any other contributed to growing distrust during the postwar period, it would be racial discrimination against African Americans and the collective political action that it eventually generated. I argue later that public trust in government began to seriously erode in the 1960s and 1970s, and I consider the possibility that rising levels of distrust were directly related to the rapid increases in street crime rates that followed.

At the end of World War II, the United States was the undisputed leader of the global economy. Although the war obviously took its toll in lives lost and resources depleted, it left the United States in a much more favorable economic position than the rest of the industrialized world. One of the real challenges faced by researchers who have examined connections between economic indicators and crime during the postwar years is that in many respects the economy seemed quite strong during the 1960s and early 1970s. But economic measures come in many varieties with their own unique characteristics. Although absolute economic measures such as poverty and unemployment were relatively favorable in the United States during the middle postwar years, relative measures such as inequality and inflation were much less auspicious. In particular, the middle postwar years witnessed substantial increases in income inequality and the highest rates of inflation of the entire postwar period.

By just about any measure, the American family has undergone extraordinary changes in the past half century. The male-dominated nuclear family, which was both the norm and the goal of most Americans following World War II, was criticized with increasing urgency during the 1960s and 1970s. Changing attitudes toward the traditional form of the family were no doubt fueled in part by enormous economic changes. As the national, and increasingly international, economy evolved during the postwar years, the family farm all but disappeared, women joined the paid labor force in record numbers, and children and ever larger numbers of young adults greatly increased the amount of time they spent in schools. As a result of growing dissatisfaction with the traditional form of the family and the changes in the family being wrought by the economy, the proportion of Americans living in single-parent households or "blended" households as well as the proportion living entirely outside of households soared. I argue later that these changes in family institutions contributed to rising crime rates. Conversely, as changes in the family slowed in the late postwar period and as alternative forms of the family became more routine, some evidence of stability could be seen by the end of the twentieth century.

Institutions and the Characteristics of Offenders

A plausible explanation of postwar crime must also account for high African American crime rates. Indeed, compared to general trends in crime, changes in African American crime rates have been especially dramatic during the postwar years. An emphasis on connections between the legitimacy of social institutions and crime trends for African Americans has immediate appeal. Given African American history, it certainly seems reasonable to conclude that, compared to other Americans, African Americans are likely to have had weaker ties to social institutions throughout the postwar period. In particular, it seems plausible to argue that, compared to others, African Americans experienced greater distrust in political institutions, greater economic-related stress, and greater changes in the structure and functioning of families during the postwar years.

Institutional Responses to Crime

It is important to point out here that Americans did not sit passively by while institutional legitimacy declined and crime rates escalated during the postwar years. Institutions are human creations, and societies develop new ones and refine old ones to meet their evolving needs.[25] The postwar period witnessed the tremendous growth and expansion in America of three institutions with direct relevance for crime control: criminal justice, education, and welfare.

These three institutions obviously differ in the directness of their connections to crime. Criminal justice institutions are the most directly linked to crime. By contrast, increasing postwar support for education and welfare was justified for many reasons in addition to, or instead of, crime control. Still, examination of both the timing of spending on education and welfare and the public policy statements made about each makes it clear that one of the main reasons these institutions received increasing support during the postwar period, especially during and after the high crime increase decades of the 1960s and 1970s, was because they were also expected to reduce crime rates. This connection is clear in the influential report, first published in 1967, of President Lyndon Johnson's Commission on Law Enforcement and the Administration of Justice: "Warring on poverty, inadequate housing and unemployment, is warring on crime. A civil rights law is a law against crime. Money for schools is money against crime. Medical, psychiatric, and family counseling services are services against crime. More broadly and most importantly, every effort to improve life in America's 'inner cities' is an effort against crime."[26]

American efforts to rebuild legitimacy and control crime by strengthening criminal justice, education, and welfare institutions were partly successful. In fact, the combined effects of declining political trust and increasing economic stress and family disintegration might well have had far more devastating effects on crime rates if the United States had not also increased support for criminal justice, education, and welfare institutions. As the strength of traditional social institutions stabilized and spending on institutions such as criminal justice and education increased, crime rates in America did eventually level off and even began to decline a bit during the twilight of the twentieth century.

• • •

These preliminary observations about institutions and postwar American crime trends should raise more questions than they answer. Before I pursue the questions raised, however, it will be useful to consider what actually happened to street crime rates. I begin Chapter 2 by exploring the major options for studying crime trends in contemporary America and then go on to consider what the best available information tells us about these trends. To help interpret the crime rates, I compare them to earlier periods of U.S. history and to crime rates for other countries. Chapter 2 sets the stage for the rest of the book by defining what a viable explanation of postwar American crime trends must explain. I then turn in Chapter 3 to differences in crime rates by gender, age, ethnicity, and race. Again, after presenting the best available data, I consider what additional insights can be gained by looking at differences in crime rates for different demographic groups. My assumption here is that by examining trends for specific subgroups we may be able to learn more about the reasons why crime rates in the postwar period behaved as they did.

Armed with a clearer picture of how crime rates developed in the postwar period, in Chapter 4 I consider the most common explanations for crime and how they compare to the crime trends themselves. This chapter explores earlier theories of crime for the benefit of readers interested in such details. In Chapter 5, I introduce the book's main argument: that overlapping declines in the legitimacy of political, economic, and familial institutions were largely responsible for the postwar crime boom. Chapter 5 also explains how institutions work and the ways in which they affect crime rates for those readers interested in the more abstract qualities of institutions.

The following chapters show how postwar American crime trends were actually related to changes in political, economic, and family institutions: Chapter 6 examines the connections between crime trends and American political institutions, focusing especially on growing levels of distrust in government and the impact of the civil rights movement. In Chapter 7, I examine how postwar crime trends are related to changes in economic stress, especially inequality and inflation. In Chapter 8, I take up the issue of how postwar crime trends are related to changes in the structure of the American family.

Having described developments in these three traditional institutions, in Chapter 9 I consider the impact of three institutions that gained much greater prominence during the postwar period: criminal justice, education, and welfare. In the final chapter, I review the conclusions afforded by the book, consider the implications of the American crime wave for other nations, and evaluate the prospects for social policies that might reduce crime rates in the future.

two

Riding the Wave
Street Crime Trends in Postwar America

Our observations can only refer to a certain number of known and tried offenses out of the unknown sum total of crimes committed.

—**Lambert Quetelet,** *A Treatise on Man and the Development of His Faculties,* **1835**[1]

The government are very keen on amassing statistics. They collect them, raise them to the nth power, take the cube root, and prepare wonderful diagrams. But you must never forget that every one of these figures comes in the first instance from the village watchman who just puts down what he damn well pleases.

—**Sir Josiah Stamp,** *Some Economic Factors in Modern Life,* **1929**[2]

Crimes are ultimately defined as such only after a complex sorting process involving some combination of suspects, victims, witnesses, and legal agents. Adding to the complexity is the fact that suspects generally have a vested interest in not being defined as criminals, or at least as serious criminals, whereas others, both in the legal system and outside of it, also have varying stakes in how incidents are defined. Small wonder that counting crimes is a difficult business.

Still, the nature of the street crimes that are the subject matter of this book impose some parameters on the number of ways they can be counted. These crimes are similar in that they each consist of an offender; a victim; and, at least for the crimes that are reported or discovered, police and other legal agents. Generally, these parameters also define the crime data that may be collected: "official" data collected by legal agents, "self-report" data collected from offenders, and "victimization" data collected from crime victims. Because the strengths and weakness of these

12

data sources are important for interpreting postwar street crime trends, I briefly consider them in the next three sections.

Official Crime Data

In large part because the federal system of the United States gives individual states a good deal of control over their internal affairs, including their legal systems, the development of national crime statistics in the United States has lagged behind their development in other industrialized Western nations. The movement that eventually resulted in the first nationwide crime data system in the United States did not begin until 1927. In that year, the International Association of Chiefs of Police formed a committee on uniform crime records and gave it the task of developing a system of standardized police statistics. After studying state criminal codes and evaluating police record-keeping practices, the committee completed a data collection plan, and in 1930 the Federal Bureau of Investigation (FBI) was given the task of collecting the first set of Uniform Crime Reports (UCR) data.

Since its inception, the basic structure of the UCR data collection system has remained remarkably consistent: Crime definitions, classifications, and modes of data collection are virtually the same today as they were in 1930.[3] The most reliable UCR data have been collected on the seven crimes that make up the original UCR crime index: murder, rape, robbery, aggravated assault, burglary, theft, and motor vehicle theft.[4]

The UCR is unique in its reliance on the voluntary cooperation of thousands of individual police departments across the country to provide crime information. In general, UCR coverage has been most complete for major metropolitan areas, in which about 98 percent of the population is now represented, and least complete for rural areas, in which about 90 percent of the population is now included.[5]

The UCR has consistently collected two main types of crime information: total crimes "known to police" and total arrests. Crimes known to police include all crimes reported to police, observed or discovered by police, or reported from witnesses or complainants. Crimes are classified as cleared by arrest, if a suspect is arrested, charged, and turned over to the courts for prosecution, or by "exceptional means." The latter term applies to situations in which the police believe that they have solved the case but have not made an arrest. Most often, cases are cleared by exceptional means when the police feel that further processing is impractical: For example, a suspect has already been arrested in another jurisdiction, a key witness refuses to press charges, or a suspect has fled the country.

The most common criticism of the UCR is that its emphasis on street crime focuses attention on offenses that are more common among minorities and the poor and less common among nonminorities and the wealthy. The incompleteness of the UCR should not be seen as a catastrophic deficiency, however. Although the seven index crimes for which the UCR includes the most complete data are only a subset of all crimes, these crimes have been of substantial policy interest in the United States throughout the postwar period. Few would argue that we should reject data on murder, for example, just because we do not have equally valid data on embezzlement.

The way in which the UCR data are collected raises additional issues, however. A strategy that takes information collected by the police and uses it to explore crime policies makes it pretty easy to tell "whose side we are on." By relying on official police data, criminologists interested in studying why people commit crime are starting with definitions of crime supplied by official agencies. From the onset of UCR data collection efforts, many observers were concerned that such a strategy ignored the possibility that these data were themselves the product of biased legal and political decisionmaking. In fact, these criticisms began to grow more urgent in the late 1950s as a broader set of social developments started to take shape. These social developments are in turn related to the rise and credibility of a second major crime data collection strategy, the self-report survey.

The Rise of the Self-Report Crime Survey

From the inception of the UCR, its crime data showed that minorities and the poor committed a disproportionate amount of street crime. Most crime theories in the early postwar period offered explanations for these differences. But as the postwar period unfolded, and especially as concern with civil rights and racial discrimination grew in the 1960s, an increasing number of researchers began to suspect that official crime data were hopelessly biased. As an alternative to official sources of crime data such as the UCR, many researchers advocated instead the use of self-report surveys. Self-report surveys had been used in the United States since the 1940s,[6] but it was the influential work of the sociologists James Short and F. Ivan Nye in the late 1950s that established self-report methods as a viable alternative to official data for the study of crime.[7]

Short and Nye administered questionnaires to schoolchildren and to institutionalized children convicted of various offenses. They found that both groups of juveniles surveyed could recall and generally would accurately report their delinquent acts to researchers. Some have compared the impact of the Short and Nye research to the controversial studies of sexual behavior by Alfred Kinsey a generation earlier: Both "revolutionized ideas about the feasibility of using survey procedures with a hitherto taboo topic."[8]

Following Short and Nye, studies based on self-report crime data quickly multiplied.[9] Less than ten years after the original publication of Short and Nye's research, a conference on self-report methods was organized and included presentations on sixteen large-scale self-report studies.[10] Self-report surveys dominated the study of juvenile delinquency in the United States throughout the 1960s and early 1970s.

Although Short and Nye's study was important because they demonstrated the feasibility of self-reported crime surveys, it was probably not feasibility alone that accounted for the sudden popularity of self-report surveys in the 1960s. Mainstream criminology theories based on UCR data generally showed that street crime was concentrated among young, urban, lower-class males—especially African Americans. As labeling and conflict perspectives gained momentum in the 1960s, many criminologists began to question the assumption that street crime was concentrated among minorities and the poor. Instead, labeling and conflict theorists argued that the explanation why more African American than white (and more poor than rich) offenders were arrested and processed by the legal system was because of selective law enforcement or outright discrimination.

Early results from self-report crime surveys fit these assumptions like a hand in a glove. For example, the criminologist Travis Hirschi, in a self-report survey of California high school students in the 1960s, found that juvenile delinquency rates for African American students were only about 10 percent higher than rates for white students.[11] Findings such as these implied that most differences between African Americans and others in UCR statistics were the result not of differences in actual behavior but rather of citizen reporting and police arrest decisions.

The National Crime Victimization Survey

A third option for collecting data on crime is the victimization survey. Victimization surveys ask samples of the general public whether they or other members of their households have been crime victims in some preceding time period. The researchers Preben Wolf and Ragnar Hauge report on a victimization survey carried out in Århus, Denmark, in 1730,[12] and the criminologist Richard Sparks relates an anecdote about a nineteenth-century police constable in England who reputedly went door to door asking villagers about crimes that had been committed against them.[13] The first systematic, large-scale national victimization survey was undertaken in the United States in the mid-1960s.

The motivation for this victim survey is clear. The United States was in the early stages of what was widely (and correctly) perceived as a crime explosion, and lacking the benefit of hindsight, no one really knew how steeply crime was going to rise before leveling off. The same distrust of official statistics that encouraged researchers to develop self-report crime surveys worked in favor of victimization surveys. In fact, victim surveys were even more appealing because of the commonsense assumption that victims would be more truthful than offenders.

In 1967, President Lyndon Johnson's Commission on Law Enforcement and the Administration of Justice approved three experimental victimization surveys. The first surveyed 511 adults living in three Washington, D.C. police districts and, shortly afterward, 293 adults in a fourth district.[14] The second surveyed 595 adults residing in two precincts in Boston and two in Chicago and 768 businesses and organizations in those same precincts.[15] The third and most extensive was based on a national sample of 9,644 households.[16] In the ten years following, several dozen similar surveys were carried out in other cities and communities (including Phoenix; Minneapolis; Boston; Toledo; Dallas; Brooklyn; and Detroit) as well as other countries (including Australia, Finland, Denmark, Sweden, and Norway).[17]

Ironically, the presidential commission that had encouraged all this activity by sponsoring the pilot victimization surveys ended up relying mostly on UCR data in its final report.[18] Nevertheless, the commissioners were favorably impressed with the potential of victimization surveys. As with self-report studies, preliminary victimization survey data showed that there was far more crime occurring in America than was indicated by official data. In fact, the pilot surveys suggested that only about one-quarter of all rapes, one-third of all burglaries, and one-half of all aggravated assaults and larcenies were being recorded in official police statistics.[19] Responding to this situation, the commission recommended more intensive efforts to gather victimization data on a regular basis.[20]

To collect these data, the commission advocated the creation of the National Criminal Justice Statistics Center. This center, later renamed the National Criminal Justice Information and Statistics Service, was created and in 1969 began to meet with representatives of the U.S. Bureau of the Census to plan a national victimization survey. The first full-scale National Crime Survey (NCS) began in July 1972—only two years after the results from the three surveys conducted by the president's commission were available. Regular national victimization surveys of approximately 120,000 households have been collected in the United States ever since.

The first NCS surveys in 1972 had two main components: a national household survey and several city-level surveys. The city-level surveys were conducted in twenty-six large central cities, thirteen of which were surveyed twice and thirteen only once between 1972 and 1975. In each city, a sample of 10,000 households containing 22,000 respondents age twelve or older was selected. In addition, a sample of 1,000 to 5,000 businesses in each city was interviewed. The city-level surveys were discontinued in 1975.

Like the city-level samples, the national sample at first included both households and businesses. The original national surveys sampled 60,000 households containing 136,000 individuals. About 50,000 businesses were originally included in the national survey, but the business component of the survey was discontinued in 1976. Thus, the only longitudinal element of the NCS that has continued from 1972 to the present is the national household survey.

The NCS surveys are based on a complex panel design; each respondent remains in the sample for three years and is interviewed every six months. One adult member of each household is asked questions about household crimes—burglary, motor vehicle theft, and larceny. If offenders come into direct contact with one of the inhabitants of the victimized household, the act is classified as a "personal crime." Personal crimes include rape, robbery, assault, and personal theft. All members of households fourteen years of age and older are interviewed about their experiences as personal crime victims during the preceding six months. Thus, the NCS includes all crimes classified by the UCR as index offenses except murder and arson. Proxy interviews are conducted with other household members for juveniles of twelve or thirteen years of age and for respondents who are too ill to be interviewed or are unavailable for interviews.

The sheer scope and size of the NCS has made it impossible for researchers to ignore. It is probably the most extensive and costly criminological data collection effort in history.[21] Between 1972 and 1977 alone, the costs of the NCS were an estimated $53 million.[22] Many additional millions of dollars have kept the survey going into the 1990s.

In 1992, the survey went through a major redesign intended to improve methods and expand the information collected.[23] The redesigned survey is now called the National Crime Victimization Survey (NCVS).[24] Survey directors have attempted to devise methods for ensuring comparability between the revised survey and earlier versions.

Comparing Crime Data Sources

I argued earlier that longitudinal data are important for understanding postwar crime trends and their origins. But this requirement severely limits our analysis options. Although the NCVS now contains data from 1973 forward, the UCR provides the only longitudinal data on street crime that include the entire postwar period. Hence, for those interested in longitudinal trends for the postwar United States, an important question becomes, how valid are UCR data?

In fact, the validity of UCR statistics has been hotly debated for more than half a century.[25] Apart from the many technical issues, the most common criticism of UCR crime statistics is what is ominously referred to as "the dark figure" of unreported crime. Stated simply, if a crime is not reported to the police or if the police purposely or accidentally fail to record or report it, it cannot show up in UCR crime statistics.

Fortunately, the systematic collection of offender self-report and victimization surveys has given us a much better understanding of the quality of UCR data. Victimization surveys generally show that the single most important influence on citizen decisions to report offenses to the police is the seriousness of the crime. Not surprising, people are most likely to report serious offenses to police. For example, past research shows that about 68 percent of robberies with injuries are reported to the police, but only about 51 percent of robberies without injuries and 25 percent of attempted robberies without injuries are reported.[26] In general, completed crimes are more likely to be reported than attempted crimes; crimes resulting in serious injury are more likely to be reported than those resulting in less serious injury; and property crimes involving larger amounts of money are more likely to be reported than those involving smaller amounts. An important implication of these findings is that the kinds of crimes missed by the UCR are generally those that are less serious.

The increasing sophistication of self-report survey data has encouraged similar comparisons with UCR data. As noted earlier, based on early self-report surveys, many criminologists concluded that rates of crime reported in self-report surveys were inconsistent with those reported by the UCR. But as data collection and analysis have grown more sophisticated, many of the apparent differences between UCR and self-report data have disappeared or diminished. For example, Michael Hindelang and his colleagues found that differences in reported crimes for young men and women increased along with the seriousness of offenses.[27] Thus, boys and girls were equally likely to report being runaways, but boys were three times more likely than girls to report armed robbery or car theft. When the researchers compared male-female self-reported rates for the most serious crimes, the results were comparable to UCR arrest statistics by gender.

Similarly, Delbert Elliott and Susan Ageton found that differences between self-report and UCR data on the proportion of crime committed by African Americans are due mostly to the types of self-report data collected.[28] In general, differences between the proportion of crimes committed by African Americans and whites for self-report data, as for UCR data, are greatest for serious offenses. Thus, for serious offenses, there is considerable similarity in results for the proportion of crime by race of the offender between the UCR arrest statistics and self-report surveys. Elliott and Ageton conclude: "While we do not deny the existence of official processing biases, it does appear that official correlates of delinquency also reflect real differences in the frequency and seriousness of delinquent acts."[29]

This brings us full circle with regard to crime statistics. In the early postwar years, research based on UCR data was increasingly regarded as hopelessly biased. During the late 1950s and 1960s, self-report survey data seemed to confirm these fears. But as victimization survey data began to accumulate in the 1970s and 1980s and self-report survey data became more sophisticated and extensive, researchers increasingly concluded that there was in fact a great deal of similarity between the crime pictures presented from these three data sources—especially for more serious crimes. The postwar research literature on the validity of the UCR data permits three main conclusions.

First, the UCR undoubtedly underestimates the true amount of crime actually being committed. Among other things, this means that it is probably more justifiable to examine trends over time than absolute rates. In other words, it is safer to conclude that crime rates doubled between periods one and two than to argue that UCR crime data accurately represented total crime occurring during either period. In this sense, my focus on crime trends is an advantage.

Second, the UCR generally offers a more accurate portrayal of more rather than less serious crimes. This means that data for murder and robbery are probably more accurate and are definitely more complete than data for assault and theft. Nevertheless, as we will see later in this chapter, trends for all seven of the street crimes analyzed here are highly correlated. This suggests that although less serious crimes may be underreported they still have shown overall postwar trends that are substantially similar to the trends observed for more serious crimes.

Finally, the weaknesses of UCR data should serve as a reminder that we must pay the greatest attention to the largest differences in trends over time. For example, if murder rates double in a ten-year period we can be pretty certain that something important is happening. We should be less impressed with minor fluctuations. With these considerations in mind, we are ready to examine postwar street crime trends.

Street Crime Trends in Postwar America

I begin this section by presenting postwar trends in the UCR measure of crimes known to police for total annual rates of murder, robbery, rape, aggravated assault, burglary, motor vehicle theft, and other theft—the traditional components of the UCR crime index.[30] I examine only murders that were intentional—as opposed to unintentional killings, such as those resulting from negligence. Robberies examined here include those in which property is seized from another person by violence or intimidation. Rapes include cases of unlawful, nonconsensual sexual intercourse.[31] Assaults include cases in which individuals confront others with the intention of

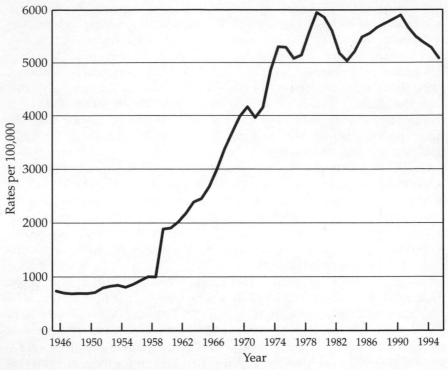

FIGURE 2.1   Total Street Crimes, 1946–1996
SOURCE: Data supplied by the U.S. Federal Bureau of Investigation, "Crime in
the United States," *Uniform Crime Reports* annual, 1946 to 1996 (Washington, DC:
Government Printing Office), includes UCR categories for murder, robbery, rape,
aggravated assault, burglary, motor vehicle theft, and larceny.

causing them serious physical injury. Cases are "aggravated" if they are
accompanied by a deadly weapon or with an intent to kill, rob, or rape.
Burglaries include cases in which individuals break into someone else's
home with the intention of committing a crime, most commonly, a theft.
Larcenies simply refer to stealing someone else's property. To standardize
for population growth, I present the rates per 100,000 Americans included
in the UCR survey of police departments for each year.

Figure 2.1 shows that following the end of World War II the UCR reported about 700 of these seven street crimes a year for every 100,000
Americans. But beginning in the 1960s, street crime rates began to dramatically increase.[32] In the twelve years from 1959 to 1971 alone, reported
street crime rates more than quadrupled. After a two-year lull, they began
to climb again, reaching a postwar high of nearly 6,000 crimes per 100,000

Americans in 1980. Overall, reported street crime rates increased eight-fold from 1946 to their postwar peak. But note also that street crime rates have been relatively flat for the last quarter of the twentieth century—they were about the same in 1996 as they were in 1975.

Of course, the behavior represented in Figure 2.1 is extremely diverse, ranging from brutal murder to petty theft. Although all types of street crime increased in the postwar period, rates of increase varied considerably for individual crimes. Moreover, combining all the crimes into a single index highlights trends for more common crimes such as theft and burglary and obscures trends for less common crimes such as murder and rape. To see individual differences between crime types, I next consider separately trends for violent and property offenses.

Violent Crimes

The UCR crime index includes the violent crimes of murder, robbery, rape, and aggravated assault. Total violent crime rates from UCR statistics showed little variation from 1946 to about 1962—hovering at about 140 crimes for every 100,000 Americans. But starting in the early 1960s, violent crime rates began to show remarkable increases. From 1960 to 1975 alone, total violent crime rates more than tripled. After a shallow decline from 1982 to 1985, the total violent crime rate again began increasing, reaching a postwar high in 1991. After 1991, total violent crime has again gone into a shallow decline, dropping by over 16 percent between 1991 and 1996.

There is also substantial variation in the frequency of the individual violent crimes that make up these trends. Aggravated assaults were the most common form of UCR violent offense in the postwar period, followed by robbery, rape, and murder. In 1996, aggravated assault rates per 100,000 U.S. residents were nearly twice as high as robbery rates, nearly eleven times higher than rape rates, and fifty-two times higher than murder rates. Thus, violent crime trends are influenced most by changes in the relatively common crimes of aggravated assault and robbery and much less by the relatively uncommon crimes of murder and rape.

Figure 2.2 shows UCR murder rates from 1946 to 1996. According to Figure 2.2, murder rates reported to the UCR went into a shallow decline in the immediate postwar years, reaching a low of 4.6 per 100,000 in both 1962 and 1963. But they more than doubled in the decade from 1963 to 1974, reaching a postwar high of 10.2 in 1980. After a seven-year decline, murder rates again rose in 1986, leaving them just under the postwar high mark in 1991. From 1991 to 1996, murder rates declined by nearly 25 percent. These recent declines left murder rates in 1996 lower than they were in 1970.

FIGURE 2.2   Murder Rates, 1946–1996
SOURCE: Data supplied by the U.S. Federal Bureau of Investigation, "Crime in the United States," *Uniform Crime Reports* annual, 1946 to 1996 (Washington, DC: Government Printing Office).

Postwar robbery rates resemble those for murder. As shown in Figure 2.3, UCR robbery rates were stable from 1946 until about 1962—in fact, rates in 1946 and 1962 were nearly identical. But robbery rates more than tripled in the next thirteen years, reaching a peak of 221 per 100,000 in 1975. After a brief decline, they again rose rapidly, reaching a postwar high of 273 per 100,000 in 1991. Following 1991, robbery rates have again declined—by about 26 percent between 1991 and 1996. These recent declines mean that robbery rates in 1996 were less than they were in 1974.

As with murder and robbery, UCR rates for rape and aggravated assault were relatively flat from the end of World War II until the early 1960s. But from 1963 to 1980, rape rates nearly quadrupled and aggravated assault rates more than tripled. In comparison to postwar murder and robbery rates, rates for rape and assault showed a steadier upward trend following their initial rise in the early 1960s. Both rape and aggra-

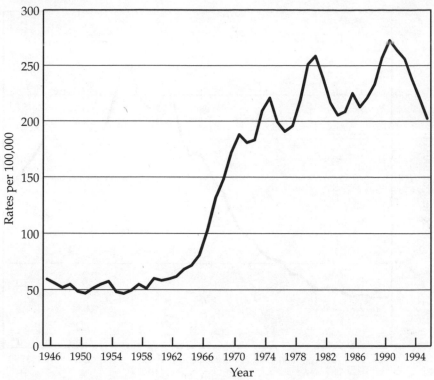

FIGURE 2.3 Robbery Rates, 1946–1996
SOURCE: Data supplied by the U.S. Federal Bureau of Investigation, "Crime in the United States," *Uniform Crime Reports* annual, 1946 to 1996 (Washington, DC: Government Printing Office).

vated assault reached their highest postwar level in 1992: 43 per 100,000 residents for rape and 442 per 100,000 residents for aggravated assault. From 1992 to 1996, rape rates declined by 16 percent and aggravated assault rates declined by 12 percent.

Property Crimes

The UCR crime index includes three property crimes: burglary, motor vehicle theft, and other theft. Although violent street crime no doubt raises the greatest public fear, property crime, in which there is no direct contact between offender and victim, is by far the most common type of street crime. In 1996, total property crimes were seven times more frequent than total violent crimes.

FIGURE 2.4   Burglary Rates, 1946–1996
SOURCE: Data supplied by the U.S. Federal Bureau of Investigation, "Crime in the United States," *Uniform Crime Reports* annual, 1946 to 1996 (Washington, DC: Government Printing Office).

Total UCR property crime rates broke the level of 1,000 per 100,000 Americans for the first time in 1960; they broke the 2,000 mark in 1963, the 3,000 mark in 1968, the 4,000 mark in 1974, and the 5,000 mark in 1979. As with violent crime trends, property crime rates were relatively constant from the end of World War II until the early 1960s and then began a rapid increase that continued with only brief interruptions until the late 1970s. Since the 1970s, rates of property crime have flattened. Thus, the rate of total property crime in 1996 was similar to the rate in 1974.

Of the three property crimes tracked by the UCR, larceny is most common, followed by burglary and auto theft. In 1996, larcenies were about three times more common than burglaries and more than five times more frequent than auto thefts. Burglary rates are shown in Figure 2.4.

As can be seen in Figure 2.4, burglary rates were at a postwar low in 1948. They rapidly increased in the 1960s and early 1970s, reaching their highest postwar level in 1980. After 1980, burglary rates steadily declined. From 1980 to 1996, these declines amounted to a 44 percent drop. By 1996, declines in burglary rates left them at a lower level than they had been in 1969.

Like burglary rates, rates for auto theft and larceny were relatively stable in the immediate postwar period. Also like burglary rates, auto theft and larceny rates increased rapidly in the 1960s. But in contrast to burglary rates, auto theft and larceny rates have not declined as rapidly in the 1980s and 1990s. Both auto theft and larceny did not reach their postwar high level until 1991 and both have declined less rapidly than burglary rates since then. Still, from 1991 to 1996, auto theft rates declined by more than 20 percent and larceny rates by almost 8 percent. Also, unlike burglary and larceny rates, motor vehicle theft rates went through a longer period of relative stability from the late 1960s to the early 1980s before moving upward again. For example, rates of auto theft were about the same in 1969 as they were in 1984.

Some Immediate Implications of Postwar Crime Trends

Taken together, postwar trends for these seven UCR crimes permit three main conclusions:

Crime and Public Perceptions of Crime

First, the crime trends support the conclusion that crime rates are only loosely related to public concern about crime. Recent media accounts of crime and public opinion polls both suggest that public concern about crime has never been higher.[33] This would seem to imply that we are currently in the midst of a serious crime wave. The crime trends presented do not entirely support this image, however. For example, the rates for murder, the most serious of all street crimes, are actually lower in 1996 than they were in 1975. In fact, the largest postwar increases in murder rates came from about 1963 to 1974. Since then, murder rates have either declined or remained fairly stable.

Trends for robbery, another crime that elicits great public concern, tell much the same story. Although robbery rates continued to increase for a longer period than murder rates, the big increases in robbery rates, like the increases for murder, came not in the 1980s and 1990s but rather in the 1960s and early 1970s. Robbery rates in 1996 were similar to rates in 1975.

Although aggravated assaults and rapes have also shown recent signs of tapering off, compared to murders and robberies they increased more steeply in the 1980s and 1990s. Both aggravated assaults and rapes have characteristics that make them especially difficult for the UCR to accurately count, however. For completed violent crimes, NCVS data tell us that rape is the least likely to be reported to police.[34] Recent trends in rape and aggravated assault and, to a lesser extent, robbery are also more likely than murder rates to be influenced by changes in police effectiveness over the last twenty years.

In a thoughtful comparison of NCVS and UCR data from 1973 to 1992, the sociologist Robert O'Brien shows that rates of violent crime from the NCVS have been essentially flat, whereas until recently UCR data have shown increases.[35] O'Brien concludes that these differences between the NCVS and the UCR are most likely produced by increasing police effectiveness, which increases UCR but not NCVS crime rates. He argues that murder is probably the best indicator of violent crime trends because it is the least likely to be affected by changing police practices—murders are almost universally reported and have long received more investigative resources than other street crimes.

In short, among violent crimes, the two most reliably reported, murder and robbery, do not support the widely held view that we are in the midst of a new crime wave. Instead, rates for both crimes increased most rapidly in the 1960s and early 1970s—more than two decades ago. Although both remain at high levels, they have actually shown substantial decreases in recent years. Aggravated assault and rape continued to increase into the early 1990s, but they too have leveled off and even declined in recent years. Moreover, compared to murders and robberies, UCR rates for aggravated assaults and rapes are more likely to be influenced by the effectiveness of police in carrying out their jobs.

Similarly, data on property crime do not universally support the image of a crime crisis in the 1990s. In fact, rates for burglary, the most serious of the UCR property crimes, reached a postwar peak in 1980. Rates in 1996 are substantially lower than they were in 1975. As with murder and robbery, the greatest increases in burglary rates happened in the 1960s and early 1970s.

Larceny and motor vehicle theft rates are more supportive of the image of a recent crime wave. Both had the highest postwar levels in the early 1990s. And, largely because of insurance requirements, auto theft is thought to be among the most completely reported of all crimes.[36] Rates of larceny and auto theft, like the five other index crimes, have recently declined, however. Larceny rates in 1996 are about the same as they were in the late 1970s; motor vehicle theft rates in 1996 are about the same as they were in the late 1980s. Moreover, both larceny and motor vehicle theft rates are strongly affected by what the sociologists Lawrence Cohen and Marcus Felson call the availability of "suitable targets."[37] That is, rising larceny and automobile theft rates are most likely influenced by the simple availability of more consumer products and automobiles. The United States may have had lower auto theft and larceny rates thirty years ago partly because there were fewer automobiles and consumer goods to steal.

Overall, these results suggest that public concern about crime is only loosely related to actual crime rates. Or more precisely, concern appears to lag behind crime rates by twenty to thirty years. Trends for these street crimes generally support the conclusion that the real crime wave began in the early 1960s but had already flattened out by the late 1970s.[38]

Similarities Between the Trends

A second striking feature of postwar crime trends is that despite variation in exact patterns the trends for different crimes are highly correlated. In a statistical analysis, I found that trends for the seven UCR index crimes from 1946 to 1995 were all closely related.[39] This finding has some potentially important implications for arguments about postwar crime trends. Most important, it suggests that whatever caused crime to increase in the postwar United States probably had very broad-gauged effects—influencing murder as well as larceny, rape as well as motor vehicle theft. More generally, the similarities in trends support the utility of seeking an explanation for these crime trends that is broad enough to account for a wide array of specific crime types.

Three Postwar Crime Periods

Finally, all of these crimes exhibit similar historical patterns. Thus, all seven crimes have low points in the early part of the postwar period. The lowest level of aggravated assault and theft was recorded in 1946, of burglary in 1948, of motor vehicle theft in 1949, of rape in 1954, of robbery in 1956, and of murder in 1962. Similarly, all seven crimes recorded highs near the end of the postwar period. Murder and burglary reached postwar highs in 1980; robbery, motor vehicle theft, and larceny in 1991; and rape and aggravated assault in 1992.

The general impression left by these patterns is that the postwar history of street crime can be divided into three broad periods based on the level and direction of crime trends: The *early postwar period*, from 1946 to 1960, is marked by low and stable crime rates; the *middle postwar period*, from 1961 to 1973, is marked by rapidly increasing crime rates; and the *late postwar period*, after 1973, is marked by high but relatively stable crime rates.

Putting the Trends into Context

Given the extensive research done on the strengths and weaknesses of the UCR, it is clear that crime rates actually did increase substantially from the beginning of the postwar period to its end and that these increases are not simply an artifact of the way UCR data are reported. But how can we put these increases into a meaningful context? We have already seen that public fear of crime is not a very precise indicator of actual crime rates. Two ways of contextualizing postwar U.S. crime trends are by comparing them to trends in earlier periods of U.S. history and to trends in other industrialized nations.

Broader Historical Trends

World War II is a formidable barrier in world history. The war affected virtually every aspect of life for citizens of many nations, including the United States. Of course, it is for this reason that it makes sense to talk about "prewar" and "postwar" history. Nonetheless, if we use the early postwar period as a baseline for our conclusions about crime trends, we get a different perspective than if we take a longer historical view of crime in America. This is because rates of street crime were at historically low levels in the United States following World War II.

The political scientist Ted Gurr, in a study of crime trends in Western democracies, concludes that the rapid increase in violent crimes in the United States in the 1960s was preceded by other periods of equally high increases.[40] The most reliable data are for murder. The sociologist Douglas Eckberg shows that U.S. murder rates from 1900 to 1933 ranged annually from seven to nine per 100,000 residents.[41] Thus, murder rates in the first three decades of the twentieth century were about the same as those observed after the 1960s. Judged from this perspective, the low murder rates of the 1940s and 1950s, rather than the high rates of the 1970s and 1980s, are the aberration. In short, current murder rates in the United States are only slightly higher than those experienced during the first third of this century.

International Comparisons

By the 1990s, there was a nearly universal perception among both researchers and the general public that U.S. crime rates were much higher than rates for other industrialized democracies. For example, the sociologist Louise Shelley concludes, "The crime patterns of the United States are unique among all developed countries in terms of the high rates of criminal behavior, the pervasiveness of the phenomenon, and the severity of the crimes that are committed."[42] Similarly, the sociologist Elliott Currie concludes, "In the severity of crime rates, the United States more closely resembles the most volatile countries of the Third World than other developed western societies."[43] Although there is much truth to

TABLE 2.1 Murder Rates (per 100,000 population) for United States and 17 Industrialized Nations, 1960 and 1991

Country	1960	1991
United States	4.7	10.4
Australia	1.5	2.0
Austria	1.2	1.3
Canada	1.4	2.3
Denmark	0.5	1.4
England and Wales	0.6	0.5
Finland	2.9	3.1
France	1.7	1.1
Germany	1.0	1.1
Italy	1.4	2.8
Japan	1.9	0.6
Netherlands	0.3	1.2
New Zealand	1.0	1.9
Norway	0.4	1.5
Russian Federation	—	15.2
Scotland	0.7	1.5
Sweden	0.6	1.4
Switzerland	0.6	1.4

SOURCE: World Health Organization, *World Health Statistics Annual* (Geneva, Switzerland, 1959, 1992).

these claims, there is also a great deal of variation by type of crime, by country, and by the year in which comparisons are made.

Because of differences in the ways countries define, record, and count crime, difficulties in collecting reliable data on crime are greatly compounded for cross-national comparisons.[44] The most accurate international comparisons for murder are probably those provided by the World Health Organization (WHO).[45] WHO data are collected from death certificates supplied by participating countries and define murder as "lethal injury purposely inflicted by other persons."[46] In Table 2.1, I compare WHO data on murder rates for the United States and seventeen other industrialized nations. Data from the Russian Federation, part of the former Soviet Union, are only available for 1991.

Table 2.1 shows that murder rates in the United States are indeed considerably higher than those for other industrialized nations. In 1991, the United States had murder rates that were more than twenty times higher than those for Japan and England and Wales and more than nine times higher than those for France and Germany. The highest murder rate among West European nations, that of Finland, is still only one-third of the comparable U.S. rate in 1991.

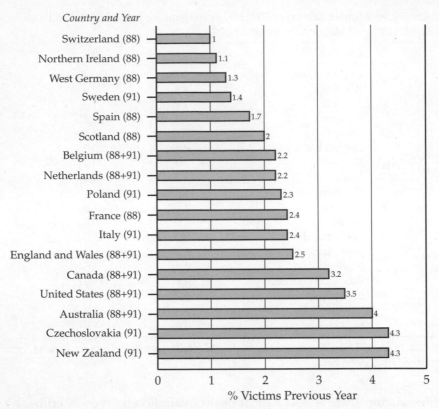

FIGURE 2.5   Annual Percentage of Burglary Victims in 17 Nations
SOURCE: Pat Mayhew, "Findings from the International Crime Survey" (London: Home Office Research and Statistics Department, No. 8, 1994), p. 3.

On the other hand, the United States had lower murder rates than the Russian Federation in 1991. Moreover, U.S. rates were much closer to European rates in 1960 than in 1991—less than twice as high as rates in Finland and about two and one-half times those of Japan.

The growing availability of victimization survey data in which random samples of citizens are asked to report their experiences as crime victims over the preceding year also allows some direct crime rate comparisons between countries. Thus far, the most comprehensive of these surveys has been the International Crime Survey (ICS) carried out between 1988 and 1991.[47] Altogether, the ICS included over 50,000 interviews completed in twenty countries. Figure 2.5 compares burglary rates for citizens of the countries that participated in the survey.

The results may be surprising for those who assume that the United States is in the midst of an unprecedented crime wave. Figure 2.5 shows that the United States ranked fourth in burglary rates—behind Czechoslovakia, New Zealand, and Australia. Canadian rates were only slightly lower than those reported in the United States In general, about 3.5 per cent of U.S. households sampled reported being the victim of a burglary in the preceding year. This was relatively high—more than twice as high as seven countries included in the survey (Sweden, West Germany, Northern Ireland, Switzerland, Japan, Norway, and Finland)—but not so different from other industrialized countries as to make the United States stand out.

Results are similar for other crimes reported in the ICS, including robberies and auto thefts. Robbery data were based on responses to the question, "During the past year, has anyone taken something from you by using force or threatening you or did anyone try to do so?" The results show that compared to thirteen Western, industrialized nations and two cities (Warsaw, Poland; and Surabaya, Indonesia), the United States had the second highest robbery rates in 1988. The highest rates—nearly twice those of the United States—were reported for Spain. In the case of auto theft, five nations had higher rates than the United States: England and Wales, Italy, Australia, New Zealand, and France. Again, U.S. robbery and auto theft rates were relatively high: Robbery rates were nearly four times those of the five nations (France, Norway, Switzerland, Northern Ireland, and Scotland) and one city (Surabaya) with the lowest rates; U.S. auto theft rates were more than double those of the five countries with the lowest rates (Finland, Belgium, Canada, Scotland, and Czechoslovakia). Nevertheless, crime rates for the United States were not as lopsided as much current public opinion seems to suggest.

Summary and Implications

The best available evidence supports the conclusion that the United States in the late postwar years had higher total rates of street crime than at any other time during the postwar period. Moreover, individual rates of robbery, rape, aggravated assault, and theft were higher in the early 1990s than at any other time in the postwar period—although it is likely that recent increases in rates of rape and aggravated assault are due at least in part to increasing police effectiveness. Murder and burglary rates reached their peak in the early 1980s, but both remain at high levels. Although crime data for the period prior to World War II are less reliable, data for murder suggest that current rates are about the same as those found in the United States in the first three decades of the twentieth century.

The United States also has relatively high street crime rates when compared to other Western democracies—although the disparities are often exaggerated. The differences are greatest for the violent offenses of murder and robbery.[48] Even for violent personal crimes, however, there is substantial variation depending on the specific crime, year, and country examined.

Clearly, although the timing of public concern about street crime in America is off—about thirty years late—it is neither unfounded nor unreasonable. The United States in the late twentieth century is experiencing a period of relatively high street crime rates, in both historical and comparative terms. But it is important to keep these crime trends in perspective. The United States had about the same rate of murder in the 1990s as it had during the first three decades of the twentieth century. Moreover, the United States in the early 1990s had lower robbery rates than Spain, lower burglary rates than Australia, and lower auto theft rates than England and Wales.

Toward an Explanation of Postwar U.S. Crime Trends

Taking into account the imperfect nature of these crime data, we can still conclude with a fair amount of confidence that a suitable explanation of postwar street crime trends in the United States must explain at least three facts: First, street crime rates increased a great deal during the postwar period. The broadest measure of this—total street crimes per 100,000 Americans—was eight times higher in 1991 than in 1946.

Second, the rates of increase were patterned. We can identify three fairly distinct crime periods in the postwar years: an early period from 1946 to the early 1960s during which rates of street crime were comparatively low and stable, a middle period from the early 1960s through the late 1970s during which street crime rates increased steadily and rapidly, and a late period from the late 1970s to the mid-1990s during which rates of street crime were comparatively high and stable.

And finally, the patterns observed are similar across crime types. Although there are substantial variations for the seven street crimes examined, the overall trends for all of the crimes are highly correlated.

Thus, we are looking for causes of crime that can account for rapid changes in crime rates, that were especially influential from the early 1960s to the late 1970s, and that had similar effects on diverse forms of street crime.

In terms of the first of these considerations, we can imagine an array of crime explanations on a continuum from those in which crime rates change most rapidly to those in which rates change most slowly. For example, most theories that claim that changes in crime rates are produced by biological drives or psychological defects would be on the slow-change end of the spectrum because we would expect these kinds of changes to happen not over months or even decades but rather over generations. By contrast, most social theories would be more consistent with the middle and rapid-change parts of the continuum. Social explanations that emphasize relatively malleable social institutions, organizations, and attitudes would be on the rapid-change part of the continuum. Social theories that attribute crime to deeply entrenched cultural values or highly stable social-structural characteristics would be somewhere in the middle of the continuum—faster than biology and psychology, but slower than other social explanations.

In terms of this crime explanation continuum, the postwar crime trends observed in the United States clearly favor explanations on the more rapidly changing end of the spectrum. After all, total street crime rates more than tripled in the two decades of the 1960s and 1970s alone. If this crime wave was produced by biological drives or psychological defects—or even by deeply held cultural beliefs passed between generations—how could it fluctuate so rapidly in such a short time?

The crime data presented previously also suggest that crime trends in postwar America have gone through identifiable stages. What was it about American society in the early 1960s that resulted so consistently in rapidly accelerating crime? Why did rates of all seven street crimes climb during this period? Just as important, what was it about American society in the 1940s and 1950s that produced such low crime rates?

The criminologists Michael Gottfredson and Travis Hirschi argue for a general theory of crime and fault researchers for implying that we need "one criminology for murder and another for robbery, and one criminology for Chicago and another for Taipei."[49] The crime data already presented support the wisdom of this criticism. Although there are some important differences in the street crime trends I presented, the similarities appear to be far stronger. My approach is to look for the common threads related to all seven of these crimes rather than to concentrate on what appear to be much smaller individual differences.

One final issue should be emphasized before we move on. The crime trends I have presented also raise important insights into the nature of our reactions to crime. The data show that the biggest increases in crime began in the early 1960s, but the rates flattened out and declined in the 1980s and 1990s. Yet, the level of public concern with crime, as demonstrated by public opinion polls and the growing importance of crime as an issue in elections, remained at very high levels in the 1990s—nearly three decades after the largest increases. This should remind us that public attitudes about crime in the United States are influenced by a great many variables in addition to (or instead of) actual crime rates.

• • •

If crime trends seem to contradict many popular assumptions about crime, the contradictions are, if anything, even greater when we consider trends by offenders' characteristics. In the next chapter, I look at postwar crime patterns for different age, gender, ethnic, and racial groups. I conclude the chapter by considering the additional implications of subgroup differences for explanations of crime in postwar America.

three

Offender Characteristics and Crime Trends in Postwar America

The danger of a conflict between the white and the black inhabitants perpetually haunts the imagination of the Americans, like a painful dream.

—Alexis de Tocqueville, *Democracy in America*, 1835[1]

If sociological theorists of crime and delinquency were to use the 'clues' provided by known correlates of criminal behavior . . . sex, race, and age group . . . theory and research might be able to advance more steadily.

—Michael J. Hindelang, "Variation in Sex-Race-Age Specific Rates of Offending," 1981[2]

Even a cursory look at America's police lockups, courts, jails, and prisons quickly confirms that a disproportionate number of individuals arrested, convicted, and sentenced for committing street crimes are young men from racial and ethnic minority groups. When official data from the UCR were the only major source of information on crime in the United States, many policymakers and researchers feared that the overrepresentation of young, minority men in the system was in large part due to the biased decisionmaking of police and other agents of the law.[3] But with the increasing availability of victimization and self-report data, the weight of evidence has shifted toward the conclusion that much of the difference in the arrest, conviction, and incarceration rates of specific gender, age, and racial groups is quite simply due to their differential propensity to commit crime.[4]

In this chapter, I examine postwar street crime trends in the United States by the offender's age, gender, and race. My assumption is that by

35

carefully documenting subgroup differences in crime rates, we may be able to learn a good deal about why overall crime trends behaved as they did.

Data on Offender Characteristics

Characteristics like age, gender, and race can affect postwar crime trends in two main ways. First, if certain categories of individuals are systematically more likely to commit crime, then trends will naturally be affected by the changing supply of these subgroups over time. For example, if young people are more prone than others to commit crime, then increasing supplies of young people as a result of changing population patterns will increase crime rates. And, second, age, gender, and race characteristics might also affect crime trends if men, young people, or members of specific racial or ethnic groups change over time the rates at which they commit crime. For example, if crime rates for females, compared to other demographic groups, increased during the postwar period, then women would be responsible for an increasing share of crime during these years. Thus, crime trends can be affected both by the supply of individuals from particular demographic groups and by their changing crime rates.

For postwar America, the supply effect is generally a more important consideration for age and race groups but a less important issue for gender groups. This is because the proportion of young people and racial groups has varied quite a bit during the postwar period whereas the proportion of women in the population has changed relatively little. For example, women constituted 49.8 percent of the U.S. population in 1940 and 51.2 percent of the population in 1995—less than a 3 percent increase.[5] By contrast, African Americans constituted 9.8 percent of the U.S. population in 1940 but 12.6 percent in 1995—a 29 percent increase.[6] Similarly, at the lowest postwar level in 1955, less than 14 percent of the U.S. population was between the ages of fourteen and twenty-four.[7] By contrast, the proportion of Americans age fourteen to twenty-four reached a postwar high of nearly 21 percent in 1976—a 50 percent increase.

Unfortunately, data options for studying crime rates by age, gender, and race in the postwar United States are even more limited than the options for studying crime trends in general. Neither self-report survey data nor victimization data are available before 1973—already after the period when the largest crime increases of the postwar period occurred. Thus, as with data on crime trends in general, the only data source that includes annual estimates by age, gender, and race for the entire postwar period is the UCR.

I explained earlier that the UCR collects two main types of data— crimes known to police and arrests. Because the crimes known to police measure depends less on the decisionmaking of police than arrests do, researchers have generally preferred this measure. But the UCR measure of crimes known to police does not report the suspect's age, gender, or race. Thus, the only U.S. crime measure that includes offender characteristics and has been collected annually for the entire postwar period is the UCR measure of arrests.

As we saw in Chapter 2, the quality of UCR data has been strenuously debated ever since they were first collected in 1930. Unsurprising, these debates have been especially sharp with regard to the accuracy of the UCR for reporting the characteristics of offenders and, most especially, for offenders' race. Perhaps the most common criticism of UCR arrest data for race has to do with the UCR's emphasis on street crimes, which critics have argued focuses attention on crimes that are more common among minorities and less common among nonminorities.[8] This is certainly an important consideration. But I find it not a very compelling reason for altogether ignoring UCR data. Although it is true that the seven index crimes for which the UCR has recorded the most complete data are only a subset of all crimes, it is also true that these crimes are of substantial policy interest.

As with the general concerns about UCR data outlined in Chapter 2, most of the criticisms of UCR data on crime trends by offender's age, gender, and race reflect concern with either citizen or police reporting. The reasons for this concern are clear. For example, if nonminorities are more likely than minorities to report crimes to police, then conclusions about crime rates by race may be erroneous. Similarly, if police arrest decisions are influenced by gender, then conclusions about crime rates by gender may also be biased.

During most of the postwar period, the UCR was the only national data source on crime and hence it was impossible to evaluate its quality by comparing it to other data sources. Fortunately, this situation changed substantially with the growing availability of victimization and self-report survey data in the 1970s. Most important, since 1973, the NCVS has provided annual comparative data on street crime victims that are independent of UCR data. Analysis of the NCVS and other victim survey data since 1973 does show some differences in reporting by subgroup characteristics. In a review of international research on the topic, the political scientist Wesley Skogan concludes that compared to men, women are more likely to report crimes, and compared to younger persons, the elderly are more likely to report crimes.[9] Skogan finds few reporting differences by the victim's race, however. Moreover, the magnitude of subgroup differences by age and gender, especially for more serious street crimes, is relatively small.

The most convincing support for the conclusion of minor differences in crime reporting is found by comparing the subgroup characteristics of offenders reported in NCVS data to the characteristics of UCR arrestees.[10] To the extent that gender, age, or racial correlates of arrest rates from the UCR are similar to offending rates for each group as measured by the NCVS (which is independent of the police), we can have greater confidence in the validity of UCR data. Indeed, systematic comparisons of UCR index arrest rates with offending rates estimated from the NCVS show substantial correspondence. The criminologist Michael Hindelang, for example, found strong similarities in the proportion of robbery and burglary offenders by age, gender, and race categories as reported by victims in the NCVS compared to the same characteristics reported in UCR arrest data.[11] Even for burglaries—where the offender is only seen by victims in 6 percent of the NCVS cases—there was a very strong correspondence between UCR arrest statistics and the NCVS survey on the offenders' characteristics.

Researchers who have compared crime rates by offender characteristics from self-report surveys and the UCR offer results similar to, if less conclusive than, those drawn from comparisons of UCR and NCVS data. For example, the sociologists Delbert Elliott and Susan Ageton found that differences between self-report and UCR data on the proportion of crimes committed by African Americans and men is due mostly to the types of self-report data collected.[12] In general, differences between the proportion of crimes committed by African Americans and whites, and men and women, are greater for more serious offenses. When these differences are controlled, there is substantial similarity between the proportion of crime by race and gender reported by UCR arrest statistics and self-report surveys.

More generally, a large and reliable body of evidence shows that crime seriousness is consistently the strongest predictor of the police decision to arrest.[13] In their comprehensive analysis of the validity of UCR reports, Walter Gove and his colleagues conclude that the most important determinant of whether a crime is reported to police and officially recorded is not the personal characteristics of the victim or the offender, but rather the perceived seriousness of the crime.[14] Hence, the available evidence suggests that UCR arrest data, especially for serious crimes and especially at the national level, provide information that reflects actual crime trends by the offenders' characteristics.

Apart from validity, however, using UCR data to measure trends in crime for different age, gender, and racial groups runs into additional problems. Since the UCR began collecting crime data in 1930, it has only provided summary data on the specific characteristics of those arrested. Thus, the UCR reports the total number of whites, males, or eighteen-year-olds arrested, but not the total number of white male eighteen-year-olds.[15] As noted in Chapter 2, the redesign of the UCR—the NIBRS—may eventually provide individual-level national data on arrestees.[16] As this book was being prepared, NIBRS data were only available for a handful of states, however, and in any event, NIBRS data will never be available for earlier years. This situation seriously complicates efforts to estimate trends for specific categories of arrestees based on their age, gender, and race.

To summarize, the UCR is the only U.S. data source that includes crime data over time on the offenders' age, gender, and race for the entire postwar period. The difficulties of using the UCR to examine these characteristics should not be minimized. Still, just as a serious archeologist would not throw out potsherds—no matter how incomplete—so, too, a responsible criminologist cannot afford to ignore the only source of national data on gender, age, race, and crime that spans the entire postwar period. In the next section, I consider postwar trends in arrest rates by age and gender before turning to a consideration of arrest rates by race and ethnicity.

Gender and Crime

The conclusion that men are disproportionately responsible for the kinds of street crimes reported here is probably the best supported assertion in all of criminology. Arrest, court, and prison statistics for the United States consistently show a massive overrepresentation of men.[17] UCR statistics show that in 1994 men accounted for more than 90 percent of murders, robberies, rapes, and burglaries; for 88 percent of motor vehicle thefts; for 83 percent of aggravated assaults; and for 67 percent of larcenies.[18] Similar differences have generally been documented for countries throughout the world.[19] The conclusion is also supported by both self-report[20] and victimization surveys.[21]

Thus, substantial differences in rates of common street crimes for males and females are well established. Moreover, given that the proportion of males and females in the U.S. population has been relatively constant during the postwar period, changes in female crime rates over time were not greatly affected by the proportion of women in the total population. Researchers have disagreed, however, on the question of whether women have been responsible for an increasing percentage of street crimes in the United States during the postwar period. Three main views can be identified.

Perhaps the most popular argument, especially in the 1970s, was that male and female crime rates were converging along with a general convergence in sex roles.[22] This view suggests that as women gain independence, confidence, and self-esteem, their crime rates generally come to resemble those of men. A leading exponent of this view is the criminologist Freda Adler, who argues, "In the same way that women are demanding equal opportunity in fields of legitimate endeavor, a similar number of determined women are forcing their way into the world of major crimes . . . formerly committed by males only."[23]

Other researchers disagree that there has been any convergence between male and female crime rates in the United States during the postwar period.[24] For example, the criminologists Michael Gottfredson and Travis Hirschi argue that increases in female crime are limited mostly to white-collar crime and are explained by the fact that women are increasingly overrepresented in occupations where such offenses are possible (e.g., in the 1990s women outnumbered men in white-collar occupations such as bank teller and clerical worker).[25] Gottfredson and Hirschi conclude that once changes in the *opportunity* to commit crime are taken into account, the differences between male and female crime rates are so widespread and consistent as to be invariant over time and space.[26]

Finally, others have argued that the convergence of male and female crime rates during the postwar period has been limited to certain types of crime.[27] Thus, in an analysis of female arrest trends from 1960 to 1990, Darrell Steffensmeier concludes that although female arrest rates have increased somewhat for property crimes, the ratio of male to female involvement in violent crime has held steady since 1960.[28]

To determine which of these explanations is most accurate for the crimes examined here, I compared trends in the ratio of female to male arrests from 1965 to 1992.[29] In general, the proportion of robberies, burglaries, larcenies, and auto thefts increased for women vis-à-vis men during this period. By contrast, aggravated assault rates showed little change, and an examination of male to female murder rates showed that women committed a smaller proportion over time. The results for robberies and burglaries are shown in Figure 3.1.

The UCR data reported here include only the years 1965 to 1992. Because I calculated the ratio of female to male crimes, a rising line means that rates for females vis-à-vis males were increasing during the years included. In general, Figure 3.1 shows that both robberies and burglaries were strongly male dominated throughout the years spanned by the data. For example, female burglary rates were less than 4 percent of male burglary rates and female robbery rates were less than 6 percent of male robbery rates in 1965. Figure 3.1 also shows, however, that the gap between men and women did narrow during the years included. By 1992, female robbery and burglary rates were about 9 percent of male robbery and burglary rates.

Of the seven index crimes examined here, the only one in which the ratio of female to male arrests showed a major decline from 1965 to 1992 was murder. Steffensmeier argues that the declining proportion of murders committed by women during the postwar period is likely related to two considerations.[30] First, the rate of instrumental, felony-related

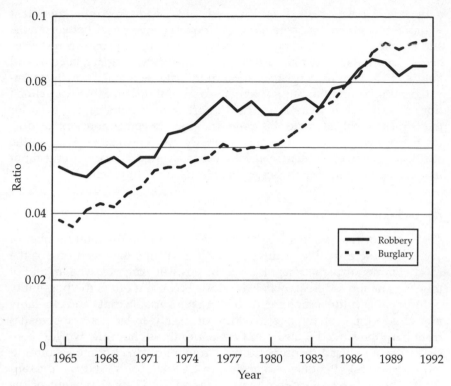

FIGURE 3.1 Ratio of Adult Female to Adult Male Robbery and Burglary Arrests, 1965–1992
NOTE: All rates for persons age 18 and over.
SOURCE: U.S. Federal Bureau of Investigation, *Age-Specific and Race-Specific Arrest Rates for Selected Offenses 1965–1992* (Washington, DC: Government Printing Office, December 1993).

killings (e.g., contract murders) increased substantially during the postwar period (from about 7 percent of all murders in 1960 to about 20 percent in 1990). Steffensmeier points out that men are overwhelmingly the offenders in these instrumental crimes. Second, compared to men, women more frequently commit murder in conjunction with noncriminal activities, especially domestic disputes. Steffensmeier argues that the decline in these types of murders for women, particularly during the 1980s, might be related to the growing availability of shelters and other services for abused women. This growth may have allowed more women to escape from rather than kill abusive men.[31] This last development might also have helped keep female aggravated assault rates relatively flat during the postwar years.

In general, postwar trends for the seven index crimes are most consistent with the conclusion that there has been modest convergence between male and female crime rates, but only for some crime types. Female arrest rates became more similar to male arrest rates for robbery, burglary, larceny, and auto theft. I found no consistent trend in the ratio of female to male aggravated assaults, and the ratio of female to male murders actually declined during the postwar years. And it is important to remember that even for the crimes in which female and male rates have become more similar during the postwar period, men are still greatly overrepresented. Thus, in the 1990s, compared to women, men were being arrested for committing about ten times more murders, robberies, burglaries, and auto thefts.

Age and Crime

The idea that changes in street crime rates are due to the total number of young people available at different points in time has been one of the most common explanations of crime in postwar America. The appeal of this explanation to researchers is obvious because it offers the possibility of forecasting future crime trends based on a variable that can be reliably measured—the evolving age structure of society. Indeed, arrest statistics from both the United States[32] and countries throughout the world[33] consistently show that a disproportionate amount of street crime is committed by youthful offenders. According to UCR statistics for 1994, persons under the age of twenty-five were arrested for 42 to 72 percent of the seven street crimes examined here.[34] For these reasons, Travis Hirschi and Michael Gottfredson argue that the relationship between age and crime is invariant across cultures, historical periods, and types of crime.[35]

As noted earlier, age adds an interesting dimension to our efforts to explain postwar crime trends because it represents a demographic category that could have contributed to postwar crime trends both in the supply of young people and in the changing frequency of crime committed by young people. Indeed, the media frequently confuse these two processes. Thus, a story about crime problems in *Time* magazine warns of the "teenage time bomb," based on projections showing that the supply of teenage "superpredators" is going to increase rapidly in the early part of the twenty-first century.[36] But these predictions are based on the alarm that has been produced by juvenile crime committed during a period in which the total proportion of young people has been relatively low. Thus, the juvenile violent crime boom of the 1990s seems to be related to changes in the motivation of youthful offenders, but the fear for juvenile crime in the future is based on projections about the expected total population of youthful offenders.

Many researchers during the postwar period have attempted to determine how the total proportion of young people in a society affects the crime rate. Depending on the specific crime types studied and the years included, researchers have estimated that anywhere from 12 to 58 percent of changes in postwar American crime rates are due to the proportion of young people in the population.[37]

In the most exhaustive review of the empirical evidence to date, Thomas Marvell and Carlisle Moody examined statistical studies that looked at the effects of age structure on rates of common types of street crime.[38] Just their review of longitudinal studies (which are the most relevant for the arguments being made here) of street crimes shows that thirty-four of fifty-seven analyses summarized (59.6 percent) found a reliable tendency for crime to increase along with increases in the proportion of youth. Only six of the studies found evidence for crime declines in relation to a rising proportion of young people. For murders, the most commonly studied of the street crimes, nineteen of twenty-four analyses examined found that murders increased significantly along with increases in the proportion of young persons. Moreover, sixteen of these nineteen studies found a "strong" or "moderate" relationship between age and murder rates whereas only one of the negative relationship studies did. Thus, there is fairly strong support for the conclusion that the supply of young persons affects crime rates, although the magnitude of this effect seems to vary considerably.

Postwar trends in the proportion of young Americans age fourteen to twenty-four are shown in Figure 3.2.[39] To allow comparisons, I also include robbery rates. Robbery provides a useful basis for comparison because, compared to other violent street crimes (i.e., murder, rape, aggravated assault), it is the crime most likely to be perpetrated by strangers.[40] As we saw earlier, however, high correlations for trends among all the street crimes means that within certain limits any of the street crimes would serve fairly well for comparison purposes.

As shown in Figure 3.2, the proportion of young Americans declined following World War II, reaching a postwar low of just under 14 percent in 1955. The proportion of young people then increased gradually, topping out at 20.7 percent in 1977. The proportion of young people then declined again, still falling slightly as this book was being prepared. These changes mean that the proportion of Americans age fourteen to twenty-four was about the same in 1996 as it was in 1960. U.S. Census Bureau projections show that the proportion of young people will increase again in the twenty-first century, with the proportion of persons age fourteen to seventeen reaching a peak in 2005 and those age eighteen to twenty-four reaching a peak in 2010.[41]

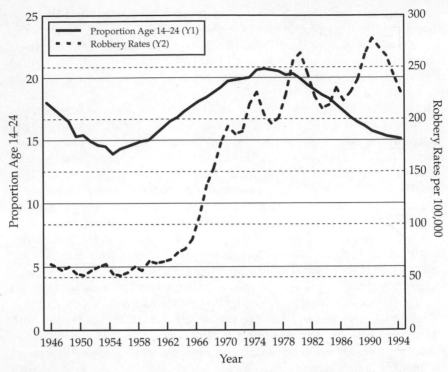

FIGURE 3.2   Proportion of Young People and Robbery Rates, 1946–1995
SOURCE: U.S. Bureau of the Census, *Statistical Abstract of the United States, 1996* (Washington, DC: Government Printing Office, 1996), p. 15.

Figure 3.2 shows a clear connection between the proportion of young people and robbery rates. As with robbery rates, the proportion of the young was relatively low following World War II, began to escalate in the 1960s, reached its peak in the early 1970s, and then declined somewhat into the 1980s and 1990s. But beyond the general contours, there are also obvious differences. Most notable, robbery rates changed more rapidly and generally a few years before or after changes in the proportion of young people. The proportion of young people did not increase as soon or as rapidly as robbery rates in the 1960s; nor did it fluctuate as widely as robbery rates did after the 1960s.

A related issue is whether the propensity to commit crime changed for young Americans during the postwar period. The idea of a "youth culture" was widely publicized during the 1960s and 1970s as the proportion of young Americans climbed. One possibility is that as this youth culture gained influence, the proportion of crimes committed by the young might

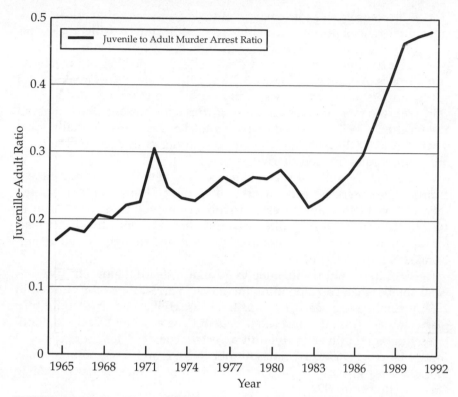

FIGURE 3.3 Ratio of Juvenile (Less Than 18) to Adult Arrest Rates for Murder, 1965–1992
SOURCE: U.S. Federal Bureau of Investigation, *Age-Specific and Race-Specific Arrest Rates for Selected Offenses 1965–1992* (Washington, DC: Government Printing Office, December 1993), pp. 158–159.

also have increased. In addition to their growing numbers, did young Americans commit a higher proportion of street crime during the postwar period?

The FBI recently published annual arrest rates for juveniles under the age of eighteen and adults over eighteen for the years 1965 to 1992.[42] By calculating the ratio of juvenile to adult arrests for these crimes, I was able to control for the fluctuating supply of juveniles over time. I estimated these ratios for all seven street crimes. In general, the ratio of juvenile to adult arrests increased for the four violent crimes (murder, robbery, rape, and aggravated assault) but declined for the three property crimes (burglary, theft, and automobile theft). The biggest changes by far were for murder rates, shown in Figure 3.3.

As with comparisons for female and male arrest rates previously, I calculated the ratio of juvenile to adult arrests here. Thus, a rising line means that juveniles are responsible for an increasing proportion of arrests whereas a declining line shows a diminishing proportion of juvenile to adult arrests. As shown in Figure 3.3, the ratio of arrests for juvenile and adult murders increased fairly steadily during the years included.

In 1965, the ratio of juvenile to adult arrests for murder stood at about 17 percent. By 1992, it topped 48 percent. Changes were especially great from 1983 to 1992—a period when adult murder rates declined but juvenile murder rates trended sharply upward.

Changes in the ratio of juvenile to adult arrests for the other violent crimes were much less pronounced, although still important. Thus, the ratio of juvenile to adult arrests for robbery moved from 76 percent in 1965 to 103 percent in 1992. Similarly, the ratio of juvenile to adult arrests for rape moved from 47 percent to 55 percent, and for aggravated assault from 32 percent to 50 percent.

Declines in the ratio of juvenile to adult arrests for the property crimes were smaller than corresponding increases in arrest ratios for murder. In 1965, juveniles were nearly twice as likely as adults to be arrested for burglary. By 1992, this ratio had fallen to about one and one-half times. Similarly, the ratio of juvenile to adult arrests for larceny fell from over 2.2 times higher in 1965 to 1.2 times higher in 1992, and the ratio of juvenile to adult arrests for motor vehicle theft fell from 3 times higher in 1965 to 2.3 times higher in 1992.

In short, there is evidence that the ratio of juvenile to adult rates of violent street crime, especially murder, increased during the postwar years. But there is also evidence that the ratio of juvenile to adult rates of property crimes declined during the postwar years.

Conclusions: Gender, Age, and Crime

In sum, excluding rape cases, the proportion of street crime arrests of women increased for four of the other six street crimes being examined here. The main exceptions were for aggravated assaults and murders: The proportion of aggravated assaults committed by women showed no clear trend, and murder arrests involving women actually declined substantially from the 1960s to the 1990s. Even for crimes in which the proportion of females arrested increased, however, males remained heavily overrepresented.

The evidence is pretty clear that the number of young Americans did have an effect on street crime rates during the postwar years—although the size of the effect is often exaggerated. The evidence for an increasing juvenile propensity to commit crime is more complex. In general, the ratio of juvenile to adult arrests increased for violent crimes and declined for property crimes. Still, the fact that the biggest changes in the ratio of juvenile to adult crime was for murder is troublesome. The growing ratio of juvenile to adult murder during the postwar period really tracks two trends. First, juvenile arrest rates for murder increased steadily throughout much of the postwar period but especially in the late 1980s and early 1990s. At the same time, adult murder rates declined a bit after reaching a peak in the mid-1970s.

Thus, young people contributed to the postwar American crime boom most clearly by the simple fact that there were more of them during much of the boom period. But they also contributed to violent crime rates, especially murder, through a growing propensity to commit crime.

Race and Crime in Postwar America

I argued previously that an understanding of street crime trends in postwar America requires that we explain the dramatic increase in African American crime rates. One way to illustrate the importance of African Americans for postwar crime trends is to imagine that the United States is not one but two countries—an African American nation composed of about 33 million inhabitants and a non–African American nation composed of about 230 million others. This imaginary African American nation would have a slightly larger population than Canada. But it would have an estimated murder rate over nineteen times higher than that of Canada and seventy-four times higher than that of Japan.[43]

An imaginary nation excluding African Americans would also greatly change total U.S. crime rates. I noted earlier that most Americans take it as a matter of course that the United States has crime rates that far exceed those of other industrialized nations. We have already seen that these claims are frequently exaggerated. But in addition, such claims leave out the fact that a large part of the difference between U.S. crime rates and rates from other nations is due to street crimes committed by African Americans.[44] If we exclude African Americans from national estimates, U.S. murder rates (5.0) would be much closer to those of Finland (3.1) and Italy (2.8).[45] U.S. robbery rates (124.2) would be lower than those of France (125.4) and Spain (166.4) and only slightly higher than those of Canada (104.20).[46] Given the disproportionate number of street crimes committed by African Americans, efforts to understand street crime trends in postwar America depend crucially on understanding African American trends.

Arrest Trends by Race and Ethnicity

I have already discussed some of the general difficulties in using the UCR to track crime trends by the offender's race and other characteristics. Estimating crime rates for ethnic and racial groups other than whites and African Americans raises additional limitations and difficulties.[47] First, the UCR does not allow an analysis of Hispanic arrest rates over time. The UCR included the category "Mexican" in 1934 but dropped it in 1941. Aside from Mexican Americans, Hispanic groups have never been separately distinguished. Second, because the UCR system is based on the voluntary compliance of police agencies, and because American Indians fall under the jurisdiction of a complex combination of native and nonnative legal entities, UCR trend data for American Indians are also problematic.[48] Third, before 1970, the UCR included categories for "Chinese," "Japanese," and "all others." After 1970, it replaced Chinese and Japanese with "Asian" and dropped the "other" category. Because many Asians were included as "others" prior to 1970, a practical consequence of these changes is that there is no obvious way of constructing trend data for Asian Americans in the postwar period based on UCR arrest statistics.

Finally, population statistics included in UCR annual reports are not broken down by race. Given that the UCR purports to be a national data set, we could still use total U.S. population by race to estimate arrest rates. The proportion of the population included in UCR reports has also changed over time, however. This is not a trivial point, especially for earlier years. For example, in 1946 UCR data were based on an estimated reporting population of 62 million at a time when the total U.S. resident population was 141 million (44 percent). By 1990, UCR reports were based on an estimated reporting population of 205 million at a time when the total U.S. resident population was 248 million (83 percent). The biggest change in UCR coverage came in 1960, when the population covered by the UCR jumped from 56 to 109 million. For total proportion of U.S. citizens included in UCR reports, the most successful year was 1985, when 86 percent of the total U.S. population was included in jurisdictions that reported complete UCR data.[49]

For these reasons, trend analysis for groups other than African Americans and whites is probably not defensible. And even with the analysis of African Americans and whites, we should proceed cautiously—especially with data from before 1960. Before turning to an examination of African American and white crime trends, I consider first what recent cross-sectional data based on UCR arrest statistics tells us about crime differences by race and ethnicity.

Cross-Sectional Arrest Rates by Race

Table 3.1 shows total arrests by offender's race for the seven street crimes tracked by the UCR.[50] In 1990, the FBI obtained complete UCR data from 10,676 police agencies, representing 204,563,914 residents—an estimated 82 percent of all U.S. residents.

Several features of Table 3.1 are worth noting. First, observe that crime rates by race follow the same sequence for all seven crimes. For each, African American rates are highest, followed by Native American, white, and Asian American.[51] These are not trivial differences. African American robbery rates are more than eleven times higher than white rates. They are more than twenty-one times higher than Asian American rates. Second, differences by race vary by crime type. The largest discrepancy by race is for robbery, in which African Americans account for 62 percent of total arrests, followed by murder (55 percent), rape (44 percent), aggravated assault and motor vehicle theft (33 percent), and burglary and theft (31 percent). In general, differences by race are greatest for violent street crimes (robbery, murder, rape) and least for property crimes involving no direct contact between victim and offender (burglary, theft).

Even allowing for the fact that UCR crime data are imperfect, these patterns raise some serious issues for policymakers. Assuming the accuracy of our worst fears about police racism and discrimination, it seems difficult to believe that police discrimination accounts for differences of the magnitude shown in Table 3.1. In fact, if police racism is at work, it might also be expected to sometimes take the form of underpolicing neighborhoods with large minority concentrations—which should result in *lower* official crime rates for racial minorities. Finally, if the results shown are mostly determined by police discrimination, we might expect this discrimination to also affect arrest rates for other racial minorities—Native Americans and Asian Americans. Research on the varying quality of different types of UCR data raises further issues.

Both critics[52] and supporters[53] of UCR data agree that its quality is generally highest for more serious crimes. This is because citizens are more likely to report more serious crimes to police and police are more likely to make arrests for more serious crimes. Following this reasoning, discriminatory behavior on the part of police might be expected to be most pronounced for the less serious crimes, in which arrests generally allow greater police discretion. Table 3.1 shows, however, that the greatest differences by race are precisely for the most serious and presumably most reliably measured crimes (murder, robbery) and lowest for the least serious and presumably least reliably measured crimes (theft, burglary).

TABLE 3.1 UCR Arrest Rates by Race, United States, 1990

Race	Murder		Rape		Robbery		Agg. Assault		Burglary		Theft		Motor Vehicle Theft	
	N	R	N	R	N	R	N	R	N	R	N	R	N	R
African American	10,645	43.2	14,384	58.3	91,164	369.6	154,838	627.8	110,181	446.7	402,526	1,632.1	71,029	287.9
Native American	133	8.3	249	15.5	486	30.2	3,588	222.7	3,054	189.5	13,460	835.4	1,279	79.4
White	8,312	5.1	18,033	10.9	53,755	32.7	235,126	143.2	242,508	147.7	866,426	527.5	105,018	63.9
Asian American1	66	2.8	276	4.6	1,039	17.4	2,865	47.9	2,961	49.5	15,381	257.1	2,321	38.8
Total	19,256	9.4	32,942	16.1	146,444	71.6	396,417	193.8	358,704	175.4	1,297,793	634.4	179,647	87.8

NOTE: $R = [a/(up)] \times 100,000$, where R is the rate, a is the number of UCR arrests by race, u is the population of reporting UCR jurisdictions, and p is the proportion of the total U.S. resident population by race.

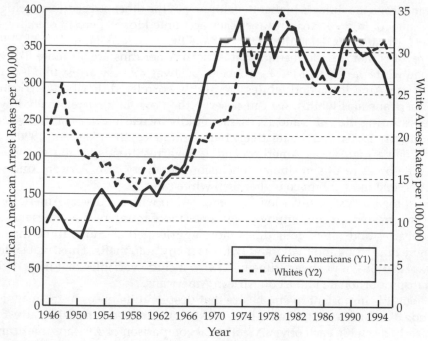

FIGURE 3.4   Robbery Arrest Rates by Race, 1946–1996
SOURCE: U.S. Federal Bureau of Investigation, *Crime in the United States,* annual reports for 1946 to 1996 (Washington, DC: Government Printing Office).

In short, even accepting the limitations of UCR arrest data, the differences in Table 3.1 are so large and exhibit patterns that are so distinctive that the hypothesis of no difference by race seems unlikely. In the next section, I turn to longitudinal comparisons for African Americans and whites—the only two groups for which trend comparisons for the postwar period are feasible.

Postwar Trends in African American and White Crime

To compare crime trends for African Americans and whites in the postwar period, I collected separate data on total arrests by race for the seven UCR index crimes described in Chapter 2. Figure 3.4 compares African American and white robbery arrest trends from 1946 to 1996. To facilitate comparisons, the figures include separate scales for African Americans (on the left side) and whites (on the right side).

Robbery provides an interesting basis for comparing African American and white crime rates because the proportion of robbery arrests of African

Americans to whites is higher than for any of the other street crimes being examined. In 1996, African Americans accounted for 58 percent of all robbery arrests reported to the UCR. Perhaps the most striking feature of Figure 3.4 is that despite the fact that African Americans are far more likely than whites to be arrested for robbery, postwar robbery arrest trends for African Americans and whites are highly correlated. For both African Americans and whites, we can observe the now familiar relatively low rates during the 1940s and 1950s, the rapidly increasing rates of the 1960s and early 1970s, and the relatively high flat rates of the 1980s and 1990s.

Comparing African American and white arrest trends for the six other UCR crimes results in similar conclusions. In every case, African American crime rates are much higher than white rates.

At their *lowest* postwar levels, compared to whites, African Americans were arrested for committing seven times more murders, five times more robberies and rapes, four times more aggravated assaults, three times more burglaries and thefts, and twice as many auto thefts. Thus, plausible explanations of postwar crime must also include variables that have had a disproportionate impact on African Americans.

But it is important to emphasize that despite differences in the magnitude of total arrests, the trend lines of African American and white arrests clearly resemble each other. A statistical comparison of African American and white rates for each of the seven crimes confirmed that the two tracked strongly together.[54] Like white crime trends, African American crime trends changed rapidly during the postwar years. African American trends also follow similar broad patterns. These patterns imply that the forces that shaped white postwar crime trends also played a major part in shaping African American postwar crime trends.

Comparing African American and white arrest rates throughout the postwar period shows a clear ordering of offenses, similar to the one already observed in Table 3.1. Compared to white rates, African American rates are generally highest for violent crimes (robbery, murder, rape, aggravated assault) and lowest for property crimes (burglary, theft, motor vehicle theft). Thus, in 1995, the ratio of African American to white arrests was more than 10 to 1 for robbery, 8 to 1 for murder, 5 to 1 for rape, 4 to 1 for aggravated assault and motor vehicle theft, and 3 to 1 for theft and burglary.[55]

Offender Characteristics and Postwar Crime Trends

As previously noted, because the UCR reports aggregate rates for individual characteristics there is no straightforward way of estimating rates for specific combinations of race, gender, and age. The NCVS, however,

TABLE 3.2   Estimated Annual Rates of Robberies per 100,000 Potential
Offenders in Each Population Subgroup, NCVS National Data, 1973–1977

Race, Gender, and Age of Offender	Robberies per 100,000 Population	Ratio of Young (18 to 20) Black Males to Others
African American Males		
18 to 20	35,030	—
12 to 17	16,663	2.1
21 or Older	7,000	5.0
White Males		
18 to 20	2,245	15.6
12 to 17	1,203	29.1
21 or Older	463	75.7
African American Females		
18 to 20	703	49.8
12 to 17	1,307	26.8
21 or Older	164	213.6
White Females		
18 to 20	71	493.4
12 to 17	212	165.2
21 or Older	33	1,061.5

SOURCE: Based on Michael J. Hindelang, "Variations in Sex-Race-Age-Specific
Incidence Rates of Offending," *American Sociological Review* (1981) 46:461–474,
468.

does allow such estimates. In a 1981 article, the criminologist Michael
Hindelang used NCVS data to estimate annual offending rates per
100,000 potential offenders for specific demographic categories based on
the offender's race, gender, and age. Table 3.2 is based on Hindelang's estimates for robberies reported to the NCVS from 1973 to 1977—just after
the largest increases in postwar crime rates had taken place. I use young
(eighteen to twenty years of age) African American men as a reference
group because they had the highest robbery rates of any demographic
group included. The ratios on the right-hand side of Table 3.2 show total
robbery rates of young black men compared to each of the other population subgroups.

We should consider two points before interpreting the data in this
table. First, I chose to illustrate this example with robbery rates, which as
we saw earlier are the most lopsided by race of all the street crimes examined here. And, second, because these data are based on victim reports,
they do not reflect total numbers of offenders but rather total numbers of
offenses. Thus, a single offender may be counted more than once.

Even with these caveats, the differences in Table 3.2 are remarkable. The most extreme comparison shows that black men age eighteen to twenty had annual robbery rates that were more than 1,000 times higher than white women age twenty-one or older. Comparing black men to white men of different age groups yields ratios ranging from fifteen to more than seventy-five times higher. Note also that estimated robbery rates for black women are considerably higher than comparable rates for white women. For example, the estimated robbery rate for black women age eighteen to twenty is about ten times higher than the rate for white women of the same age group. In fact, black women age twelve to seventeen have higher estimated robbery rates than white men of the same age group.

Although Hindelang generally found the greatest differences for robbery estimates, estimates for rape, aggravated and simple assault, and personal larceny show the same general patterns between race, gender, and age subgroups. Thus, compared to estimated offending rates for young (eighteen- to twenty-year-old) white men, estimated rates of offending for young (eighteen- to twenty-year-old) black men were six times higher for rapes, three times higher for assaults, and twenty-one times higher for personal larcenies. Also, as with robbery comparisons, black women age twelve to seventeen had higher estimated assault rates than white men in the same age group. Black women in both the twelve-to-seventeen and eighteen-to-twenty age groups had higher estimated rates of personal larceny than white men in the same age groups.

In Chapter 2, I concluded that a convincing explanation of postwar crime trends for the United States had to explain rapid, highly correlated changes in street crime rates, especially increases from the early 1960s to the mid-1970s. My review of crime trends by age, gender, and race provides three additional requirements. First, a plausible explanation of postwar crime should account for the increasing proportion of crimes (with the exception of murder and aggravated assault) committed by women during the postwar period. Analysis of gender, age, and race subgroups provides the additional insight that a disproportionate part of this increase is likely due to the changing behavior of young, black women.

Second, a plausible explanation of postwar crime trends must explain why the young committed a disproportionate number of street crimes throughout the postwar period. Hindelang's data suggest that in particular we should be concerned with explaining the behavior of young, black men.

Finally, a plausible explanation of postwar crime trends must account for the fact that street crime rates have been substantially higher for African Americans than whites throughout the postwar period.

● ● ●

Having described the contours of postwar U.S. street crime trends by gender, age, and race, I am now ready to turn to the task of explaining these trends. My strategy is to begin by considering the implications of the crime trends for the most common explanations of postwar crime. In the next chapter, I consider several of these common explanations and how well they fit what we now know about crime trends.

four

Evaluating Common Explanations of Crime

The central conservative truth is that it is culture, not politics that determines the success of a society. The central liberal truth is that politics can change a culture and save it from itself.
—**Daniel Patrick Moynihan,** *Family and Nation,* **1986**[1]

Based on the previous three chapters, we now know quite a bit about the requirements for a plausible explanation of the observed changes in postwar American crime rates. We know that we are looking for an explanation that can account for the sometimes rapidly changing crime trends. We know that we are looking for a historically contingent explanation that is congruent with steady low crime rates in the early postwar period, rapidly increasing crime rates in the middle postwar period, and steady high crime rates in the late postwar period. And we know that a convincing explanation of postwar crime must be able to account for street crime rates of the young, of men, and of African Americans that are consistently higher than rates for older individuals, women, and whites—especially in the high crime increase decades of the 1960s and 1970s.

Common Theories of Crime

We can begin by dividing the most influential explanations of crime into two broad traditions, depending on whether they emphasize individual-level or social explanations. Models of individual responsibility can in turn be divided into two main categories: biological and psychological perspectives and rational choice perspectives.

Individual-Level Perspectives

Biological and Psychological Perspectives. Biological and psychological theories have a long history in criminology, encompassing an extremely varied group of crime explanations. The pioneering work of the Italian physician Cesare Lombroso in the nineteenth century suggested that criminals were physically different from law-abiding citizens and that these differences were proof of the biological basis for criminal behavior.[2] In the century after Lombroso's work was first published, influential biological and psychological perspectives linked crime rates to feeblemindedness or low intelligence, chromosomal abnormalities, learning disabilities, biochemical imbalances, autonomic nervous system malfunctioning, and various personality disorders.[3] Typical of this work was a biological theory of crime advanced in the 1960s that proposed that men with an extra Y chromosome might have an elevated propensity to engage in crime.[4] Based on this work, researchers estimated that the frequency of XYY chromosomes is about 1 per 1,000 in the general population of males but about 1 to 2 percent (ten to twenty times larger) in the institutionalized male population.[5]

But the rapidity of change in postwar crime trends presented earlier raises obvious problems with biological and psychological perspectives such as these. Stated simply, if common crime is the result of slowly evolving biological characteristics or deep-seated psychological characteristics, how can it have doubled in only ten years (1960 to 1970) and tripled in twenty years (1960 to 1980)? Because changes in crime rates were even more rapid for some gender, age, and race subgroups, common biological and psychological explanations seem even more problematic here. Thus, in just fifteen years—from 1959 to 1974—African American arrest rates for robbery nearly tripled. How could biological or psychological characteristics of African Americans change so dramatically in such a short time frame? Although differences are not as great for changes in female crime rates during the postwar period, the changes observed raise similar issues for women.

Interestingly, biological and psychological theories have undergone major transformations in recent years that may yet provide insights into the kinds of rapid crime changes observed in the postwar United States. More recent research has moved away from strategies that examine the direct effects of such biological characteristics as an extra chromosome on criminal behavior and toward perspectives that emphasize instead a complex interplay between social, psychological, and biological processes. Thus, in a recent review for a national panel on preventing violence, Paul Frederic Brain notes that research linking hormones to crime is moving beyond "the highly simplistic view that hormones simply switch aggression on and off," to recognition of the importance of the interaction of hormones and environmental factors, social experience, and other biological factors in the generation of aggression and violence.[6]

Recent research by evolutionary biologists,[7] evolutionary psychologists[8] and biologically oriented sociologists[9] supports the conclusion that social factors may strongly affect biological and psychological characteristics that in turn increase or decrease the propensity for violence and crime. For example, in a recent study of over 4,000 adult men who were members of the armed forces, the sociologists Alan Booth and D. Wayne Osgood show that soldiers who had completed more years of schooling, who were more likely to attend meetings of clubs and other organizations, who had more job stability, and who were married all had lower testosterone levels. Testosterone levels and these measures of social integration were in turn related to levels of adult deviance.[10] Recent studies such as this one strongly suggest that biological and psychological effects are mediated by the social environment.

A related version of this argument is being advanced by evolutionary psychologists such as Martin Daly and Margo Wilson.[11] Daly and Wilson argue that all human beings have basically the same evolutionarily produced human nature. When confronted with varying environmental conditions, this human nature produces a predictable range of behavioral responses, including crime. For example, during evolution, men have competed for status to gain access to women. Thus, status has persistently contributed to reproductive success for men. Daly and Wilson point out that if certain types of violent behavior are in turn related to male status, then under the right environmental conditions, such violent behavior may have a "selection advantage."[12] This kind of argument uses human genetic characteristics as a way of understanding the potential impact that changing environmental conditions may have on violent behavior and crime.

Rational Choice Perspectives. Rational choice perspectives assume that human beings have relatively stable preferences or interests, that they weigh the benefits and costs of behavioral alternatives, and that they behave so as to maximize the ratio of benefits to costs.[13] This perspective emphasizes that certain crime control strategies have a predictable impact on crime by raising the costs of criminal behavior or the benefits of noncriminal alternatives.[14]

The main options for increasing the "costs" of criminal behavior in postwar America have involved greater support for the various components of the criminal justice system. Rational choice perspectives argue that criminal behavior will be less common when the severity and certainty of punishment are increased.[15] Although the evidence is far from perfect, longitudinal studies of postwar crime rates in America have generally confirmed that higher levels of punishment do reduce crime rates.[16]

Rational choice perspectives are also consistent with the idea that crime can be reduced by increasing the rewards of noncriminal behavior. Thus, researchers frequently argue that a wide range of social programs for the poor can reduce crime and delinquency rates by reducing discontent and economic stress.[17] Although far fewer researchers have examined connections between welfare spending and crime than relations between punishment and crime, there is some evidence for a connection in postwar America. For example, in an analysis of U.S. metropolitan areas in the 1970s, the sociologist James DeFronzo found that cities with higher levels of public assistance to poor families also have lower rates of homicide, rape, and burglary.[18] Similar conclusions are reported for cross-national comparative research on violence against children.[19]

Rational choice perspectives are appealing for explaining the rapidity of postwar crime changes—variables that should affect rational choice decisionmaking such as incarceration rates and welfare spending went through periods of rapid change during the postwar years. Moreover, rational choice perspectives are attractive for explaining both the rapid increase in crime during the middle postwar years and the more gradual crime declines in the late postwar years. But although valuable, rational choice perspectives do not seem to have had as much of an impact on crime as proponents would lead us to expect.

Rational choice perspectives on punishment undoubtedly scored their greatest American policy successes in the late postwar period when all forms of legal punishment in the United States reached unprecedented new heights. These historic increases in punishment have undoubtedly had an impact on crime rates. Yet, despite massive increases in the scope and severity of punishment, crime rates remain at much higher levels today than they were during the years of relatively low punishment in the early postwar period. Although connections between welfare spending and crime are probably more indirect, connections here too are weaker than might be expected from a purely rational choice perspective.

Rational choice predictions about the impact of punishment and welfare spending on crime rates seem even more problematic when applied to African American crime rates. Given the unprecedented rates of legal punishment experienced by African Americans in the 1980s and 1990s, rational choice perspectives would suggest major declines in African American street crime rates. But as we have already seen, African American street crime rates remain much higher than rates for other groups and much higher than African American crime rates during earlier periods.

Similarly, although welfare spending has disproportionately affected African Americans in the postwar period, African American crime rates have clearly not responded as much as might be expected.

Although recognizing the usefulness of these perspectives, many researchers point out that broad versions of rational choice perspectives make assumptions about human behavior that simply do not fit all individual cases. For example, the criminologist Charles Tittle points out that individuals frequently misperceive reality and act in ways that they may consider beneficial, even though their behavior might be perceived as irrational to a more objective observer.[20] Furthermore, Tittle argues, the costs and benefits of different actions vary from individual to individual and situation to situation. The sociologist Amitai Etzioni expresses these relationships more generally: "People typically do not render rational decisions. They brush their teeth but do not fasten their seat belts; they continue to smoke twenty years after the Surgeon General's report; they purchase costly, unsuitable life insurance and pay stock brokers for useless advice."[21]

Similarly, there is ample evidence that street criminals frequently operate in ways that seem irrational to a disinterested observer. Thus, they most often commit crimes close to their own homes; they frequently victimize people they know, who are presumably more likely to be able to identify them; and they often commit crimes while they are under the influence of drugs or alcohol and not performing as well as they might.[22] Others have pointed out that rational choice perspectives may work better in particular situations. For example, rational choice perspectives may be more relevant for instrumental crimes that result in immediate gains rather than for more expressive types of crime.[23]

A related criticism is that rational choice perspectives usually assume that people are motivated only by the desire for self-satisfaction and are little influenced by moral values.[24] Indeed, a good deal of criminology evidence contradicts this assumption. For example, in a survey conducted by the criminologists Harold Grasmick and Donald Green, respondents were asked if they had committed various crimes in the past and if they thought they would do so in the future.[25] Next, respondents were asked to estimate the chances that they would be arrested by the police if they committed each of these crimes. The researchers measured respondents' moral commitment by asking them to indicate how morally wrong they thought each crime was. The results showed that both deterrence reasoning and moral commitments affected the respondents' predispositions to commit crimes.

Etzioni also criticizes rational choice perspectives for assuming that individuals are free-standing agents who make their own independent choices, little influenced by the social collectivities to which they belong.[26]

This conclusion is contradicted by decades of social research demonstrating the importance of social organizations and cultures on criminal behavior.

But although the conception of the perfectly rational individual, operating with little concern for moral issues and uninfluenced by broader social pressures, is obviously overdrawn, a general emphasis on the ability of social systems to change the rewards and benefits of crime is nevertheless useful. In later chapters, I explore the effect of criminal justice punishments and welfare system rewards on postwar American crime rates.

Social Explanations

In contrast to individual explanations, social explanations look to society to explain crime. Five main themes characterize the most common of these explanations: stigmatization produced by criminal labeling, strain produced by economic stress and blocked opportunities, cultures rewarding crime and deviance, the declining effectiveness of social control, and the impact of criminogenic crime situations.

Labeling Theories. The hallmark of labeling theory is the assertion that crime is not an objective property of certain behavior but rather a definition constructed through social interaction. Labeling theorists draw heavily on symbolic interaction theory, especially as developed in the 1920s and 1930s by the sociologists Charles Cooley, W. I. Thomas, and George Herbert Mead. Symbolic interactionists contend that people develop images of themselves early in life through their interaction and communication with others. Symbols—words or gestures that signify ideas, persons, or things—are crucial in this process because they form the basis of human interaction. Language is the most important system of symbols. Symbolic interactionists argue that through language and other types of communication, people constantly change and reconstruct their images of themselves and others.

Labeling theory applies the insights of symbolic interactionism to the study of law and social control by focusing on the social interaction between alleged criminals and official agents making criminal allegations. Thus, it is primarily a theory of how people come to be identified as criminal or deviant and the consequences of these processes for those so labeled.

In his influential 1963 book on marijuana users, the sociologist Howard Becker argues, "Deviance is *not* a quality of the act the person commits, but rather a consequence of the application by others of rules and sanctions to an 'offender.'"[27] Becker and other labeling theorists argue that legal sanctions are not always or even usually applied when laws are broken, that many and perhaps most people who break the law are never identified, and that other people who do not break the law are nonetheless treated as criminals. Thus, the central theme of labeling theory is that law is not applied to suspects because of their criminal behavior but rather because of their differential power to resist labels.[28]

At its extreme, labeling theory implies that the crime statistics I presented earlier are little more than a record of stigmatization and discrimination against less powerful members of society—that they reflect not actual criminal behavior but rather the coercive power of governments to label the least powerful among us. Thus, the surest way to reduce crime is to furnish stronger legal and procedural safeguards for those defendants with the fewest resources: presumably, the poor, racial and ethnic minorities, and women. Viewed in this way, labeling theory would suggest that street crime rates should be highest when discrimination against the least powerful members of society is greatest.

Labeling theories run into obvious difficulties when applied to the crime trends presented earlier. If official crime rates are mostly the product of discrimination and differential treatment, then we must be willing to argue that compared to the 1940s, the 1990s were far more discriminatory toward less powerful social groups. But this argument is contradicted by civil rights gains of the 1960s and 1970s and by the subsequent rights revolutions for minorities, women, gays, the disabled, the elderly, and others. If official statistics are produced mostly by discriminatory treatment, we must explain why crime rates increased so dramatically during a period that by all accounts offered increased civil rights safeguards. And as with individual explanations, labeling theory seems especially problematic when applied to postwar crime trends for African Americans. If discriminatory treatment causes crime, then we must be willing to argue that African Americans are experiencing worse discrimination in the 1990s than they were in the 1940s and 1950s. We must also explain why African American crime rates seem to have escalated most rapidly at precisely the time that African Americans appear to have won some of the most important civil rights victories of the postwar period.

Labeling theory also runs into difficulties in explaining crime rates by gender. The most common labeling explanation of gender differences in crime is based on the idea that official bias grounded in paternalistic notions of "chivalry" accounts for the lopsided criminal justice processing outcomes for men and women.[29] But this argument is contradicted by evidence showing that, at least for some crimes, girls are more harshly treated than boys by the criminal justice system.[30] It also seems to be at odds with the fact that female rates for several types of street crime have been increasing at the same time that women seem to have made important advances in gaining equal treatment.

But despite difficulties with specific labeling predictions about the impact of discrimination and stereotyping on criminal justice processing outcomes, the symbolic interaction roots of labeling theory are important for the argument I develop here. If justifications for obeying rules and laws are socially constructed, we have a possible explanation for the rapid changes in crime rates actually observed during the postwar period. Under the right circumstances, social constructions should be capable of relatively rapid change. Moreover, symbolic interaction theory could be helpful for explaining the consistent differences found between African American and white crime rates in postwar America. Instead of arguing that crime rates are socially constructed and hence not real, however, I argue that it is the meaning, significance, and even possibility of committing crime that is socially constructed.

Strain Theories. Strain, breakdown, or social disorganization theories can be traced most directly to the French sociologist Emile Durkheim's assessment of the transition from traditional to modern society: A well-organized society integrates members into the whole, provides them with a sense of community, and offers them realistic goals and aspirations. When there is a breakdown in social organization, informal sources of social control—family, work, school, voluntary organizations—lose their ability to channel individuals into conventional behavior.[31] The resulting disorganization or "anomie" frees social actors to engage in a wide variety of antisocial behavior, including crime.[32]

The American sociologist Robert Merton applied these ideas specifically to the United States.[33] Merton argues that deviance and crime in the United States are produced by a social structure that bombards Americans with the goal of monetary success but does not equally distribute legitimate opportunities for attaining this goal.[34] In direct contrast to individual crime theories, Merton claims that criminal motivation does not result from the flaws, failures, or free choices of individuals. Instead, he argues, there is an exaggerated emphasis on the goal of monetary success in the United States coupled with weak support for the idea that only socially acceptable means should be pursued for achieving this goal. Merton's observation that "a cardinal American virtue, 'ambition,' promotes a cardinal American vice, 'deviant behavior,'" suggests that high crime rates are a standard feature of U.S. society because of an obsessive preoccupation with achieving the "American Dream."[35]

Strain theorists argue that legitimate opportunities to obtain financial success are not equally distributed throughout society. Instead, inequality in access to legitimate opportunities puts differential strain on individuals, depending on their economic background. Lower-class individuals face the greatest strain; upper-class individuals face the least. Children from poor families are taught to strive for economic success and to judge themselves against this standard. When they find that they are blocked from legitimately achieving this goal because they are excluded from the best schools, do not have the necessary connections to get a good job, and lack the cultural background to enter a middle-class lifestyle, many of them turn to crime. Thus, the criminologists Richard Cloward and Lloyd Ohlin argue, lower-class juveniles who fail to secure an adequate education have little chance of improving their circumstances and the resulting frustration leads them to crime.[36]

When tested against the crime trends reviewed earlier, strain explanations face several difficulties. To begin with, Merton's original formulation of strain theory suggests that strain is a more or less permanent feature of American society.[37] The inordinate emphasis in America on getting ahead at any cost explains why crime rates in the United States are so high compared to other Western democracies—now as in the past. The data presented in Chapter 2 show that crime rates in the postwar period have been anything but constant, however. If American society has always placed an inordinate emphasis on getting ahead and has always provided unequal access to this goal, we are faced with explaining the historically low crime rates of the 1940s and 1950s.

The strain theory argument that crime increases when individuals are blocked from full participation in economic opportunities also seems problematic when viewed against the rapid increases in crime rates during the middle postwar years. In fact, as we have seen, critics of liberal crime explanations were quick to point out that crime rates increased dramatically during the 1960s and early 1970s, a period of apparently rapid economic expansion and growth in the United States.[38] By contrast, crime rates were relatively stable during the 1980s, a period when the United States faced the greatest economic depression of the postwar period. Economic strain can be measured in many ways. One possibility that I explore later is that compared to absolute measures of economic stress, measures that emphasize economic inequality may be better predictors of postwar crime trends.

Strain theory perspectives that emphasize increased access to educational opportunity also seem problematic for the postwar years. In particular, access to education seems to have increased at about the same time as the postwar crime boom.

These problems with strain explanations are generally compounded when African American crime rates are considered. Compared to others, African Americans should face especially great "strains" because of their disadvantaged economic and social position. In fact, Merton recognized this possibility in his original formulation of anomie theory, arguing that African Americans face even greater economic stress than lower-class whites.[39] But if strain causes crime, we must explain why African American crime rates exhibited the largest increases at exactly the time—the 1960s and early 1970s—when African Americans appear to have made the greatest economic, social, and educational gains of the century.

Despite these difficulties, strain explanations of crime also have several characteristics that make them especially helpful for explaining the crime trends described earlier. First, Durkheim's original perspective underscores the basic role of legitimacy in maintaining social order. Agreement on fundamental rules and the essential fairness of the social order is critical to social organization. Without this agreement, a wide variety of antisocial behavior is more likely. I argue in the next chapter that part of the explanation for rapidly rising crime rates in the postwar period was a decline in the amount of trust Americans had in their political institutions.

Second, Merton's work in particular highlights the importance of economic institutions for predicting criminal behavior. And at the heart of Merton's anomie theory is the assumption that relative perceptions of deprivation—rather than absolute measures of economic well-being—are most closely linked to crime. I consider connections between economic change and crime rates in the chapters that follow.

Finally, Cloward and Ohlin's version of strain theory suggests that high crime rates are directly related to limitations surrounding "legitimate avenues" of access to "conventional goals," including education.[40] Although the impact of educational attainment on crime has been complex, educational institutions, like crime, changed rapidly during the postwar period. I argue later that expanding access to educational institutions helped reduce postwar street crime rates.

Cultural Deviance Theories. Cultural deviance theories argue that criminals are enmeshed in social systems that reward conformity for illegal rather than legal behavior. Thus, the individual criminal may actually be conforming, but to a set of rules that are at odds with the standards of the larger society. The most influential form of this argument is found in the pioneering work of the sociologist Edwin Sutherland, who argued that individuals learn to become criminal in the same way that they learn to play bridge or to speak German.[41] Thus, individuals may indeed commit acts that are criminal by the standards of some other group, say, middle-class citizens, but they do not commit acts that are criminal by their own standards—they simply have learned different standards from the criminal elements of society with which they have, through their own misfortune, had close contact.

The idea that crime is a learned response is appealing in that it can provide a mechanism to explain the relatively rapid changes in crime rates observed in postwar America—certainly learned behavior could be expected to change more rapidly than average intelligence or physiological characteristics. But cultural deviance views of street crime are not very helpful for explaining why there were such pronounced increases and decreases in criminal learning during different parts of the postwar period. If criminals learn criminal behavior the same way noncriminals learn acceptable behavior, we must explain why the amount of criminal learning increased so dramatically during the 1960s and 1970s and why it paused or declined in the 1990s.

Cultural deviance theories might have some special relevance for African American postwar crime experiences. Many researchers have relied on this perspective to explain the development of an inner-city African American "underclass."[42] The crime trends we have observed seem to be at odds, however, with interpretations that see the underclass as a deeply entrenched cultural system that produces high crime rates generation after generation.[43] Again, if African Americans share a highly stable culture that promotes crime, we must then explain how this culture resulted in especially rapid changes in African American crime rates. Moreover, cultural deviance theories do not seem to offer a ready explanation for the timing of African American crime rate increases. Again, we must explain what it was about black subcultures that explain the rapid increases in crime rates in the 1960s and the leveling off and decline of African American crime in the 1980s and 1990s.

Control Theories. Following especially the work of Emile Durkheim, control theorists argue that individuals are freed to commit crime when their ties to the conventional social order are weak or broken.[44] In the late 1800s, Durkheim concluded, "The more weakened the groups to which [the individual] belongs, the less he depends on them, the more he consequently depends only on himself and recognizes no other rules of conduct than what are founded on his private interests."[45] Building on Durkheim's conception of the social bond, the sociologist Travis Hirschi developed an influential social control theory that argues that delinquency and crime will be reduced for individuals with stronger attachments to others, greater commitment to conformity, and more involvement with and belief in law-abiding behavior.[46]

Like learning theories, social control explanations of crime seem to have merit for explaining the crime trends presented earlier. Most notable, the common social control argument that juveniles and young adults with strong attachments to their families[47] and schools[48] are less likely to engage in delinquency is well supported. And there is certainly much evidence to suggest that families and schools underwent considerable change in the United States during the 1960s and 1970s.[49] When considered in the context of the crime trends presented earlier, however, social control theories also leave some important questions unanswered. Assuming for a moment that crime is the result of a weakening of social bonds between individuals and their families, neighborhoods, and schools, we must still explain what changes in society caused this decline and we must explain why social bonds were weaker in the 1990s than in the 1950s.

The social control argument also seems to have some promise for explaining postwar African American crime trends. In fact, the argument that African American crime rates are directly linked to weakened family structures has been common throughout the postwar period. Thus, in his 1960s analysis of the African American family, Senator Daniel Patrick Moynihan, who was a congressional staff member at the time, argued that federal policy in the United States must increase the stability of African American families.[50] There is also much evidence to suggest that for African Americans living in inner cities, other important informal social control mechanisms, including integration into neighborhoods, school, and work, deteriorated during the postwar period.[51] Although these arguments are plausible, however, as with explanations aimed at the general population, social control explanations specific to African Americans do not explain why the weakening of social attachment to the family, schools, and the community occurred when it did.

One of the major contributions of both social learning and social control theories is their emphasis on families for controlling crime. I examine the connections between changes in family institutions and postwar crime trends in later chapters.

Situational Theories. A diverse group of sociological theories of crime emphasize the role of situations in facilitating crime.[52] For example, Lawrence Cohen and Marcus Felson's "routine activities" theory argues that crime is more likely when crime targets are more attractive, less well guarded, and more frequently exposed to motivated offenders.[53] These authors further assert that these situational elements have changed in the United States since World War II. For example, as Americans spend more of their time away from the home, opportunities for several types of street crime correspondingly increase. Cohen and Felson calculate a measure of time spent away from the home (they call it a "household activity ratio") by estimating the proportion of households that contain women working in the outside labor force or non–husband-and-wife living arrangements. They then demonstrate that as this ratio increased in the postwar United States there were significant increases in rates of homicide, robbery, rape, assault, and burglary. Similarly, they show that postwar property crime rates have been affected by such mundane variables as the total availability of automobiles and the lightness and portability of electronic gadgets.

The assertion of situational theorists that postwar crime trends are produced in large part by the relative supply of "capable guardians" and "suitable targets" seems promising in that these are variables that clearly can and did rapidly change. Moreover, situational theories have been important for expanding the focus of criminology beyond simple criminal motivation. For example, Cohen and Felson's concept of guardianship underscores the critical importance of informal social control in regulating criminal behavior.

But situational theories, like learning and social control theories, do not offer a ready explanation for the observed timing of observed changes in crime rates. For example, what was it about the 1960s that so reduced the effectiveness of guardianship or increased the "suitability" of targets? It seems unlikely that the situational variables identified by Cohen and Felson were not also changing when crime rates were low and constant in the 1940s and 1950s or relatively high and constant in the 1980s and 1990s. By concentrating on the supply of suitable crime situations, situational theorists end up treating all motivated offenders as equally motivated and all capable guardians as equally capable. I argue later that both the motivation of offenders to commit crime and society's effectiveness at guarding against it changed in important ways during the postwar period.

Toward an Explanation of Postwar American Crime Trends

In short, each of the crime explanations summarized here has strengths and weaknesses for explaining the street crime trends we have actually observed during the postwar period. Common biological and psychological explanations are problematic because crime rates changed too rapidly. Rational choice perspectives are not so much wrong as less right than we would expect. Thus, despite low levels of punishment in the 1940s and 1950s, crime rates remained low, whereas unprecedented levels of punishment in the 1980s and 1990s have had only modest effects on crime rates. Biological, psychological, and rational choice perspectives all seem especially problematic with regard to explaining rapidly changing African American crime trends.

Labeling theory's general emphasis on the socially constructed nature of crime definitions seems quite useful as a general framework for explaining the rapidity of change during the postwar period. But with the specific emphasis of labeling on the effects of biased and discriminatory criminal justice processing, the theory seems unable to explain why crime rates were low during the politically repressive 1950s and much higher following the major advances made in civil rights for disadvantaged groups after the 1960s.

The emphasis of strain theory on the perceived fairness of social institutions as well as access to economic and educational opportunities is helpful. Strain theories that argue that the United States is a criminogenic society because of its emphasis on monetary success are contradicted, however, by the enormous changes in crime trends during the postwar period. Strain theories are also contradicted by the fact that crime rates seem to have increased at one of the most prosperous times in U.S. history (the 1960s) but held stable or declined during one of the worst economic depressions of the postwar period (the early 1980s).

Cultural deviance and control theories may provide useful insights into the individual-level mechanisms by which crime rates developed but offer few concrete suggestions about why national crime rates fluctuated when they did. For example, if crime is learned behavior or if it increases in the absence of effective social controls, why did this learning and these controls change so dramatically in the early 1960s? And as with earlier perspectives, what explains the timing of African American crime trends?

Situational theories are important for moving criminology beyond a simplistic reliance on criminal motivation. Situational theories emphasize the importance of informal social control and surveillance in explaining crime rates. But situational theories seem unable to explain the crime surge of the 1960s or the decline in crime in more recent years.

In short, despite difficulties, I believe that these theoretical perspectives go a long way toward providing a framework for explaining postwar crime trends in the United States. To summarize, the emphasis of labeling theory on the social construction of human societies is useful for explaining how postwar crime rates changed so rapidly. Rational choice perspectives underscore the centrality of criminal justice and, to a lesser extent, welfare systems in regulating crime. Strain theories illustrate the fundamental importance of economic, political, and educational institutions for controlling crime. Cultural deviance theories emphasize the importance of socialization in reducing criminal motivation. Social control and situational theories emphasize the importance of informal social control systems in regulating crime. And cultural deviance and social control theories suggest the centrality of families to crime control.

• • •

I have tried to demonstrate in this chapter some of the major strengths and weaknesses of prior theories of crime for explaining the postwar crime trends I described in earlier chapters. In the next chapter, I build on these earlier theories by advancing my own explanation for street crime trends in the United States. The linchpin that links my arguments to these earlier theories of crime is the social institution.

five

Crime and Social Institutions

. . . we are moral beings only to the extent that we are social beings.
—**Emile Durkheim,** *Moral Education,* **1903**[1]

The most profound decisions about justice are not made by individuals as such, but by individuals thinking within and on behalf of institutions.
—**Mary Douglas,** *How Institutions Think,* **1986**[2]

Chapters 2 and 3 showed that a plausible explanation of postwar American crime trends must account for rapid change; for the distinctive crime patterns observed for the early, middle, and late postwar years; and for the high crime rates for men, the young, and African Americans. The review of prior theories in Chapter 4 provided a list of variables and concepts that seem promising, including the impact of economic and political variables and changes in the family and criminal justice, education, and social welfare policies. After I spent a good deal of time studying the crime trends and the common theories, I concluded that the single concept that best tied the various threads together was that of the social institution.

Social institutions begin to develop whenever the interpretation of routine human actions comes to be mutually shared.[3] Thus, the process of institutionalization starts as soon as two or more individuals reciprocally agree on a particular way of doing things and mutually reinforce this agreement.[4] For example, a wife and husband may reciprocally agree, or tacitly recognize, that the wife will henceforth sleep on the right side of the bed and the husband on the left. This territorial recognition may govern their behavior for years and one or the other partner may be upset when violations occur. When such couples travel, they may automatically gravitate to their familiar sides of unfamiliar beds. Although far more complex, the norms and roles associated with major social institutions like the family or the economy are ultimately based on the same kind of mutual, self-reinforcing agreements.

But I should hasten to point out a fundamental difference between the process of institutionalization that results in shared agreement about which side of the bed to sleep on versus the institutionalization resulting in long-term social institutions like the family and the economy. Although individuals play a major role in creating the thousands of small routines that shape their daily lives, institutions like the family and the economy exist prior to and outside of individual experiences. The family was there before specific individuals were born into it and it will presumably be there long after they die. The social theorists Peter Berger and Thomas Luckmann point out that this historical feature of traditional institutions like the family gives them a "character of objectivity."[5] In other words, these long-standing institutions confront individuals as separate from them—objective, undeniable, and real.

Institutions, then, are the patterned, mutually shared ways that people develop for living together.[6] These patterns include the norms, values, statuses, roles, and organizations that define and regulate human conduct. Institutions encompass proper, legitimate, and expected modes of behavior.[7] They are guides to how we should live and conduct our affairs, daily reminders of the conduct that we hold to be either acceptable or unacceptable.[8]

Because institutions channel human behavior into socially acceptable spheres, they are at the center of social life. In particular, institutions are critical for increasing predictability among societal members. This is because institutions provide a limited range of appropriate behavior whereas the range of inappropriate behavior is limitless. This role of institutions in increasing the predictability of everyday life has far-reaching implications. At the interpersonal level, strong institutions encourage the growth of trust.

Trust increases predictability by allowing individuals to act based on their perception that others are likely to perform particular actions in expected ways.[9] For example, predictability allows an automobile driver to proceed forward when a traffic light turns green, based on the assumption that drivers coming from lateral directions will appropriately slow down and stop for a red traffic signal.

The street crimes examined here represent a particularly serious form of unpredictability and thus an important threat to trust. These connections can be seen clearly in the now-legendary low crime rates found in postwar Japan.[10] Low crime rates in Japan allow the Japanese, even in large cities, to feel comfortable being away from their homes, in public places, at night. They also allow individuals to show less concern about protecting their private property. Bicycles and other easy-to-steal items that are carefully guarded in many societies are frequently left unprotected in Japan. When crimes do occur, consistent public cooperation with the police and the legal system generally results in high clearance rates. Taken together, these characteristics make even urban Japan a relatively crime-free, mostly predictable place. This in turn fosters high levels of public trust, even among strangers.

At a societal level, predictability is closely related to what researchers call "social capital."[11] Just as physical capital refers to the tools and machinery necessary to engage in productive enterprises, social capital refers to the creation of opportunities and capabilities through socially structured relations between individuals acting in groups.[12] Although social capital is less tangible than physical capital, it is arguably more important.[13] Social capital accumulates in relationships of trust between individuals in a society.[14] Societies in which individuals follow the rules of social institutions and can assume that others will probably also follow the rules develop a fund of social capital. Again, crime can seriously undermine a society's social capital.

Institutions are arguably the most important of all human creations. They allow societies to endure over time as individuals are joined or replaced by new members. Thus, institutions serve the same purpose for humans as instincts do for other species: They channel our behavior into forms that help us satisfy basic collective and individual needs.[15] In fact, because humans have relatively underdeveloped instincts, we are especially dependent on institutions for our survival. Instead of relying on messages genetically transmitted from the past, humans are guided in large part by institutional rules that are passed from one generation to the next.[16]

This dependence on institutions has important implications for all human behavior, including crime. On the one hand, it allows institutions to change rapidly in response to environmental changes. But because institutions are little more than socially constructed agreements, they are fragile compared to the nearly automatic, "hard-wired" responses produced by biological instincts.

Institutional Legitimacy, Change, and Crime

I argued earlier that to fit postwar trends a plausible explanation of crime must be capable of accounting for rapid change and must generally support the timing of trends and the established subgroup differences in rates of offending. The sociologist Talcott Parsons, who defined institutions as the "structurally stable element of social systems," is undoubtedly the most influential proponent of the view that institutions evolve slowly and steadily.[17] But this view of institutions as changing only slowly has generated much disagreement.[18] For example, in an influential 1961 article, the sociologist Dennis Wrong criticized the Parsonian view of institutions as presenting an "oversocialized" conception of human behavior.[19] Wrong was critical of an image of people as near automatons, perfectly socialized, overwhelmingly sensitive to the opinions of others, and nearly always obedient to consensually developed norms and values. Wrong argued that an exaggerated emphasis on social responsibility presents an inaccurate model for human behavior because it nearly eliminates the possibility for conflict and change.[20]

In fact, one of the great advantages of institutions over biologically rooted instincts is that institutions provide the flexibility necessary to meet the demands of a changing environment.[21] Thus, under the right circumstances, institutions could be expected to change rapidly enough to account for the fluctuations observed in postwar American crime rates.

At the same time, this is not to argue against the substantial stability and persistence of social institutions over time. Individuals clearly do not act just as they please. The sociologist Mark Granovetter nicely captures this view of human action as midway between total determination and ungoverned spontaneity: "Actors do not behave or decide as atoms outside a social context, nor do they adhere slavishly to a script written for them by the particular intersection of social categories that they happen to occupy."[22]

To fit the street crime rates presented earlier, changes in social institutions must also be able to account for the high crime rates of men, the young, and African Americans. In each case, I think they can. In all Western industrial societies, and certainly in the postwar United States, behavioral options for women provided by institutions are more constrained than those for men. Whether we consider work, dating, marriage, or recreation, compared to men, women have had fewer behavioral choices. There is no reason to think that gender-based institutional constraints on crime are any different than they are for other behavior. To the extent that women gained greater freedom from institutional controls during the postwar period, the observed modest increases in most forms of female street crime would be expected.

Indeed, the "power-control" theory of delinquency developed by the sociologist John Hagan is largely consistent with this interpretation.[23] Hagan argues that because, compared to sons, daughters are disproportionately the objects of strong parental social control, they grow up with less of a preference for deviance and risk taking.[24] Hagan concludes that the greater likelihood of delinquency among boys than girls and, later, the greater chance of crime among men than women is primarily a product of the stricter patterns of parental control imposed on daughters compared to sons.[25]

As we saw in Chapter 3, age contributed to the postwar American crime boom because the supply of young people increased and, at least for violent crimes, because the proportion of crimes committed by young people increased. Each generation must face the ongoing requirements of socializing, regulating, and protecting a new generation of young people. Having a large number of young people places greater demands on all social institutions with regard to satisfying these requirements. In fact, the challenges might have been even greater in postwar America because of the unique rise of a "youth culture." My assumption is that, in general, compared to older people, younger people are likely to be less well integrated with, connected to, and controlled by social institutions.

Given the history of African Americans, it certainly seems defensible to argue that, compared to other Americans, they are likely to have had weaker ties to social institutions throughout the postwar period. It also seems plausible to argue that these already weak ties would have been further frayed during the postwar period by confrontations arising out of the civil rights movement and the Vietnam War, by continuing economic disadvantages, and by the wholesale disintegration of the African American family.

Institutional Legitimacy

As I argued earlier, behavioral options for nonhuman animals are severely restricted by their instincts. Consider the basic differences in two types of encounters: a cat confronting a mouse and a group of college students meeting a professor for the first class of the semester.[26] When a cat sees a mouse, there is presumably something in the cat's congenital equipment that tells it what to do. It gives chase without reflection. We might even be concerned about the health of a cat that was uninterested in pursuing mice.

In some ways, the behavior of students on the first day of the semester is equally predictable. Professors can walk into new classrooms filled mostly with strangers that they have never met; begin talking; and have the entire group of strangers take seats, finish their conversations, pull out papers and pens, and begin taking notes. Superficially at least, the institutional rules of college classrooms function in very much the same way that the cat's genetic makeup does.

But even though the behavior of students and a professor meeting for the first time is substantially constrained by institutionalized rules, this behavior always has comparatively more leeway than that of cats and mice. There are many circumstances that can jeopardize the predictable behavior of professors and students on the first day of the semester that are not problematic for cats and mice—protests over tuition increases, concern about policies of the university, a bomb scare, or perhaps doubts about the competence or ethical suitability of a particular professor. In general, institutions are most effective at regulating human conduct when they are perceived or assumed by participants to be legitimate.

The sociological pioneer Max Weber defined legitimate power (or "authority") as "the probability that certain commands (or all commands) from a given source will be obeyed by a given group of persons"[27] and added that a basic criterion of legitimate power is a "minimum of voluntary submission."[28] All societies face the ongoing problem of legitimizing their rules and laws and transmitting this legitimacy to succeeding generations. Legitimation is the process of explaining and justifying the rules to new societal members.[29]

Many theorists who have thought about the nature of legitimacy have argued that individuals follow social rules mostly because they believe in their moral validity.[30] And indeed, this is often the case. Weber points out, however, that individuals may also attribute legitimacy to rules for other reasons, including their fear of punishment, their respect for tradition, their religious beliefs, or simple expediency.[31] Most often, the legitimacy of rules is simply taken for granted; the rules are so deeply ingrained that they are never even consciously challenged.[32]

The success of institutions in regulating behavior depends of course on the specific type of behavior in question. Behavior in any society can be placed on a continuum ranging from acts that are universally condemned to acts the wrongfulness of which generates a great deal of disagreement. In general, institutions are most effective in regulating behavior for which there is widespread agreement. The street crimes I examine in this book represent behavior that is almost universally condemned by society. We do not find, for example, organized social groups campaigning for the legalization of murder or robbery.[33] Thus, the commission of these crimes are clear instances in which institutions failed to properly channel the behavior of one or more societal members.

How Institutions Regulate Crime

Before I move on, it would be useful to consider how institutions actually regulate crime. In general, institutions limit crime in three interrelated ways: by reducing individual motivation to commit crime, by supplying effective controls to curb criminal behavior, and by providing individuals with protection against the criminal behavior of others.

Because institutions are primarily responsible for teaching children what is right and what is wrong, what is appropriate and what is inappropriate behavior, they have a direct linkage to our motivation to commit crime. The most obvious institutional connection here is the family. Through socialization, families teach children the differences between appropriate and inappropriate conduct.[34] These lessons are of course enforced by social sanctions, both positive and negative. For example, families may reinforce acceptable behavior with praise, love, and support and punish unacceptable behavior with criticism, ostracism, or expulsion. But the impact of institutions on reducing criminal motivation is not limited to families. Thus, economic and political institutions may reduce individual motivation to commit crime simply by convincing individuals that they are fair, just, and worthy of respect.

Institutions also regulate behavior by providing social control. As used here, social control refers to all the mechanisms aimed at compelling individuals to adhere to institutional rules.[35] Thus, social control is extremely broad and far-reaching in its effects.[36] It tells us what crime is, how we are to respond to it, and what is right and wrong about it.

Social control can be further divided into informal and formal sources.[37] Informal social control refers to sanctions imposed by individuals or groups who are not acting directly on behalf of official political agencies and includes especially the influence of family, friends, and neighborhood residents. By contrast, formal social control refers to the control of individuals acting on behalf of official legal and political agencies, including especially police, judges, prison guards, and prosecutors.

Researchers have long recognized that informal social control is usually more effective than formal control. Over two centuries ago, the social philosopher Jeremy Bentham noted that fear of detection prevents crime in large part because of its consequences for "reputation and the desire for amity."[38] In other words, formal sanctions generally deter criminals because they are enforced in everyday life by informal sanctions. This means that societies with little crime are nearly always those with effective informal social control.[39] The sociologist John Braithwaite describes these societies as those "where people do not mind their own business, where tolerance of deviance has definite limits, where communities prefer to handle their own crime problems rather than hand them over to professionals."[40]

This description should make it clear that formal social control is likely to be far less effective in the absence of smoothly functioning informal social control. Indeed, as the effectiveness of informal social control erodes, citizens fearful of the lawlessness of others often demand increasingly punitive formal social control.[41] But as the political scientist Robert Putnam argues in his research on civil society in Italy, this strategy is usually lost in a vicious circle because "heavy-handed government . . . is itself enfeebled by the uncivic social context . . . [whereas] light-touch government is effortlessly stronger because it can count on more willing cooperation and self-enforcement among its citizenry."[42]

Not only is formal social control generally less effective than informal social control, it is also considerably more expensive. Family and friends are rarely paid for exercising social control over their loved ones, whereas police, courts, litigation, and prisons all require significant sums of money.[43] The social commentator Francis Fukuyama points out that societies that are forced to rely increasingly on formal social control to govern themselves are imposing a kind of tax on all forms of social activities.[44] Instead of ensuring civility through institutions that are based on informal ties of respect and affection (like families), these societies increasingly rely on buying formal social control through more lawyers, police, and prison guards.

The sociologist Mark Granovetter uses the term "embeddedness" to describe the social relations that link individuals to institutions and thereby regulate their behavior.[45] Embeddedness provides a useful metaphor for how social control works. What keeps individuals from smashing windows and grabbing the new electronic equipment they desire but cannot afford? Most individuals are embedded in a complex web of social connections that either make them think long and hard before making such a move or simply provide enough surveillance to make such a move difficult. For most people, the first social hurdles to crime are informal: the potential embarrassment they will face when their misdeeds become known to their families—spouse, children, parents, and other relatives. Beyond the family, there is the shame associated with those with whom they work or attend school, members of their church or military company, civic or fraternal organizations to which they belong, and so on. Finally, in addition to all of these informal sources of social control, there is the formal legal system itself, with its threats of arrest, legal processing, and punishment. Most individuals, then, are embedded in social networks that usually serve to channel their behavior into noncriminal paths.

In addition to regulating the motivation to commit crime and surrounding individuals with social controls, institutions can also reduce crime by directly protecting individuals from criminal victimization. Thus, families, communities, businesses, and schools can play an important role in guarding their individual members from the criminal behavior of others. Likewise, legal institutions in society, especially the police, are justified in large part by their ability to protect citizens from crime.

In general, then, institutions suppress crime by enmeshing individuals in social systems that reduce their motivation to commit crime, by increasing the effectiveness of those who are informally or formally expected to regulate their criminal behavior, and by protecting individuals from the criminal behavior of others. In a smoothly functioning society, these elements are inextricably related. Thus, individuals who are well socialized in effect serve as their own social control agents. Strong social control reduces motivation and the need for protection; weak motivation makes social control and protection less important; strong guardianship may compensate in part for high levels of motivation and ineffective social control. Succinctly stated, as institutions lose their ability to regulate their members, more individuals are more motivated to behave as they please, less successfully controlled by others for behaving as they please, and less effective in protecting institutional members from others who behave as they please.

Most often, people follow institutional rules effortlessly and without much (if any) thought, simply because the rules represent the right things to do—as when students automatically realize that on the first day of class they are expected to take a seat, stop talking among themselves, and take notes. But as the legitimacy of institutions declines, correct behavior does not happen as effortlessly.[46]

Individuals in societies with institutions that have less legitimacy feel freer to break group rules than individuals in societies with stronger institutions. Moreover, individuals in low-legitimacy societies are likely to have less contact with others who struggle to keep them obeying the rules or protect them from the rule breaking of others. In short, as the hold institutions have over individuals declines, institutional effectiveness in controlling crime is correspondingly weakened.

Crime and Social Institutions

If we think of institutions as nothing more than shared rules that regulate our conduct in recurrent situations, we may conclude that there are thousands (or even millions) of institutions in any given society. But obviously, some institutions are more important than others for controlling criminal behavior. I concentrate in this book on three social institutions that have been among the most frequently linked to crime by policymakers and researchers in the past: political, economic, and familial.

I refer to these three institutions here as "traditional" in the very limited sense that all three are long-established mechanisms for regulating crime. I argue that these three institutions have been especially important in explaining the historically low crime rates enjoyed by the United States in the early postwar period, the rapid increase in crime in the middle postwar period, and the stabilization of crime rates in the late postwar period. In subsequent sections, I contrast these three institutions with more recent institutional developments with relevance to crime control.

The development of political, economic, and family institutions is not entirely accidental. Just as instincts allow other animals to provide for their basic needs, these three institutions have developed and survived in part because they satisfy fundamental human needs.[47] Political institutions are primarily responsible for mobilizing and distributing resources for collective goals. They include the entire governmental apparatus: the legislature, the judiciary, the military establishment, and the administrative agencies that implement governmental decisions. Political institutions have direct responsibility for crime control and the lawful resolution of conflicts.[48] They are also responsible for maintaining social order, providing channels for resolving conflicts, and protecting citizens from foreign invasion.

Economic institutions are responsible for societal adaptation to the environment.[49] Economic institutions include those organized around the production and distribution of goods and services.[50] The economy is responsible for satisfying the basic material requirements for human survival: food, clothing, and shelter. Economic institutions also include a stratification system that ranks individuals in a social hierarchy of rewards and responsibilities.

For centuries, families in human societies have been chiefly responsible for the socialization of children. The sociologist James Coleman describes family institutions as "primordial" because, unlike other social institutions, they are based in part on a social organization that develops through birth and blood ties.[51] In addition, the family has traditionally had primary responsibility for regulating the sexual activity of its members, caring for and nurturing children, and seeing to the needs of the infirm and the elderly.[52]

I maintain that crime rates in postwar America have been strongly influenced by the declining legitimacy of political, economic, and family institutions. But of course, these three institutions vary a great deal in their history, scope, and exact connections to crime. I argue later that the declining legitimacy of political institutions is due mostly to a rise in political distrust, linked especially to a series of social movements and protests beginning in the 1960s. The declining legitimacy of economic institutions is due especially to increases in economic inequality and inflation. And the decline in the legitimacy of family institutions is a product of a postwar rebellion against the two-parent, male-dominated family, buttressed in part by a radical transformation of the economy. In the next three sections, I consider in more detail the specific links between postwar American crime rates and each of these three traditional institutions.

Political Institutions and Crime

Because political institutions in most societies are officially responsible for the control of crime, they have a special primacy in efforts to explain it. I argue that connections between political institutions and crime in the postwar United States are most directly linked to the trust Americans have had in their political system.[53] Growing distrust in political institutions in America threatened their legitimacy, increasing the motivation of individuals to commit crime and reducing the effectiveness of social control mechanisms.[54]

A large and diverse criminological research literature supports the conclusion that people who believe more strongly in the basic legitimacy or fairness of laws are less likely to violate them.[55] There is a good deal of disagreement among researchers, however, about the extent to which the legitimacy of political institutions is in turn related to this belief in the importance of complying with laws. The most effective arguments against such a connection have been made by resource mobilization theorists,[56] who argue that collective political action is clearly distinguished from crime by both the motives of participants and the degree of organization necessary.[57] Proponents argue that crime, unlike collective political action, is largely amoral and requires little in the way of organization to sustain it. Offenders are not striking out against an unjust system or righting wrongs when they commit crime. Rather, criminal motives are limited to the immediate short-term gains provided by the act itself.[58]

I disagree with the view that crime is unrelated to the legitimacy of political institutions for two main reasons. First, as I show in the next chapter, there is much evidence to suggest that the motives of offenders in committing crime vary a great deal and that crime often does in fact have a moral dimension. Both interviews[59] and ethnographic studies of street crime[60] suggest that offenders frequently select targets and justify their behavior on moral or ethical grounds.

Second, as I argued earlier, crime rates in a society are determined not only by the motivation of offenders but also by the effectiveness of social control and guardianship. Social control efforts in particular are likely to be closely related to the legitimacy of political institutions. When members of a society begin to doubt the fairness of their political institutions, even if they do not themselves violate laws, they become less enthusiastic agents for the social control of others. Parents, families, and neighborhoods do less to defend rules and respond less harshly to rule violations. Formal punishment by the legal system is less threatening and carries less of a stigma when it is applied. Social controls of every type are weakened by political institutions that lose their legitimacy.

At the end of World War II, the United States entered a period in which its citizens reported unprecedented levels of trust in the honesty, fairness, and integrity of American political institutions. There was widespread support for the war effort; high levels of respect for politicians and judges; and enough popular support to carry General Dwight D. Eisenhower, a military hero, into the presidency in 1952. But this trust began to erode substantially in the late 1950s and early 1960s. The civil rights movement led the way by exposing long-standing racial injustices in American society. Further erosion accompanied the divisive war in Vietnam, a series of widely publicized political scandals, and the rights based revolution that followed in the wake of the civil rights movement. Moreover, because political institutions are chiefly responsible for crime control, rising crime rates themselves no doubt further undermined political legitimacy. By the 1990s, there was evidence that the level of public trust in political institutions had stabilized, but at a much lower level than in the early postwar period. I argue that the declining legitimacy of political institutions in the postwar period was directly related to rising street crime rates.

Economic Institutions and Crime

Declining economic legitimacy can be expected to increase street crime rates in two main ways: by increasing the motivation of potential offenders to commit crime and by reducing the effectiveness of social control aimed at crime prevention and punishment. Perhaps the most obvious connection between economic legitimacy and criminal motivation is captured by the prosaic observation that compared to the more well-to-do those with less property and wealth simply have more to gain by committing crime. A large number of studies confirm that compared to the wealthy the less economically advantaged are more likely to commit street crimes of every type.[61]

As reviewed earlier, the idea that economic deprivation increases criminal motivation is also central to strain theories. The sociologist Robert Merton argues that individual behavior is strongly influenced by the intersection of the goals individuals in a given society are taught to value and the means to these goals that each society puts at their disposal.[62] The conditions for strain are present when the poor are constantly informed through social contacts and the media of the aspirations they should value but at the same time are blocked from legitimately satisfying these aspirations. Merton argues that some individuals who want to be financially successful but lack access to the legitimate means to become so simply shortcut the system by turning to crime.

Several other influential explanations of crime are closely related. For example, the sociologist Albert Cohen argues that economic stress experienced by inner-city juveniles leads to a loss of self-esteem, which in turn results in increasing rates of juvenile delinquency and crime.[63] Similarly, Richard Cloward and Lloyd Ohlin argue that an economic system that blocks some juveniles from legitimate participation produces a sense of injustice in these juveniles, resulting in higher crime rates.[64] In fact, a large body of research confirms that compared to nonoffenders criminal offenders consistently report feeling that their economic opportunities are severely limited.[65]

Although most criminology research on the link between economic legitimacy and crime has focused on the impact of legitimacy on the offender's motivation, the declining legitimacy of economic institutions may also reduce the effectiveness of informal and formal social control. Those who believe that economic institutions are unfair or unjust might be reasonably expected to have less interest in helping to control or regulate the criminal behavior of others.

I argue that the legitimacy of economic institutions in the postwar United States was weakened directly by the growing strains the economy imposed on Americans. These strains were increasingly shaped by global economic trends. At the end of World War II, the United States entered an era of unprecedented economic prosperity. The war jolted the U.S. economy out of a devastating depression and matched the undamaged industrial plants of the United States against the war-torn factories of Europe and Japan. America became a supermarket to the world.

The economic picture had changed considerably by the 1970s. Economic inequality grew substantially, inflation reached new heights, corporate downsizing resulted in thousands of closures and firings, and companies increasingly "outsourced" high-paying industrial jobs to lower-wage nations. The resulting economic stress and uncertainty reduced the legitimacy of economic institutions, thereby increasing individual motivation to commit crime and reducing the effectiveness of social control in preventing crime and apprehending and punishing criminals. As we shall see later, however, economic effects on crime in postwar America have been complex; although some common economic indicators such as inequality and inflation have had relatively consistent effects on crime, others, such as unemployment and average income, have been more erratic.

Economic institutions may also be related to the selective increases in crime rates for young Americans and African Americans. The income gap between older and younger persons increased substantially from the early postwar to the late postwar period.[66] Rising Social Security benefits and increased pension coverage lifted a large share of the elderly from the bottom of the economic distribution. By contrast, children moved in the opposite direction, and at the end of the twentieth century they are more likely than at any other time during the postwar period to occupy the lowest income levels.[67] Although the postwar period witnessed the tremendous expansion and growth of a relatively affluent black middle class, there is also disturbing evidence as the century draws to a close that many African Americans are being left behind by these economic improvements.[68] Recent survey data show that compared to whites African

Americans are considerably more likely to link crime and other social problems directly to the economy.[69]

Family Institutions and Crime

Like political and economic institutions, family institutions can reduce crime by regulating the motivation of offenders and providing effective social control. In addition, the family can play a special role in protecting its members from the criminal activity of others. Throughout human history, families have been the primary institution for passing social rules and values from one generation to the next.[70] In fact, there is evidence that the nuclear family has become increasingly important in child rearing in industrialized nations during the twentieth century, as the importance of extended families, church groups, and community members in raising children has diminished.[71] With few exceptions, children have more frequent and longer contacts with family members than with others, and family contacts are generally earlier and more emotionally intense than other contacts. The family has long been the major social institution for teaching children right from wrong, instilling moral values, and emphasizing the importance of law-abiding behavior. This socialization role of families means that they are critical for training children to respect and abide by criminal laws.

Families also control crime by directly regulating the behavior of their members. Families may limit the delinquent behavior of their children by restricting their activities, by maintaining actual physical surveillance over them, and by knowing their whereabouts when they are out of sight.[72] But perhaps even more important, families often control the behavior of children simply by commanding their love and respect. A good deal of research confirms that children who care about their family are more likely to avoid behavior that they know may result in shame, embarrassment, or inconvenience for family members.[73]

Families are also an important crime-reducing agent through the guardianship that they provide their members. Thus, families may reduce the criminal victimization of family members by protecting them from property crimes such as burglary and theft and by shielding them from the potential physical harm of unwanted suitors and would-be molesters, muggers, and rapists.[74]

Even as parents in America assumed an ever-expanding share of the moral and economic burdens for their children's social development and success as adults,[75] there were major declines in the legitimacy of the traditional two-parent, male-dominated family. Two related processes were especially important. The first was a growing challenge to the traditional form of the family.[76] As the feminist movement gained momentum in the

1960s, women and many men increasingly came to regard the traditional two-parent family as a bastion of male dominance.[77] Occurring almost simultaneously and related in complex ways was a growing movement toward greater sexual freedom and experimentation outside of marriage. In response to these two developments came an explosion of alternatives to traditional family living arrangements.

Although it is important not to overstate the homogeneity of the American family directly following World War II,[78] the aggregate changes were nevertheless substantial. In 1946, less than a third of women were in the paid labor force, divorce rates were low, and only 11 percent of American households contained individuals with no family connections. After the 1960s, rates of divorce, children born to unmarried parents, and single-parent families rapidly increased and the total number of Americans living entirely outside of families skyrocketed.

Revolutionary changes in the economy also contributed substantially to the declining legitimacy of the traditional American family. The economist Shirley Burggraf notes that in the past 200 years the United States has had a series of three successive economies.[79] In the "frontier" economy, women were largely dependent on men for both economic and physical survival. Staying alive in this economy required physical activities such as hunting, farming, and fighting that men had long dominated. In the "industrial" economy, which was in full bloom at the conclusion of World War II, it became possible for women to support themselves, albeit at relatively low economic levels, in caretaking, clerical, retail, and processing jobs. Women remained dependent on men in the industrial economy for earning better wages, however.

In the "postindustrial" economy that has steadily emerged after World War II, job success is increasingly based on knowledge, information, and service skills and has less direct connection to physical strength. Although this transformation is far from complete, the developing postindustrial economy increasingly depends on tasks at which women are as naturally adept as men.

Taken together, these and other related economic changes have led to a major "depopulation" of American homes during the postwar period. The steady movement of men away from agricultural labor at home to positions in the paid labor force, which had already begun in earnest during the industrial revolution, continued to gain momentum during the postwar period. Simultaneously, women joined the paid labor force in record numbers during the postwar years. Finally, the amount of time children and young adults spend in schools continued to accelerate. Changes in the extent of male agricultural employment, female labor force participation, and schooling have totally restructured the American family. No matter how we look at it, the average American man, woman, and child spent considerably less time in households that contained other family members at the end of the postwar period than at its beginning.

If economic changes affected the legitimacy of traditional families, changes in family institutions have also had major effects on the legitimacy of economic institutions. In particular, the rapid increase in the proportion of children living in female-headed families has been closely associated with substantial postwar increases in poverty among children. Changes in the form of families have also encouraged economic polarization. Both the proportion of families with no earners and families with two earners greatly increased during the postwar period.[80] No-earner families have risen along with increases in female-headed families and rising retirement rates. The growth of two-earner families has coincided with the rapid increase in female labor force participation.

In short, the institutionalized model of a two-parent family with a husband working for pay and a wife running the household became far less common in America during the postwar period. These changes have been complex and can be measured in a variety of ways. All, however, lead to the same general conclusion: During the postwar period, the legitimacy of the traditional family declined enormously. Moreover, the new forms of family and nonfamily living that increasingly replaced it have thus far not developed the same levels of legitimacy that the traditional family enjoyed during the early postwar period. I argue that these changes in the family increased crime rates by reducing the effectiveness of socialization, social control, and guardianship.

New Institutional Reactions

Of course, societies facing new challenges do not necessarily sit idly by as traditional institutional arrangements falter. Certainly crime is a problem that has generated a wide variety of institutional responses in postwar America.[81] As political, economic, and family institutions lost legitimacy, Americans greatly expanded their support for other social institutions that were promoted in part as crime reduction mechanisms. The most important of these new or expanded institutional commitments during the postwar period have been criminal justice, education, and welfare institutions.

Although criminal justice institutions have obviously been a part of American efforts to control crime throughout U.S. history, the size and scope of criminal justice institutions grew enormously in postwar America. As the legitimacy of political institutions declined, the United States relied increasingly on formal criminal justice institutions to maintain law and order. Directly following World War II, Americans spent only $255 a year (in inflation-adjusted dollars) on all levels of federal, state, and local law enforcement. They spent a little over $100 a year at all governmental levels for corrections. By the early 1990s, per capita spending on police had increased sevenfold and per capita spending on corrections had increased nearly twelvefold.

Similarly, as the legitimacy of traditional family institutions continued to decline, Americans relied increasingly on educational institutions to perform responsibilities that were once performed by families. Moreover, the age of those attending educational institutions expanded greatly from a relatively narrow range of children from about six to seventeen years of age to encompass much younger children and older juveniles and young adults. As children spend a greater proportion of their childhood and adolescence in schools, there are increasing pressures on schools to transmit basic cultural standards to children as well as to control and protect them.

Although much less extensive than either criminal justice or educational institutions, welfare institutions in the United States also grew enormously during the postwar period. Total public spending at the local, state, and national levels on welfare (in inflation-adjusted dollars) increased tenfold from 1948 to 1992.[82] Welfare institutions were justified primarily as reducing economic stress, but many observers have pointed out that their ameliorative effects have also been aimed at least in part at reducing crime.[83]

An Institutional Model of Postwar Crime Rates in America

I have summarized these rather complicated relationships between social institutions and crime in Figure 5.1. The rectangular box on the left-hand side of Figure 5.1 reiterates my predictions about declining institutional legitimacy. Political legitimacy in postwar America was threatened especially by a rising distrust of political institutions and by several highly organized and frequently violent social movements. Economic legitimacy was challenged most directly by rising economic inequality and inflation. Family legitimacy declined in response to a series of ideological challenges to its traditional male-dominated form as well as radical economic changes that increasingly pulled men, women, and children out of households.

Declining political, economic, and family legitimacy increased crime by both increasing the motivation of individuals to commit crime and reducing the effectiveness of informal and formal social control. In addition, the decline in traditional family institutions made them less effective in protecting their own members.

The rectangular box on the right-hand side of Figure 5.1 shows the three main institutional responses to declining legitimacy and increasing crime rates: criminal justice, education, and welfare. In general, these three institutions decrease crime by reducing the motivation of would-be offenders and by increasing the effectiveness of social control. In addi-

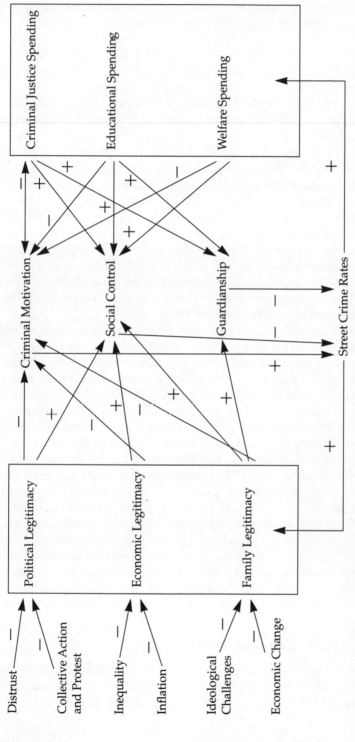

FIGURE 5.1 Institutional Change, Legitimacy, and Postwar Street Crime Rates

tion, criminal justice and, to a lesser extent, educational institutions can reduce crime by providing some level of protection to citizens.

Figure 5.1 also shows effects leading from crime back to the three traditional and three newer social institutions. These connections are especially clear for political legitimacy. Because citizens look directly to political institutions to control crime, rapidly rising crime rates provide additional justification for declining trust in political institutions. Compared to political institutions and crime, the connections between economic and family institutions and crime are less obviously reciprocal. Still, there is evidence that rapidly increasing crime rates can affect economic and family institutions. In particular, rising crime rates influence economic conditions by raising the costs of crime control and by discouraging business investments.[84] Similarly, rising crime rates and rates of punishment affect family structure by changing patterns of courtship, marriage, and family functioning.[85]

Crime rates in postwar America also had obvious reciprocal effects on criminal justice, education, and welfare institutions. As crime rates increased, Americans responded by spending more on all three of these social institutions. But as we shall see later, the mix of support for the three institutions varied a good deal over time.

Figure 5.1 should make it clear that sorting out the effects on crime of traditional institutions and more recent institutional initiatives is complicated by the fact that their effects are often interrelated. For example, West European nations seem to have avoided some of the crime-generating forces of declines in traditional social institutions in the postwar years by greatly increasing their spending on social welfare.[86] Similarly, the United States countered major changes in traditional institutions in part by massive increases in spending on criminal justice and education.

Although my main focus in this book is on three institutions that have traditionally been important in regulating crime and three more recent institutional responses to crime, there are no doubt other social institutions that affected postwar American crime rates. For example, religion, neighborhood and community organizations, voluntary associations, and media and mass communication have all been suggested as important determinants of postwar crime trends.[87] Although I by no means claim that the six institutions examined here exhaust the possibilities for institutional effects on crime, I argue that these six institutions have been especially influential in producing the crime trends observed in postwar America.

The Timing of Postwar Institutional Changes

Now that we have considered trends in both postwar crime rates and levels of institutional legitimacy, it would be useful to summarize the historical interaction between crime rates and institutions during the postwar

Early Postwar
High Legitimacy of Traditional Institutions → Low, Stable Crime Rates

Middle Postwar
Declining Legitimacy of Traditional → Rapidly Rising Crime
  Institutions   Rates

Late Postwar
New Institutional Responses; Stabilization → Stable or Declining Crime
  of Traditional Institutions   Rates

FIGURE 5.2   Longitudinal Relationships Between Institutional Legitimacy and Street Crime in Postwar America

period. Figure 5.2 presents a general overview of the timing of changes in these institutions and crime rates.

Figure 5.2 shows relationships between institutions and crime for the three periods identified in previous chapters. As we have seen, the early postwar period was characterized by low, stable crime rates. I argued earlier that these crime rates were directly related to the legitimacy of traditional institutions. In particular, crime rates were held down by high levels of trust in political institutions, low levels of economic inequality and stress, and the highly institutionalized form of the traditional male-dominated family. The legitimacy of these traditional institutions began to decline in the late 1950s and radically declined in the 1960s and early 1970s. I argue that these changes triggered the street crime wave of the 1960s and 1970s.

American society responded to the institutional legitimacy crisis in part by increasing its support for education, welfare, and criminal justice institutions, especially during and after the middle postwar years. By the late postwar period, these initiatives began to put downward pressure on crime rates. Moreover, the legitimacy of political, economic, and family institutions had stabilized, albeit at low levels compared to the early postwar period. By the 1990s, crime rates had flattened and even begun to decline a bit.

I have purposely portrayed the time periods listed in Figure 5.2 broadly. Such a depiction is appropriate because the timing of reactions to crime varied by institution and the timing of crime stabilization varied by crime type. In general, support for educational and welfare institutions increased earliest, followed by increased funding for more punitive forms of criminal justice. These patterns probably reflect the fact that support for educational and welfare institutions were affected by many concerns besides controlling crime. It seems highly likely that spending on education and, to a lesser extent, welfare institutions would have increased in the postwar period even without rising crime rates as a justification.

●   ●   ●

Having described a general model of how changes in six major social institutions were related to postwar American crime rates, I am now prepared to consider more specifically the relationships between each of these institutions and crime trends. I examine the three traditional institutions first before turning to the more recent institutional responses to declining legitimacy and increasing crime rates. In the next chapter, I evaluate postwar connections between crime and political institutions. My specific concern here is to determine the extent to which street crime rates were affected by changing levels of trust Americans had in their political institutions during the postwar period.

six

Crime and American Political Institutions

In the long run, this nation cannot have it both ways: either it will carry through a firm commitment to massive and widespread political and social reform, or it will become a society of garrison cities where order is enforced with less and less concern for due process of law and the consent of the governed.

—Jerome Skolnick, *The Politics of Protest*, 1969[1]

What is clear is that a society perceived to be unjust will earn no loyalty or commitment from its citizens. Such a society is doomed, in the end, to destroy itself.

—Charles Handy, *The Age of Paradox*, 1994[2]

. . . crime in the last analysis is a form of rebellion.

—Elvin H. Powell, "Crime as a Function of Anomie," 1966[3]

During the late evening hours of June 4, 1944, General Dwight D. Eisenhower, Supreme Commander of the Allied Expeditionary Forces, made the final decision to begin the D day invasion of the beaches of Normandy.[4] Operation Overlord, the Allied invasion of German-occupied France, was unprecedented in its scope. In a single day, 175,000 soldiers and their equipment, including 50,000 tanks, armored bulldozers, and motorcycles, were transported across sixty to a hundred miles of open water and landed on a hostile shore against fierce enemy resistance.[5] They were either carried or supported by 5,333 battleships, landing ships, and other craft and by nearly 11,000 bombers and fighter planes.[6] In twenty-four hours, nearly 5,000 soldiers lost their lives and thousands more were wounded.[7]

Military operations, along with legislatures, criminal and civil justice systems, and the administrative agencies that implement governmental decisions, can all be included under the general heading of political institutions. Imagine the level of trust in political institutions that was necessary to organize and execute the D day invasion. And yet, memoirs and eyewitness accounts show that most of the young Americans who risked their lives said little about the possibility that their government could be acting deceptively when it sent them to the beaches of Normandy in the predawn hours of June 6, 1944.[8] In fact, as we have already seen, institutions operate most efficiently when their legitimacy is automatic, unquestioned, taken for granted.

The major role of political institutions in societies is to mobilize people to get things done. This of course goes much more smoothly when individuals voluntarily cooperate with institutional goals. Most of the young men who took part in the D day invasion went willingly into battle. In fact, it is hard to imagine staging an event like the D day invasion without a substantial amount of voluntary compliance. As the historian Stephen Ambrose observes, for all the industrial capacity, organizational planning, and military preparation that went into D day, in the end its success came down to the independent efforts of "a bunch of eighteen-to-twenty-eight-year olds."[9]

In this chapter, I explore the relationship between crime trends and the legitimacy Americans bestowed on their political institutions during the postwar period. My main purpose is to examine the possibility that declining legitimacy of political institutions was associated with the postwar crime boom. I argued earlier that a decline in the legitimacy of political institutions can increase individual motivation to commit crime and can reduce the effectiveness of informal and formal social control in preventing crime. At the same time, rising crime rates can further erode the legitimacy of political institutions.

Political Institutions and Crime

The thinking of U.S. policymakers and researchers about the relationship between political legitimacy and crime went through a fundamental change during the postwar period. Prior to the 1960s, most researchers assumed that measures of political legitimacy such as protests, riots, and other types of collective political action naturally increased along with crime rates. As discussed in Chapter 4, these perspectives were variously referred to as "strain," "anomie," or "social disorganization" theories. Regardless of the specific title employed, all of these related theories assumed that crime and collective political action in a society are positively related because both flow from some form of underlying social breakdown or crisis.[10]

Social breakdown perspectives can be traced most directly to Emile Durkheim's arguments that well-organized societies integrate members into the whole by providing them with a sense of community and offering them realistic goals and aspirations.[11] But when there is a breakdown in social organization, social institutions lose their ability to channel individuals into conventional behavior. The distinguishing feature of this breakdown is the declining legitimacy of social norms. Thus, Robert Merton concludes, "When a high degree of anomie has set in, the rules once governing conduct have lost their savor and their force. Above all else, they are deprived of legitimacy."[12] As a result, individuals are freer to engage in a wide variety of antisocial behavior, including crime, protest, and civil disobedience.[13]

But after the mid-1960s, this view of the association between political legitimacy and crime was increasingly discredited. The most articulate of these challenges came from resource mobilization theorists,[14] who argued that protests and other forms of collective political action were different from crime because political action requires both access to resources and the development of a well-defined organizational structure.[15] Thus, the sociologist Anthony Oberschall concludes, "Collective action is not anomic tension release, but purposive and political."[16] Because protests and crime have different requirements, resource mobilization theorists reason that perspectives that assume that both arise from similar social forces are incorrect.

Although producing a less unified and cohesive set of theoretical expectations than social breakdown or resource mobilization theorists, some researchers claim that under the right circumstances challenges to political legitimacy might actually reduce crime. At least two versions of this argument can be identified. A "safety valve" model holds that if declining political legitimacy is translated into marches, protests, and other forms of collective action, these reduce crime by offering alternative outlets for dissatisfaction. An example of this thinking is provided by Frederic Solomon and his colleagues, who argue that civil rights campaigns in the United States in the 1960s reduced African Americans' crime rates by providing more legitimate avenues for their anger and frustration.[17]

In a related argument, others have claimed that declining rates of protest and other types of collective action can increase crime by reducing the number of legitimate protest outlets. Thus, the French theorist George Rude argued that as populist agitation burned out in nineteenth-century Europe the lower classes responded by committing more crime.[18] The sociologist Donald Black makes a similar argument, pointing out that much crime is an effort to seek justice by those who are blocked from legitimate mechanisms of redress.[19]

Reassessing the Political Legitimacy-Crime Linkage

Although resource mobilization views have dominated recent thinking about political institutions and crime, the conclusion that crime and political legitimacy are unrelated may be premature. Resource mobilization theorists generally dismiss the possibility of a link between crime and political legitimacy because of their a priori assumption that crime, unlike collective action, has no moral dimension.[20] This view can be traced back to Karl Marx, who includes common criminals in the *Lumpenproletariat*, described as "the 'dangerous class,' the social scum, that passively rotting mass thrown off the lowest layers of the old society."[21]

The conclusion that crime has no moral dimension is also frequently supported by criminologists. For example, in a review of several different types of common crime, Michael Gottfredson and Travis Hirschi conclude that crimes like murder, robbery, and rape "have no larger purpose" beyond the immediate gains they provide.[22] They arrive at this conclusion by carefully examining evidence describing how street crimes are actually carried out. For example, prior research suggests that typical robberies involve offenders who are using alcohol or drugs at the time of the offense, have engaged in little or no planning, most often choose victims in areas close to where they live, and rarely realize any long-term financial gain as a result of the crime.[23] Thus, the authors reason that offenders are not committing crime to strike out at injustice or any other higher purpose. Rather, they conclude that common crimes are committed simply because they are easy, exciting, and provide immediate gratification.[24]

As I argued in Chapter 4, descriptions of crime such as the one given by Gottfredson and Hirschi are an important antidote to rational choice assumptions that criminal behavior invariably reflects rational decisionmaking. But the conclusion that because street crime is less than perfectly rational it is also devoid of moral choices does not necessarily follow. For example, I referred earlier to a survey by Grasmick and Green showing that respondents cited moral considerations as well as deterrence issues in describing their decisions about committing crime.[25] Similarly, the sociologist Donald Black shows that many crimes express deeply held grievances by one person or group against others.[26] Black points out that these offenders persist in seeing their criminal actions as just, and he argues that in such cases, although offenders may appear to be acting irrationally, they might more accurately be regarded as "martyrs."[27] Black describes "collective liability" as the practice of holding all people in a particular social category responsible for some past or current injustice and claims that the practice occurs in modern as well as in traditional societies.[28]

Ethnographic data on street crime offenders confirms that they frequently select targets and justify their behavior on moral or ethical grounds.[29] Thus, Elijah Anderson, in a study of urban offenders, concludes, "Many feel wronged by the system, and thus its rules do not seem to them to be legitimate."[30] Similarly, the sociologist Jack Katz argues that homicides are often committed by offenders who are convinced of the moral correctness of their behavior, are resigned to their fate, and patiently await the arrival of the police.[31]

In contrast to their assumptions about crime, resource mobilization theorists often portray the behavior of those who directly challenge political institutions as being universally moral and meaningful.[32] For example, Margaret Abudu and her colleagues describe African American ghetto violence of the 1960s as "a form of attempted communication"[33] and conclude that looting and burning are "as politically relevant as either voting or writing one's congressman."[34] Similarly, H. L. Nieburg argues that to dismiss "extreme and violent political behavior . . . as erratic, exceptional, and meaningless . . . is to deny the role of violence in creating and testing political legitimacy."[35]

Such views downplay the possibility that collective action varies in political significance; that although some may protest for political reasons, others may have more complex motivations, ranging from personal gain to simple enjoyment. For example, studies of prison riots suggest that riots are not only occasions to express political grievances but also opportunities for revenge and even recreation.[36]

Although social breakdown theorists have mostly defended associations between crime and political action in terms of the similarity of the effects of declining political legitimacy on individual motivation to commit either crime or protest, a more important connection between crime and political action may well be the impact that political legitimacy has on the effectiveness of informal and formal social control. That is, declining legitimacy of political institutions may simultaneously increase levels of crime and collective action by changing the attitudes of individuals who may never engage in either.

In the previous chapter, I argued that institutions prevent crime in part by embedding individuals in a web of social responsibilities and obligations. When members of a society begin to doubt the fairness of legal and political institutions, they are likely to become less enthusiastic supporters of the rules and laws promulgated by these institutions. Parents, families, schools, and neighborhoods will do less to defend rules and will respond less harshly to rule violations. Formal punishment by the legal system will be less threatening and will carry less of a stigma when it is applied. Social control of every type will be weakened by institutions that have lost their moral validity. It therefore seems logical to expect that these changes could lead to increases in crime and, under the right circumstances, to increases in organized collective political action as well.

Although politically inspired social movements and crime have generated an enormous amount of interest individually, there is relatively little research on the connections between the two. An exception is research on nineteenth-century France by Charles Tilly and his associates.[37] In an analysis of French departments (i.e., provinces) in 1841, 1846, and 1851, Abdul Lodhi and Tilly concluded that the number of participants in politically motivated violence was unrelated to rates of either personal or property crimes for the same period.[38]

But in contrast to the conclusions of Tilly and his collaborators, the political scientist Ted Gurr has found that "crime waves"—sharp increases in crimes of violence and theft—coincided with episodes of civil strife in London, Stockholm, New South Wales, and Calcutta during various periods of the nineteenth and twentieth centuries.[39] Similarly, in a study of racial disorders in 119 American cities in the 1960s, Joel Lieske found that high levels of criminal activity were significantly associated with race riots.[40]

Measuring Political Legitimacy

To fit the street crime trends described previously, I am looking for evidence that the legitimacy of political institutions began the postwar period at high levels, declined rapidly in the early 1960s, and then flattened out in the late 1970s. I am also interested in whether, compared to whites, African Americans showed lower levels of support for political institutions throughout this period and especially during the high-crime decades of the 1960s and 1970s.

Given the abstractness of the concept, measuring levels of political legitimacy in a society presents a challenge. I begin by considering briefly some of the major postwar historical events that shaped American trust in political institutions. I then consider evidence for how public trust in political institutions changed during the period. I examine changes in public attitudes toward politicians and consider how changes in the field of criminology itself reflected rising levels of distrust in political institutions during the postwar period.

Several commentators have argued that rising rates of litigation and declining levels of political participation in a society are also measures of declining political legitimacy.[41] Accordingly, I next compare litigation rates to crime rates in the postwar period and briefly consider several other measures of political participation. Finally, many argue that the single greatest threat to political legitimacy in postwar America has been race-based discrimination. Therefore, I conclude the chapter with an examination of how the civil rights movement and the rights-based revolution that followed it have been related to crime trends in America.

Entering the Age of Distrust

After the global changes wrought by World War II, the United States emerged in 1946 as the military and economic leader of the Western world. The devastation experienced by Europe and Japan left the United States as an almost unchallenged economic power. But the unique position of the United States was not based only on economic hegemony. After all, the United States had just fought and won the "good war." As the social observer Studs Terkel points out, for many World War II represented clear moral choices—good versus evil; right versus wrong.[42] This extraordinary level of trust was never again attained in the subsequent wars and military actions in which the United States was involved during the postwar period.

The widespread popular support for World War II was of course solidified by a decisive American victory. The importance of the war as a focal point for American solidarity was demonstrated by the enormous popularity of General Dwight D. Eisenhower. Despite strong popular support and even a large number of prominent Democratic backers, Eisenhower steadfastly refused the Republican nomination for the presidency in 1948.[43] He gave in to the pressure in 1952, however, and won the greatest presidential landslide election since the overwhelming victory of Franklin Delano Roosevelt in 1936. In the heady years following World War II, it is little wonder that many commentators envisioned this period as the dawn of the "American Century."[44]

But of course, history rarely cooperates with such predictions for long. Even in the seeming tranquillity of the 1950s, seeds of political discontent were germinating. Rising alienation and youthful restlessness were evident in popular films like *The Wild One* with Marlon Brando (1954), *The Blackboard Jungle* (1955) with Glenn Ford, and *Rebel Without a Cause* (1955) with James Dean. Although the kinds of deviance reported may now seem relatively minor, in the early 1950s endless local newspaper stories related incidents of growing juvenile misbehavior and delinquency.[45] And although there was much to cheer about in the United States following World War II, it was also becoming painfully obvious that not all Americans had the same cause for celebration.

The Civil Rights Revolution

Undoubtedly, the greatest single threat to the legitimacy of American political institutions during the early postwar period was the growing urgency of protests against race-based segregation and discrimination. Boycotts of public buses in the 1950s were the opening salvo in what the sociologists J. Craig Jenkins and Craig M. Eckert call "the first sustained challenge to white supremacy in the South since the installation of Jim Crow in the late 19th century."[46] Student sit-ins, protests, freedom rides, and mass action campaigns pressured federal courts to desegregate public facilities and interstate transportation in the early 1960s and eventually forced Congress to pass the Civil Rights Acts of 1964 and 1965 and the courts to more vigorously enforce the Fourteenth Amendment's equal protection clause.[47] The success of the civil rights movement in using the courts to open up public and later private institutions to African Americans made litigation a strategy of choice for other excluded groups, including women, the elderly, the disabled, homosexuals, people accused and convicted of crimes, Latinos, and immigrants.[48]

As the 1960s wore on, peaceful protests and demonstrations gave way to riots and urban violence. Even legislative changes that would have been considered revolutionary in an earlier epoch were unable to stop the rising tide of discontent. Less than a week after the 1965 Voting Rights Act was signed by President Lyndon Johnson, on the evening of August 11, a highway patrolman arrested a young African American man for speeding in the Watts neighborhood of Los Angeles. Called to the scene to control a gathering crowd, one police officer used a billy club to strike an African American observer and another police officer dragged a young African American woman into the street. After the police left, a rapidly growing crowd started throwing rocks at passing automobiles, attacked several white motorists, and began to set cars on fire. Two days later, following the decision of city officials not to mediate the increasingly volatile confrontation between the police and local residents, crowds began looting, firebombing, and vandalizing buildings and cars. As a result of the six-day Watts riot, thirty-four African Americans lost their lives, nine were seriously injured, and $35 million dollars' worth of property was destroyed.[49] In the days and weeks that followed, riots broke out in cities across America.

The War in Vietnam

As the militancy of the civil rights movement grew and spread, the war in South Vietnam was also escalating. In January 1962, there were only about 2,600 American soldiers and advisors in Vietnam.[50] Three years later, this number had grown to 184,000.[51] And huge increases followed: There were 385,000 soldiers by the end of 1966; more than 485,000 by the end of 1967; and more than 536,000 by the end of 1968. American military forces eventually dropped an estimated 3.2 million tons of bombs in Vietnam—more tonnage than was used during all of World War II.[52]

In January 1968, the North Vietnamese mounted the Tet Offensive—a series of surprise attacks on cities throughout South Vietnam, including the capital at Saigon. Many American viewers were shocked by media photographs of enemy troops who had actually penetrated the walls of the U.S. embassy.[53] Although American generals claimed that the Tet Offensive was a military victory for the United States, its obvious extensiveness seriously undermined public confidence in just how well war efforts were actually going.[54] If the U.S. Army could not even protect the nation's embassy, other official claims about the war began to also seem less credible.

As protest against the Vietnam War grew more forceful, resistance to the war increasingly overlapped with civil rights–related protests. This was hardly a surprising development, given that African Americans were far more likely than other groups to be drafted, to serve, to be wounded, and to die in Vietnam.[55] The Reverend Martin Luther King, Jr., publicly spoke out against the Vietnam War for the first time in 1966.[56] King talked in general terms about the possibility that growing U.S. involvement in the war was limiting social programs to combat poverty. By the time King was assassinated in 1968, his relatively moderate position on Vietnam was already losing ground to more radical voices, such as those of Black Panther party leaders Stokely Carmichael and Eldridge Cleaver. Cleaver directly linked U.S. involvement in Vietnam with U.S. suppression of African Americans at home: "Blacks . . . all over America could now see the Viet Cong's point: Both were on the receiving end of what the armed forces were dishing out."[57]

In stark contrast to the perceived clear-cut victories of World War II two decades earlier, the Vietnam War produced a seemingly endless series of setbacks, tragedies, and polarizing debates. Opposition to the war became increasingly bitter, vocal, and widespread. Because the military draft allowed deferments for college students whose families could afford to pay for education, it further polarized Americans by economic class and race. Growing resistance to the war convinced Lyndon Johnson not to seek a second term in the White House, paved the way for the election of Richard Nixon, and greatly changed the face of American politics for decades to come. In the end, the Vietnam War severely undermined Americans' trust in their political institutions.

Watergate and Other Political Scandals

Scandals also reduced the legitimacy of American political institutions during the middle postwar period. In September 1973, following a highly publicized grand jury investigation, Vice President Spiro Agnew was charged with accepting payoffs from contractors he had favored while serving first as executive for Baltimore County and then as governor of Maryland. On

October 16, Agnew resigned in exchange for a Justice Department agreement to let him plead nolo contendere to income tax evasion.[58]

But the defining event in postwar political scandals was set into motion more than a year earlier with a burglary at a Washington, D.C., hotel. On June 17, 1972, at 2:30 a.m., five men loaded with electronic surveillance gear were arrested and charged with breaking into Democratic Party headquarters at the Watergate Hotel.[59] At first, President Richard Nixon's press secretary dismissed the news as "a third-rate burglary attempt." But once the burglars were caught, President Nixon and his top aides repeatedly broke laws to cover up their involvement. They resisted efforts to investigate the crimes by claiming "national security" and "executive privilege." They paid "hush money" to keep the burglars quiet. They authorized illegal wiretaps on journalists and officials whom they distrusted. They even pressed the CIA to block the FBI's investigation of the Watergate break-in. In the end, secret Oval Office recordings would confirm that President Nixon himself lied repeatedly in speeches to the American public. Finally, on August 8, 1974, President Nixon appeared on national television to announce his resignation.[60]

Although no president since Nixon has been seriously threatened with impeachment, investigations of possible presidential misdeeds have become common after Watergate. Watergate-style inquiries have included the business dealings of Bert Lance, President Jimmy Carter's budget chief; illegal aid to contra rebels in Nicaragua during the presidencies of Ronald Reagan and George Bush; and Whitewater and campaign finance investigations during the presidency of Bill Clinton.

Declining Political Legitimacy in Postwar America

Beyond gauging public reactions to specific historical events, such as the Watts riot or the Watergate cover-up, systematic evidence about how the legitimacy of political institutions has changed in postwar America can be divided into attitudinal and behavioral categories. With regard to attitudinal evidence, in the next two sections I review information drawn from a unique series of national opinion surveys and briefly consider how assumptions about political institutions have changed among criminology researchers during the postwar years. To examine behavioral evidence about public trust in government for the postwar period, I examine trends in voting behavior; civil litigation; and civil rights–related collective action, including protests and riots.

Attitudes Toward Government

The political scientist Warren Miller has collected information from biennial national election opinion surveys since the 1950s.[61] These national studies can shed some light on trends in the level of trust Americans have in their political institutions. Perhaps the most direct evidence comes from a series of surveys from 1958 to 1996, in which Miller and his colleagues asked respondents, "How much of the time can you trust the government to do what is right?" Figure 6.1 shows the proportion of African Americans and whites who answered "Most of the time" or "Just about always" to this question.[62]

Figure 6.1 shows a dramatic decline from 1958 to 1996 in the amount of trust Americans say they have in the federal government. Trust in the government was highest in the 1950s and early 1960s. In 1958 and 1964, more than 70 percent of white Americans reported that they trusted the federal government to do what was right most of the time. But rates plummeted in the 1960s and 1970s. By 1980, only about a quarter of white Americans said that they trusted the federal government to do what was right most of the time. In the 1980s and early 1990s, levels of trust have been relatively low but stable.

Both African Americans and whites showed high levels of trust in government in the late 1950s and early 1960s. Interestingly, the proportion of whites and African Americans who expected the federal government to do what was right most of the time was almost identical in 1964—the year before Congress passed landmark civil rights legislation. Rates declined rapidly after 1964 for both African Americans and whites. African American rates of trust fell farther and faster than white rates, however. White rates, but not African American rates, increased somewhat in the 1980s, during the presidential administration of Ronald Reagan.

Of particular interest is the period from the early 1960s to the early 1970s—the period when street crime rates in the United States dramatically increased. Figure 6.1 shows that from 1964 to 1974, the proportion of white Americans with high trust in the federal government plunged by 40 points: from 78 to 38 percent. The drop for African Americans was even steeper, declining from 77 percent in 1964 to 18 percent in 1974.

A related way of tracking levels of trust Americans have in their political institutions is to examine their attitudes toward elected officials. From 1958 to 1996, the national election surveys asked Americans whether they agreed with the statement, "Quite a few people running the government are crooked." The proportion who thought quite a few were crooked, from 1958 to 1996, is shown for whites and African Americans in Figure 6.2.

According to Figure 6.2, the proportion of Americans believing that politicians are crooked begins the postwar period at relatively low levels—26 percent for whites, 22 percent for African Americans. It then increases sharply in the late 1960s and early 1970s. For African Americans, the proportion believing that quite a few politicians are crooked more than triples in just five years—from 1968 to 1972. For whites, the increase is less dramatic but nevertheless rises by 60 percent from 1968 to 1974. Since the 1970s, levels of dis-

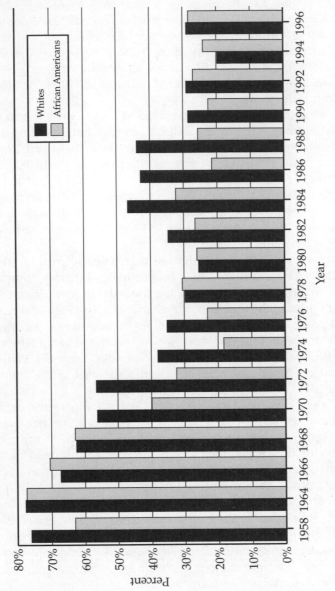

FIGURE 6.1 Percent of Americans Who Trust Their Government, 1958–1996

Percent of Americans who answer, "Most of the time" or "Just about always" to the question, "How much of the time can you trust the government to do what is right?"

SOURCE: *Warren E. Miller, American National Election Studies Cumulative Data File, 1952–1996* (Ann Arbor, MI: Center for Political Studies, 1996).

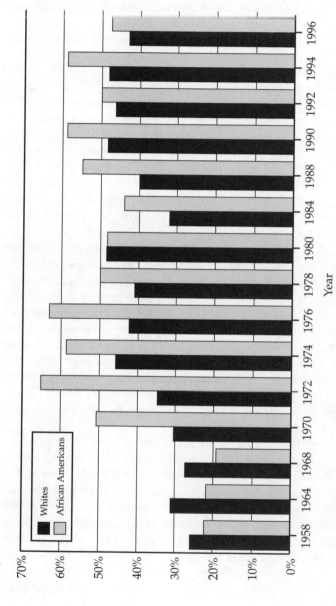

FIGURE 6.2 Percent of Americans Who Believe Government Officials Are Crooked, 1958–1996

Percent of Americans who agree with the statement, "Quite a few people running the government are crooked"

SOURCE: Warren E. Miller, *American National Election Studies Cumulative Data File, 1952–1996* (Ann Arbor, MI: Center for Political Studies, 1996).

trust have leveled off but remain at high levels—in the 1990s the proportion of both white and African American citizens who believe that politicians are crooked is about twice as high as it was in the late 1950s.

In fact, a wide variety of measures examining attitudes toward American political institutions summarized in the National Election Survey data tell pretty much the same story. From the 1950s to the 1970s, both African Americans and whites were more likely to feel that their political representatives were paying less attention to their needs and wishes, that their representatives were only interested in getting elected, that their vote didn't make much difference, and that they had little say in how their government was being run. And for each of these trends, I found a pattern of greatest trust in the early postwar period, declining trust during the 1960s and early 1970s, and then relatively stable but low levels of trust in the 1980s and 1990s. Moreover, compared to white levels of trust, African American levels are generally lower and dropped more rapidly during the crucial crime increase decades of the 1960s and 1970s.

Cross-sectional survey data on postwar African American attitudes and attitudes toward violence and protest further distinguish African American and white attitudes toward politics and change. In a comprehensive, national study of attitudes toward violence published in 1969, at the height of race-related postwar urban violence, Monica Blumenthal and her associates found that 20 percent of white American male respondents and almost 50 percent of African American male respondents felt that "some violence" was justified to bring about political change.[63] In general, compared to white men, black men were more skeptical that political changes would happen without violence; were more angry about delays in political changes; and were more willing to justify violence, injury, and property damage to attain social change.[64]

Similarly, in research based on a national sample of 1,049 Americans interviewed in 1977, the sociologists John Hagan and Celesta Albonetti found that black Americans were considerably more likely than white Americans to believe that the American legal system is unjust.[65] In particular, compared to white respondents, black respondents were more likely to believe that police, courts, and lawyers treat poor suspects worse than well-to-do suspects, that juries and judges are biased and unfair, and that courts do not treat blacks and other minorities the same as whites. Moreover, Hagan and Albonetti found the greatest differences in perceptions of injustice for blacks and whites among a relatively well-off group of professionals and managers.

Political Attitudes and Criminology Research

Interestingly, parallel changes in attitudes toward political institutions can be observed in mainstream criminology research. Like other citizens, most criminologists entered the postwar period with a great deal of trust in political institutions. This trust is evident both in the research questions addressed by criminologists and in the general tone of criminological studies in the postwar period.

From the beginning of an indigenous American criminology at the University of Chicago in the 1920s until the rise of labeling and conflict perspectives in the 1960s, mainstream American criminology was mostly concerned with discovering the causes of criminal behavior.[66] This research on criminal behavior implied trust in legal and political institutions because it usually took them for granted. As mainstream criminology concentrated on explaining why individuals commit crime, it spent relatively little time examining the processes by which individuals are selected and processed as criminals.

A fundamental trust in political institutions is also evident in the style of most mainstream criminology writing immediately before and after World War II. The clear tone of such influential classics as Clifford Shaw and Henry McKay's social disorganization theory and Edwin Sutherland's differential association theory is one in which political institutions are fundamentally sound but crime is a problem that needs to be studied and controlled. Although social problems are identified as critical in crime causation, they are presented as amenable to repair. In fact, the role mainstream criminology reserved for itself during this period was to provide the necessary research to make these repairs possible. Thus, high levels of trust in political institutions among criminologists largely corresponded to a period of relatively low crime rates.

As a new generation of criminologists came of age in the 1960s, the contrast could hardly be more profound. Labeling and conflict theories, the most influential of the "new" criminologies, were based on the fundamental premise that researchers cannot simply trust governments to do what is right or best for their citizens—especially their less powerful citizens.[67] Instead of studying why people commit crime, beginning especially in the 1960s many criminologists urged that we study how the legal system affects the unfortunate souls who happen to fall within its grasp. Political distrust increased among criminologists at about the same time that distrust was also rising in the larger society.

But even as criminological trust in political institutions seemed to be reaching a low ebb in the late 1970s, countertrends were evident. Most notable was growing dissatisfaction with criminology research focused on the unfairness of the system to the exclusion of strategies aimed at understanding and preventing crime.[68] This perspective is clear in the political scientist James Q. Wilson's influential 1975 book, the principal focus of which is on understanding why people commit crime.[69] By the 1990s, there were unmistakable signs that criminology was in an eclectic period in which basic distrust in political institutions remains alongside and sometimes in conflict with a new appreciation for the potentially devastating impact that crime can have on both individuals and social systems. This new eclecticism has corresponded to crime trends that are either stable or declining.

Although both national survey data on attitudes toward political institutions and attitudes among mainstream criminologists evident in their research are largely consistent with postwar street crime trends, it might be the case that attitudes about political institutions changed in ways that resembled crime rates, whereas actual behavior with regard to these institutions did not. In the next section, I consider several behavioral indicators of postwar trends in American trust in political institutions.

Untrustworthy Actions

The sociologist Robert Bellah and his colleagues have argued that civil litigation in a society is one measure of citizens' trust in their political institutions.[70] In fact, litigation not only reflects declining trust in political institutions but most likely also further reduces public trust.[71] At the most basic level, litigation indicates citizens' unwillingness to accept the informal decisions or outcomes of the institutions in which disputes arise.[72]

Civil Litigation Trends.   Figure 6.3 shows the total number of civil cases filed in U.S. courts annually, from 1946 to 1995. To facilitate comparison, I have included postwar robbery trends. In general, the total number of civil cases filed is relatively low in the immediate postwar period, escalates rapidly in the late 1960s and especially in the 1970s, and then flattens out or declines in the 1980s and 1990s. The fewest civil filings were recorded in 1948; the most in 1985. These cases represent a wide variety of actions: lawsuits against corporations for dangerous products, against businesses for job discrimination, against prisons for civil rights violations, against drug companies for defective treatments.

Civil rights cases are an especially interesting measure of political distrust because they represent situations in which individuals or groups of individuals directly challenge the way they are being treated by fundamental social institutions. Comparisons between total civil rights cases initiated in U.S. courts with postwar street crime trends provide very similar conclusions to those observed for civil cases in general.[73] Total civil rights cases were at very low levels in the early postwar period. In 1946, there were only forty civil rights cases heard in U.S. courts. But the annual rate accelerated rapidly in the 1960s. From 1960 to 1970, total civil rights cases initiated in U.S. courts increased by more than fourteen times—from 280 to 3,985. Rapid increases continued after the 1970s. Total annual cases initiated passed 10,000 per year in 1975, 20,000 per year in 1986, and 30,000 per year in 1994.

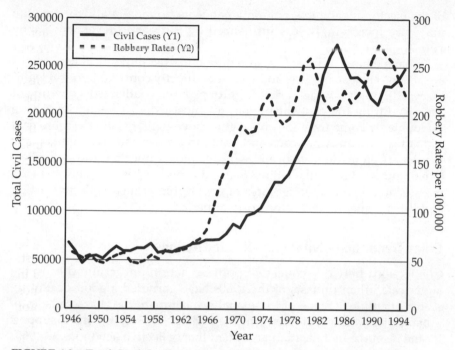

FIGURE 6.3   Total Civil Cases Filed in U.S. District Courts and Robbery Rates, 1946–1995
SOURCE: Administrative Office of the United States Courts, Statistics Division, Analysis and Reports Branch, Washington, DC, *Annual Report to the Director*, reports for 1946–1995 (Washington, DC: Government Printing Office).

In general, both total civil litigation and specifically civil rights litigation show trends that are quite similar to those exhibited by street crime rates: low in the 1940s and 1950s, rapidly increasing in the 1960s and 1970s, tapering off but remaining at historically high levels in the 1980s and 1990s.

Political Participation.   Several other measures of civic participation are also generally consistent with postwar crime trends. In a democratic society, voting is a fundamental measure of institutional trust. Rates of voting in the United States, never high compared to other nations, have nevertheless fallen during the postwar period. In the 1964 presidential election, 78 percent of eligible Americans voted. By the 1988 elections, this percentage had dropped to 70 percent. Similar changes in voting participation are reported at the local and state levels.[74] Participation in the major political parties has also declined. "Independents" now constitute 40 percent of the electorate, and even nonindependents nominally affiliated with a party are increasingly less influenced by the party ticket when they vote.[75]

Perhaps the most direct measure of public trust in political institutions are actions such as protests and riots that directly confront political legitimacy. Although a wide variety of groups have challenged government policies during the postwar period, the most extensive challenges have undoubtedly come from the civil rights movement. Efforts to secure civil rights for African Americans and, later, to protect the civil rights gains that had been made have been by far the most important form of collective political action in the United States during the postwar period. In the next section, I compare measures of civil rights–related collective action and street crime trends for the postwar period.

Crime Trends and Civil Rights–Related Actions

Connections between collective political action and crime during the large-scale urban protests of the 1960s have garnered a good deal of research attention.[76] Some of these analyses compare the characteristics of urban rioters and nonrioters, whence perhaps derives the main support for the resource mobilization argument that collective action in the 1960s was unrelated to crime. Several of these comparisons suggest that rioters were more racially conscious and politically sophisticated than nonrioters but were similar to nonrioters in background characteristics, including criminal record, income, marital status, education, and occupation.[77] But other researchers claim that these comparisons are flawed. For example, Abraham Miller and his associates argue that early studies had serious methodological errors and that when these errors are corrected rioters were at the bottom of their communities in both social integration and economic resources.[78]

In any event, the finding that those who participate in riots and protests are different from those who commit common crimes does not necessarily demonstrate that aggregate levels of collective behavior and crime are unrelated. Robert Merton's anomie theory provides a clear demonstration. Anomie theory suggests that dislocations in society contribute to a wide range of conflictual behavior, including crime and protest.[79] But it does not argue that the same individuals are necessarily responsible for both activities. Rather, individuals of certain backgrounds commit crime whereas those of other backgrounds may rebel or retreat to drug or alcohol use.[80]

Perhaps the most common method for examining trends in social movement activities is to calculate total "event counts" based on analyses of newspapers likely to cover such events.[81] I was able to obtain annual

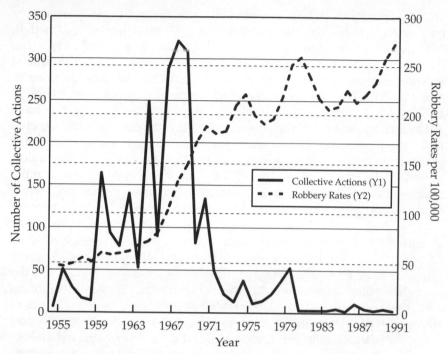

FIGURE 6.4   Collective Action Events and Robbery Rates, 1955–1991
SOURCE: Gary LaFree and Kriss A. Drass, "African American Collective Action and Crime, 1955–1991," *Social Forces* (1997) 75:835–853. Reprinted with permission.

event counts, from 1955 to 1991, for civil rights–related riots, protests, marches, rallies, sit-ins, demonstrations, economic boycotts, and other direct actions from an analysis of *The New York Times Annual Index*.[82] I excluded institutionalized political actions like court cases and lobbying efforts; "symbolic actions" like press conferences and speeches; efforts to mobilize resources such as membership drives and fund-raisers; simple announcements about organizational changes; and reactions to direct action. In Figure 6.4, I compare trends in total protests and other direct actions to trends in robbery from 1955 to 1991.

As shown in Figure 6.4, collective action rates increased rapidly from the late 1950s through the late 1960s and then declined just as rapidly in the early 1970s, remaining close to zero in the 1980s and 1990s. When superimposed against robbery rates, we can see that collective action and crime both began their rapid increases at about the same time. But collective action dropped off much more rapidly than crime rates after the 1970s.

This overall pattern is shown even more dramatically if we concentrate only on riots, the most violent of direct actions. Most race-related riots in the postwar United States occurred in a narrow window of only about five years. Starting in 1966, the total annual number of riots increased rapidly, reaching a postwar zenith of 287 only two years later, in 1968. Thereafter, the number of riots declined just as rapidly, totaling only six in 1972.

Thus, compared to total measures of civil rights–related actions, total riots form a narrow spike that reaches a peak in the late 1960s. As with the other measures of declining political legitimacy reviewed previously, however, the placement of this spike is clearly linked to street crime trends—it comes precisely at the moment when street crimes underwent their steepest postwar increases. From 1965 to 1971, the prime years for urban rioting, total rates for the seven street crimes reviewed previously increased by 70 percent.[83] Increases in some individual crimes were even more dramatic. For example, during the same six-year period, robbery rates increased by two and one-half times.[84]

These results clearly contradict the argument that increases in rates of collective political action reduced crime by providing a "safety valve." Instead, rates of crime and collective political action increased rapidly and at about the same time. Similarly, the trend data do not support George Rude's argument that crime increases as direct political action burns itself out.[85] On the contrary, the results show that crime rates increased most dramatically at the same time that collective action rates did. When collective action rates later declined, crime rates remained stable, declining only slowly and much later.

Thus, although trends in the total number of civil rights–related actions are clearly correlated to trends in levels of political trust, levels of litigation, and street crimes for the early and middle postwar years, they diverge considerably during the late postwar years. In particular, political distrust, litigation, and crime have all remained at historically high levels whereas measures of direct action and riots declined sharply in the 1970s. Two considerations probably account for this divergence.

First, as resource mobilization theorists have convincingly argued, direct forms of collective action depend on resources and organizational structure that are difficult to sustain. For example, economic boycotts, marches, demonstrations, sit-ins, and protests all require a relatively high degree of organization and commitment. By contrast, street crime requires little or no organization and resources, litigation is fueled at least in part by the rules that govern it, and attitudes expressed in public opinion surveys require no serious commitment.

Second, social control efforts were no doubt more effective against relatively organized and highly visible collective action than they were against street crime. Thus, tough law enforcement virtually wiped out urban rioting after the late 1960s[86] but had much more limited success in eliminating or even seriously reducing street crime rates.

Based on comparisons between levels of collective political action and street crime only, I find the strongest support for a special type of asymmetrical relationship: From the 1950s to the early 1970s, rates of collective action and crime for both African Americans and whites were closely related but moved increasingly in opposite directions as rates of collective action plummeted while crime rates held steady in the 1970s. The early positive relationship between collective political action and crime is consistent with social breakdown arguments that collective action and crime spring in part from similar social forces. But the growing negative relationship between collective action and crime after the early 1970s is consistent with resource mobilization arguments that, compared to crime, collective political action requires more resources and organization to sustain and therefore declines more rapidly.

Taken together, these results underscore the fact that the meanings assigned to collective political action and crime are both related and historically situated. Thus, collective action during the 1950s and 1960s established a "vocabulary of motives" that could be used by offenders to justify or "neutralize"[87] their criminal actions. For example, the speech of the inner-city residents studied by Elijah Anderson is filled with references to discrimination and social injustice.[88] Moreover, as I noted previously, these justifications are likely to have a major impact not just on the motivation of potential offenders but also on the effectiveness of informal and formal social control efforts. Conversely, politicians and policymakers are adept at the use of metaphors about crime and the construction of "moral panics" to discredit social activism aimed at bringing about political reform.[89]

Most likely, the success of both efforts to see crime as politically justified and to see political action as nothing but crime are historically contingent. For example, the portrayal of street criminals as "political prisoners" was undoubtedly more successful during the height of the civil rights movement in the mid-1960s than during the near absence of direct action by the civil rights movement in the 1990s. Similarly, the ability of officials to define rioters as criminals is likely to be more successful during the Los Angeles riot of 1992—when street crime remained high but direct political action had virtually disappeared—than during the Watts riot of 1965.

Summary and Conclusions

Overall, I argue that declining levels of political legitimacy in postwar America are clearly related to street crime trends. The rapid growth of street crime in the 1960s and 1970s coincided with major increases in levels of political distrust. My hunch is that criminology researchers, like other Americans, were also affected by these trends. I think anyone who was involved in criminology research during the postwar period would have a hard time arguing that criminologists as a group were more trustful of political institutions in the 1960s and 1970s than they were in the 1940s and 1950s.

It is perhaps impossible to determine fully the extent to which levels of political distrust were in turn affected by specific historical events like the Vietnam War or the Watergate scandal. Most likely such historical events were both determinants and conduits of wider political attitudes. For example, note the very different way that evidence of presidential philandering has been interpreted by the media and the public in the case of President John F. Kennedy in the high-trust period of the early 1960s compared to the case of President Bill Clinton in the low-trust period of the 1990s.

The explosion of civil litigation and the drop in levels of political participation are also clearly correlated with postwar street crime trends. Like street crime rates, civil litigation rates were at low levels in the early postwar period, increased rapidly in the middle postwar period, and flattened out at relatively high levels in the late postwar period.

The relationship between crime trends and direct measures of collective political action associated with the civil rights movement is more complex. Collective action rates, like crime rates, were generally low during the early postwar period and increased rapidly during the middle postwar years. But collective action rates declined much more rapidly than crime rates after 1970. My interpretation of these patterns is that street crime and direct political action had similar causes—both were related in part to the declining legitimacy of American political institutions. But direct political action declined much more rapidly than street crime because it takes more organization and resources to maintain social movements than street crime and because governments are likely to be more successful at controlling collective action than street crime. These arguments seem especially relevant to riots—the most violent form of collective political action.

Although additional research is needed to reach definite conclusions, there is evidence that levels of political distrust may explain in part why African American street crime rates have been higher than rates for other groups, both historically and during the crime boom of the middle postwar years. In fact, given the nature of African American history, it would be hard to imagine that, compared to other groups, African Americans would not have greater distrust of American political institutions. It also seems plausible that distrust levels would have grown among African Americans as the frustrations and setbacks of the civil rights movement mounted in the 1960s and 1970s.

To fit my arguments, changing levels of political legitimacy should also correspond to the slowing and eventual decline of crime rates in the 1990s. Again, I think they do. Recent opinion surveys show that trust in government is not greatly improving, but it is also not getting any worse. Levels of litigation in the United States are also not experiencing the same rapid growth that occurred in earlier decades and there are increasingly influential moves to add new restrictions to various forms of civil litigation. Perhaps most important, there is no organized collective political action that remotely resembles the scope of the civil rights movement or the antiwar protests of the early and middle postwar period.

● ● ●

When viewed against the backdrop of the postwar years, changes in attitudes toward American political institutions must be regarded as sweeping. Still, changes in individual relationships to economic institutions were no less dramatic. In the next chapter, I consider how major economic changes during the postwar period were related to crime trends.

seven

Crime and American Economic Institutions

A house may be large or small; as long as the surrounding houses are equally small it satisfies all social demands for a dwelling. But if a palace rises beside the little house, the little house shrinks into a hut.
—**Karl Marx and Frederic Engels, "Wage Labor and Capital," 1955**[1]

What good is it to be allowed to eat in a restaurant if you can't afford a hamburger?
—**Martin Luther King, Jr.**[2]

Downtown Atlanta, like several other large cities in the United States, now includes a system of pedestrian walkways that connect large hotels with conference facilities and shopping areas. There are no doubt many reasons why these connecting tunnels between major central city destinations are attractive: They provide shelter from summer humidity, spring rain, and winter cold. They allow pedestrians to avoid the pollution and city noises that usually envelop the downtown area. But walking through these transparent plastic tubes also produces an eerie reminder of the gap between "the haves" and "the have-nots" in America.

As lines of the haves move in air-conditioned comfort between upscale restaurants, trendy shops, and luxurious hotels, down below the homeless and the poor continue to go about the gritty business of survival in urban America. A thin sheet of plastic separates middle-class comfort and predictability from lower-class grime and uncertainty. Whether a conscious planning move or not, the tunnels allow walkers to block out many of the ongoing social problems that continue unabated just beneath their feet.

But blocking out poverty, unemployment, and inequality has become an increasingly difficult task in most urban areas in the United States at the end of the twentieth century. Anyone exploring inner-city America in

114

the 1990s could scarcely avoid passing homeless men and, frequently, women and children, panhandling for spare change, sleeping in alleyways, trudging down sidewalks with loaded shopping carts, or carrying torn bedrolls and rucksacks.

Crime and Economic Institutions

The idea that crime is associated with economic institutions can be traced back to antiquity,[3] and it has probably been the single most influential explanation for crime in postwar America. The attraction of this argument is not hard to understand. It appeals to common sense because even a cursory tour of the criminal justice system demonstrates that most of the individuals being processed by the police and the courts or doing time in prisons are near the bottom of the economic distribution. Economic explanations are also appealing in that they appear to target factors more amenable to repair than explanations based on biological predispositions or psychological drives. Beginning with the influential Chicago school of criminology in the 1920s, the idea that crime could be reduced through social programs that alleviate economic deprivation has been a popular theme in the United States.

Economic explanations clearly pass the first requirement for explaining the postwar crime trends described previously, because, like crime rates, economic conditions have changed rapidly during the postwar period. Following World War II, the United States was the undisputed leader of the global economy. By the late 1940s, American companies were making 50 percent of the world's manufactured goods[4] and 45 percent of the world's steel.[5] The United States owned two-thirds of the world's gold reserves. Moreover, federal spending in the United States during the war encouraged technological innovations. From 1940 to 1950, the United States was responsible for an incredible 82 percent of all major inventions and discoveries worldwide.[6] These developments left the United States in a uniquely favorable economic position during the early postwar years.

But the economic picture changed considerably by the late 1960s. Basic industrial production dominated by the United States following World War II was among the first areas to suffer: The U.S. lead in textiles, iron, steel, and chemicals greatly diminished. Seeking higher profits and less competition, U.S. companies increasingly "outsourced" high-paying industrial jobs in these areas to lower-wage nations.[7] As economic changes accelerated, the influence of labor unions steadily declined and the high wages associated with unions also eroded.[8]

Changes that began in traditional manufacturing and production areas spread to other parts of the economy. The United States encountered increasingly stiff competition even in newer, high-technology industries that it once virtually monopolized, such as robotics, aerospace, and computers.[9] By the early 1990s, some commentators were seriously predicting that Japan—a country with only half the population of the United States on a landmass about the size of Texas—would soon overtake the United States as the world's largest economy.[10]

But not all economic news for the United States in the late postwar years was bad. By 1996, the federal spending deficit had been reduced to the lowest level since 1979.[11] In 1994, the poverty rate began to fall for the first time in five years and income inequality began a modest decline.[12] In 1997, unemployment reached the lowest level since 1973.[13] Moreover, economic strains were showing up in most major industrialized trading partners of the United States. Even the Japanese economy, which had seemed invincible during much of the postwar period, began to show severe signs of stress in the mid-1990s, including negative rates of economic growth, deflation, and a severe stock market crash.[14] In short, the magnitude of economic change experienced by the United States and its industrialized trading partners in the last half of the twentieth century appears to be as dramatic as the fluctuations in crime rates that we have already considered.

Economic arguments also offer an appealing explanation for the gap between African American and white crime rates. Regardless of the economic indicator examined, African Americans began the postwar period at a tremendous disadvantage. Compared to whites, African Americans had higher rates of poverty, unemployment, and joblessness and lower average incomes for both individuals and families. These considerations were critical in the Great Society programs of the 1960s that aimed to provide African Americans with greater access to economic opportunities.[15] And indeed, although African Americans remained behind on most economic indicators in the 1990s, the postwar period was also marked by the growth of a large and affluent African American middle class.[16]

But despite the commonsense appeal of economic explanations for postwar crime rates, the exact connections between the economy and crime are far from clear.[17] In fact, the sometimes-unpredictable response of crime to economic conditions in the postwar period had a major effect on the thinking of policymakers and researchers about crime, particularly following the crime wave of the 1960s. James Q. Wilson was one of the first social scientists to recognize and publicly comment on this weak connection. Wilson called the crime boom beginning in the 1960s "the paradox" of "crime amidst plenty," and made much of the fact that crime rates appeared to be increasing at the same time that the economy was flourishing.[18] Speaking for many researchers, the economists Sharon Long and Anne Witte concluded their comprehensive review of the link between crime and macroeconomic conditions by noting that prior research provides only "weak support" for simple connections between economic measures and crime.[19]

The relationships between economic stress measures and crime trends seem especially problematic for African Americans. Thus, under an openly discriminatory system that overtly blocked African Americans from full economic participation in the 1940s and 1950s, African American crime rates were lower than at any point in the postwar period. Conversely, during the middle postwar years when African Americans seemed to be experiencing major improvements in access to educational and economic opportunities, African American crime rates were nevertheless booming. Obvious problems with the simple argument that increasing economic opportunity for African Americans would automatically reduce crime no doubt explain why relatively few policymakers still clung to the pure version of this hypothesis by the late postwar period.[20]

Conclusions about the relationship between crime and economic institutions are complicated by a plethora of relevant studies, many with contradictory conclusions. The dominant theoretical tradition, however, has been some version of strain theory.

Strain Theories

Robert Merton's anomie theory is undoubtedly the most influential of the postwar strain theories.[21] Merton argues that individual behavior is strongly influenced by the intersection of the goals individuals in a given society are taught to value and the means to these goals that each society puts at their disposal. The conditions for anomie are present when members of some segment of society (e.g., poor persons, minorities) are constantly informed through social contacts and the media of what goods and services they should aspire to possess, but at the same time they are blocked from legitimately obtaining these goods and services. In short, Merton argues that when a high degree of anomie has set in, laws are deprived of their legitimacy.[22]

In principle, these processes should operate in all societies, but, as noted in Chapter 4, Merton believes that the United States is exceptional in its single-minded emphasis on monetary success goals. This emphasis is frequently illustrated with "Horatio Alger" stories in which individuals of humble origins nevertheless attain great financial success through their hard work and sacrifice. But of course, not all individuals from humble backgrounds end up being financially successful. In fact, the United States is highly stratified by wealth and income, so that access to legitimate opportunities for attaining economic success depend in part on the family into which a given individual is born. Merton argues that some individuals who want to be financially successful but lack access to the legitimate means to become so simply shortcut the system by turning to crime.

The perfect example is the gangster, which Merton used to illustrate his original theory. Merton claims that the mobster Al Capone represents "the triumph of amoral intelligence over morally prescribed 'failure,'" because Capone turned to crime when he was blocked from pursuing legitimate channels of upward mobility.[23] Thus, Merton argues that being blocked from legitimate economic participation in a society that emphasizes monetary success above other goals increases individual motivation to commit crime.

Several other influential explanations of crime are closely related. The sociologist Albert Cohen argues that economic stress experienced by inner-city juveniles leads to a loss of self esteem, which in turn results in increasing rates of juvenile delinquency and crime.[24] Similarly, Richard Cloward and Lloyd Ohlin—whose arguments about crime became an important research justification for President John F. Kennedy's New Frontier programs of the 1960s—argue that an economic system that blocks some juveniles from legitimate participation produces a sense of injustice in these juveniles, resulting in higher crime rates.[25]

Although most strain theorists have emphasized the effects of strain on the motivation of would-be offenders, there is also a long-standing research tradition emphasizing the way that economic stress can undermine the ability of families and communities to control the criminal behavior of their members. The best-known version of this argument is the social disorganization model that originated at the University of Chicago in the 1920s.

Examining Chicago neighborhoods, the sociological pioneers Clifford Shaw and Henry McKay observed that areas characterized by great economic hardship generally had high rates of population turnover and population heterogeneity.[26] The authors reasoned that economically depressed areas have high rates of population turnover mostly because residents move out as soon as they can afford housing elsewhere. The constant flow of the wealthiest citizens out of impoverished areas and their replacement with migrants and immigrants increases the heterogeneity of neighborhoods.

Population turnover and heterogeneity in turn reduce the effectiveness of social control in three main ways. First, because residents expect to move soon, they have fewer interests in participating in long-lasting community institutions. Individuals are more likely to decide that investing time and energy in neighborhoods that they will soon be leaving is pointless. Second, because social connections in these neighborhoods are weak and constantly changing, residents are unlikely to develop strong informal sources of social control. Neighbors are less likely to know each other and less interested in regulating the behavior of other members of their community. And finally, the heterogeneity of these communities in itself impedes efforts to solve neighborhood problems and achieve common goals.[27] As economically more stable families flee poorer neighborhoods, they are likely to be replaced by an extremely heterogeneous group of recent immigrants and migrants from other countries and regions. These individuals may not even agree on what constitutes proper behavior in their neighborhood, let alone be able to organize effectively to maintain low-crime communities.

Although strain theories are important in that they explicitly consider the impact of social institutions on crime, they face a major problem when it comes to explaining the crime boom of the 1960s and 1970s: Crime increased dramatically under what seemed to be conditions of low economic strain. One possible explanation for this seeming anomaly is that prior research has not emphasized the most appropriate measures of economic stress.

Absolute and Relative Economic Stress

One useful way of categorizing different types of economic stress is to distinguish between absolute and relative measures. Absolute measures generally refer to how individuals or groups of individuals are doing in comparison to some fixed level of economic well-being. For example, for many years the U.S. government has attempted to measure the total number of Americans who live in poverty, or are below "the poverty line." Similarly, many researchers have estimated how rates of unemployment in a given community or society are related to crime rates.[28] In both cases, the usual expectation is that absolute increases in levels of poverty or unemployment will result in crime increases.

By contrast, relative measures of economic stress emphasize how one individual or group of individuals is doing compared to other individuals or groups. The most common type of relative economic stress measure examined by criminologists has been economic inequality.[29] The expectation here is that as economic inequality increases, crime rates will also increase. Because inflation is likely to have a much greater impact on persons on fixed or minimum wages than on higher-income individuals, it may also serve as a relative measure of economic stress.[30]

An emphasis on relative rather than absolute measures of economic stress for explaining crime trends seems justifiable for at least two reasons. First, as Karl Marx and Frederick Engels observed more than a century ago, because "our desires and pleasures spring from society . . . they are of a relative nature."[31] Thus, urban muggers in major U.S. cities today may have access to economic resources only imagined by nonoffending residents of, say, Albania or Haiti or rural eighteenth-century America. Yet, these same individuals may experience substantial feelings of deprivation compared to the relatively affluent individuals who surround them or whom they regularly see portrayed in the media.

Second, absolute measures of economic stress may mask changes at the margins of the income distribution that are likely to affect crime trends. For example, a society that makes tremendous strides in per capita income may simultaneously experience increased economic inequality or inflation. Conversely, the quote from Marx and Engels at the beginning of this chapter suggests that frustration and unhappiness may nevertheless remain low in societies in which everyone is equally poor. In fact, we might expect changes at the margins of the income distribution to be especially important in predicting behavior such as street crime, which is most often linked to people at lower income levels.

The distinction between absolute and relative measures of economic stress may also help to clear up some of the apparent contradictions between postwar crime trends and measures of economic stress. In general, there appears to be more support for connections between crime and relative rather than absolute measures of economic stress. For example, in an exhaustive review of the literature, the criminologists George Vold and Thomas Bernard conclude that prior research does not conclusively demonstrate that crime rates increase along with absolute measures of economic stress such as the number of poor or unemployed persons.[32] At the same time, Vold and Bernard argue that economic inequality has been a much more consistent variable in explaining crime rates.[33]

Similarly, several studies have shown that crime rates in the United States have generally increased along with inflation during the postwar period. Thus, in a detailed longitudinal analysis of homicide, robbery, and burglary rates in the postwar United States, Joel Devine and his colleagues conclude that inflation increases crime by reducing the effectiveness of social control, both through the additional stress it causes families and communities and through its effects on government's ability to spend money to deter crime and alleviate economic suffering.[34] In a recent analysis of the same three street crimes, my colleague Kriss Drass and I also found that increases in inflation were consistently associated with increases in robbery, homicide, and burglary rates during the postwar period.[35]

Summary: Economic Stress, Legitimacy, and Crime

Economic explanations of street crime have long been popular. Strain theories bring institutional considerations to bear by arguing that economic stress results in anomie, normlessness, or a sense of injustice that in turn increases individual motivation to commit crime and reduces the effectiveness of informal social control systems. Economic institutions with little legitimacy are less successful at convincing individuals of the importance of behaving lawfully. Declining economic legitimacy can also have a corrosive effect on the ability of families and communities to control their members.

Strain theories have had difficulty, however, explaining the rapid crime increases during the American crime boom of the 1960s. One possibility that I explore later is that, compared to absolute measures of economic stress like median income and poverty, relative measures like inequality and inflation may be more closely connected to economic legitimacy and crime trends.

Economic Legitimacy and Crime in Postwar America

As in earlier chapters, we are looking here for explanations that can fit what we already know about trends in postwar street crime rates: that is, relatively low, stable rates during the early postwar years (1946 to 1960); rapidly increasing rates during the middle postwar years (1961 to 1973); and relatively high yet stable rates during the late postwar years (1974 and later). As before, I also consider whether additional insights can be gained by evaluating separately the experiences of African Americans. In this regard, I am looking for evidence of how economic trends might help explain higher crime rates for African Americans throughout the postwar period as well as during the especially rapid acceleration of African American crime rates in the middle postwar years.

The Early Postwar Period, 1946–1960

Economists are generally in agreement that the United States entered an era of unprecedented economic prosperity immediately following World War II.[36] One of the principal forces driving this prosperity was rising labor force productivity. Between 1947 and 1959, the growth of output per hour worked in private businesses in the United States averaged 3.3 percent per year.[37] This high growth rate translated into rapidly rising real wages. For example, in 1949, a typical male worker in his late twenties could look forward to an average income increase of an incredible 64 percent over the next ten years.[38] Moreover, these steadily rising wages were coupled with low inflation rates. Inflation did heat up briefly when the Korean War began in 1950, but a year of mild recession was sufficient to snuff it out.

At the same time, inequality between workers actually decreased during the early postwar years. The economists Claudia Goldin and Robert Margo show that from 1940 to 1950, wage dispersion between the highest- and lowest-paid 10 percent of the U.S. labor force declined by more than 25 percent.[39] Goldin and Margo conclude that this "great compression" of wages was probably a result of the short-term impact of wartime demand for less-skilled labor combined with longer-run changes in the demand for educated workers. The nation's demand for less-educated workers soared in the 1940s as World War II drew millions of workers into the military and into factories to support the military. At the same time, the supply of highly educated workers increased. This meant that, all things being equal, the ability of the more highly educated to command larger salaries was diminished. Goldin and Margo contend that these changes helped produce the "steel belts" in the 1940s that would become the "rust belts" of the 1980s. Although wage inequality began to rise somewhat in the 1950s, it remained at relatively low levels until the rapid increases experienced in the early 1970s.

Thus, in both absolute and relative economic measures the early postwar years might be seen as a textbook example of what we might expect of an economy in a society enjoying low crime rates: low unemployment and inflation, high productivity and wages, declining inequality.

The Middle Postwar Period, 1961–1973

If economic trends in the early postwar years seem to fit crime trends nearly perfectly, economic trends in the middle postwar years posed a challenge for American criminologists that ended up fundamentally reshaping both research and policy on crime for decades to come. The central problem is well expressed in James Q. Wilson's 1975 challenge to criminologists to explain "the paradox" of "crime amidst plenty."[40] Indeed, in many respects the economic picture of the United States in the middle postwar period was even more favorable than it had been in the early postwar years. Productivity declined slightly in the 1960s but remained at historically high levels. A typical working male in his late twenties in 1959 would see his real income grow by 49 percent over the decade of the sixties.[41] These trends are illustrated in Figure 7.1, which shows median income for American men in inflation-adjusted dollars from 1947 to 1995. To allow easy comparison, I include robbery rates for the same period.

Figure 7.1 clearly demonstrates the vulnerability of common strain theory explanations based on the connections between economic stress and crime in the middle postwar period. As shown in Figure 7.1, inflation-adjusted income for American males *grew* steadily from 1960 to 1973—about the same time as the postwar crime boom. In fact, it didn't just grow, it exploded. From 1960 to 1973, median income of American men 14 years and over, in inflation-adjusted dollars, rose from just over $19,000 to more than $26,000—a 35 percent increase. As we have seen previously, during these same years total street crime rates more than doubled.

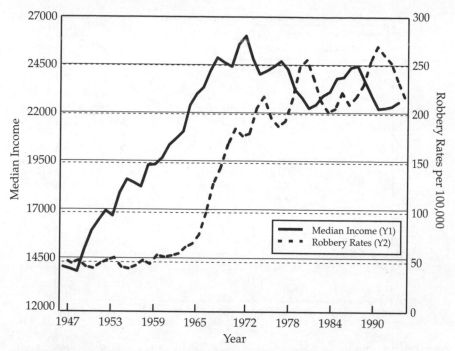

FIGURE 7.1 Trends in Median Income of Males and Robbery Rates, 1947–1995 (in 1995 Dollars)
NOTE: Males 15 years and over beginning in 1980 and males 14 years and over for previous years.
SOURCE: U.S. Bureau of the Census, "Money Income in the United States: 1995," *Current Population Reports,* Series P-60, No. 193 (Washington, DC: Government Printing Office, 1996), p. B-12.

These relationships between income and street crime are not unique to this particular measure. Kriss Drass and I found the same basic relationship for several other absolute measures of economic stress, including median family income, median income of adult men in the year-round full-time labor force, and proportion of families below the poverty line.[42] The trends are somewhat more complex for unemployment and joblessness rates—mainly because these rates fluctuate more rapidly than measures of income and poverty. Nevertheless, the overall trends for unemployment were generally quite favorable during the 1960s and early 1970s. After 1961, unemployment declined more or less steadily for the rest of the decade, falling from 6.7 percent in 1961 to 3.5 percent in 1969.[43]

But relative measures of economic stress for the middle postwar years present a very different picture. Kriss Drass and I estimated a measure of family income inequality based on applying an interquartile range[44] to in-

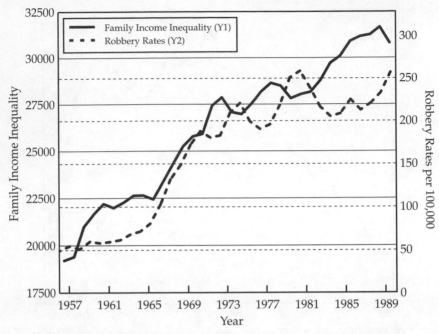

FIGURE 7.2   Trends in Family Income Inequality and Robbery Rates, 1957–1990
(in 1990 Dollars)
SOURCES: U.S. Bureau of the Census, "Money Income of Households, Families
and Persons in the United States, 1987," *Current Population Reports,* Consumer Income Series, P-60, No. 162 (Washington, DC: Government Printing Office, 1987);
U.S. Bureau of the Census, *Current Population Reports,* Series P-60, No. 184 (Washington, DC: Government Printing Office, 1993).

come distributions for each year from 1957 to 1990.[45] Figure 7.2 shows the
results. As before, I include robbery trends to allow easy comparison.
    As shown in Figure 7.2, the gap between the top quarter of male in-
come earners and the bottom quarter of male income earners was about
$19,000 in 1957 (in inflation-adjusted 1990 dollars). Income inequality in-
creased steadily during much of the postwar period. By 1990, the gap between the top and bottom quarters of male income earners had risen to
about $31,000. Increases in income inequality were especially great dur-
ing the 1960s and early 1970s. From 1960 to 1973 alone, the income inequality measure rose from $21,654 to $27,867—a 29 percent increase.
    As with economic inequality, trends in inflation during the middle
postwar years suggest large increases in economic stress. Figure 7.3
shows changes in the rate of inflation for the United States based on the
consumer price index, from 1948 to 1995. Again, to allow comparisons, I
have superimposed robbery rates for the same period.

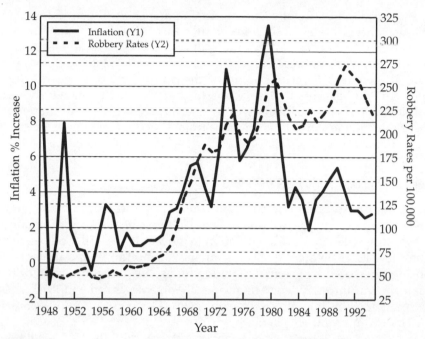

FIGURE 7.3   Annual Percentage Increase in Inflation and Robbery Rates, 1948–1995
SOURCE: Economic Report of the President, *The Annual Report of the Council of Economic Advisors* (Washington, DC: Government Printing Office, 1997), p. 348.

Inflation trends clearly demonstrate how absolute indicators can suggest increasing economic prosperity at the same time that more relative economic indicators signal growing economic stress. It was precisely during the period of high prosperity and full employment in the United States that rates of inflation began to accelerate.[46] As the administration of President Lyndon Johnson simultaneously expanded spending on social programs and decided to fight an increasingly costly war in Southeast Asia, inflationary pressure began to build. As shown in Figure 7.3, inflation fluctuated considerably in the early postwar period. In 1948, inflation jumped by 8 percent as the economy heated up following the war and again by 8 percent in 1951 as mobilization for the Korean War spurred inflation. But in the early 1960s, inflation began a steady upward trend, reaching a postwar high of 13 percent in 1979. Inflation then cooled off again in the 1980s and 1990s. Inflation remained at 3 percent or less from 1990 to 1995.

Thus, compared to absolute economic stress measures like average income, relative measures of economic stress such as income inequality and inflation appear to match crime trends better during the middle postwar years. Although critics of economic strain perspectives such as James Q. Wilson concentrate on absolute economic measures like median income to conclude that crime was booming during a very favorable economic period, relative measures of economic strain provide a quite different picture. In general, the crime boom of the middle postwar years corresponded with an economy that was strong in absolute terms but showed considerable weakness in relative terms. Compared to absolute measures, these relative measures of economic strain are better predictors of street crime trends.

The Late Postwar Period, 1974–1996

In summing up economic conditions after 1973, the economist Frank Levy offers one word: "awful."[47] The declining health of the economy was first signaled by growing inflation in the late 1960s. Inflation began to rise a few years before the major Vietnam War buildup[48] and it was seriously exacerbated by President Lyndon Johnson's decision to pay for the Vietnam War through deficit financing.[49] Worse news came in 1973 when the economy was hit with two supply shocks—one in food and the other, and more important one, in oil.[50]

In October 1973, the state of Israel was attacked by its Arab neighbors on the Jewish holiday called Yom Kippur. Arab nations placed an embargo on oil as part of their war effort. A hitherto-ineffective cartel called the Organization of Petroleum Exporting Countries (OPEC) agreed to raise the benchmark price of Saudi "marker crude" oil from $3 to $5.11 a barrel. This measure proved to be so successful that in January 1974, OPEC raised the price again to $11.65 per barrel. By 1974, these shocks caused annual inflation to increase by nearly 13 percent (see Figure 7.3).

The combination of rapidly increasing energy prices and growing economic instability helped cause productivity to decline, a condition that generally continued into the early 1990s.[51] Again, if we take a fictional average man in his late twenties in 1973, he could expect his income to remain basically unchanged for the next twenty years.[52] As we saw in Figure 7.1, median male income in inflation-adjusted dollars was actually lower ($22,562) in 1995 than it had been in 1967 ($23,313). Growing unemployment added to the developing economic doldrums of the 1970s and 1980s. The country reentered a recession, with unemployment reaching 8.5 percent in 1975, a postwar high.[53]

The structure of the labor market also underwent fundamental changes during the late postwar period. In particular, urban areas in the 1970s and 1980s, especially in the Northeast and North Central regions, lost large numbers of jobs in industries that formerly paid relatively high wages to low-skilled workers.[54] Many service jobs in large cities were also lost.[55]

Economic inequality also increased appreciably in the 1970s and 1980s.[56] The economists William Goldsmith and Edward Blakely point out that the share of aggregate family income earned by the poorest one fifth of U.S. families fell by 16 percent between 1973 and 1989 alone.[57] Average income also fell for the next three-fifths of families. Since the early 1970s, wages of less-skilled workers have declined and, especially during the 1980s, employers increased pay differentials between workers with and without college training and between workers with more and less experience.[58] These trends have held across virtually all sectors of the economy. By contrast, incomes rose for the richest fifth of U.S. families and the richest 1 percent of U.S. families gained the most.

The distribution of real disposable family income (that is, income after taxes are deducted and transfer payments are added) worsened even more dramatically between 1977 and 1990. The economists Goldsmith and Blakely offer two generalizations: "Poorer families grew relatively poorer; and the disparities increased more rapidly in the most recent period."[59] Of particular note, a 1991 report from the U.S. Congress shows that the real value of family income (that is, families' purchasing power after removing the effects of inflation) declined for the poorest half of all families from 1979 to 1989.[60]

Part of this growing inequality relates directly to changes in the relationship between education and wages. The economists John Bound and George Johnson note that during the 1980s there was a precipitous rise in the relative wages and earnings of workers with high levels of education.[61] The average wage of a college graduate increased relative to the average wage of a high school graduate by over 15 percent from 1979 to 1988. The high school to elementary school wage differential also increased substantially.

By the early 1990s, there was mounting evidence that the United States was moving in the direction of two separate societies defined by economic well-being. Robert Reich, former Secretary of Labor in the Clinton administration, has argued that the U.S. economy can be divided into four parts: symbolic analysts, routine operators, personal service providers, and everyone else.[62] Reich defines symbolic analysts as workers who deal with numbers and ideas, such as lawyers, doctors, and computer programmers. Reich refers to this group as the "fortunate fifth," because by the 1990s this 20 percent of the U.S. economy had a higher after-tax income than the other four-fifths of the economy combined.

But as this book was being prepared, there were continuing changes in the economy and some indication that we may be entering a new period in the postwar relationship between economic institutions and crime. As the United States approaches the millennium, there are indications of improvement in relative economic measures. In particular, inflation was held under 3 percent during the first half of the 1990s, and in 1995 and 1996 the United States experienced modest declines in inequality rates.[63] It is too early to be certain but provocative to consider the possibility that these changing economic conditions are partly responsible for the downturn in street crime rates that the United States is experiencing at the end of the twentieth century.

African Americans, Crime, and the Postwar Economy

Thus far, I have concentrated on general relationships between economic stress and crime trends. I next want to consider whether we can gain any further insights by considering differences in trends for African Americans and whites. In many ways, the relationship between economic conditions and crime for African Americans in the postwar period is similar to the general relationships already observed—only more so. I can illustrate by again examining postwar income data. Figure 7.4 shows median income for black males and white males from 1948 to 1995.

Not surprising, median income for black men was substantially lower than median income for white men during the entire period spanned by the data. On average, annual income for whites was more than $9,000 higher than that for African Americans during this period. In general, median income for both black men and white men increased most sharply just before and during the large increases in crime in the 1960s and early 1970s. Since the early 1970s, median income for both groups has been either flat or declining.

Figure 7.4 raises two points that seem counterintuitive in terms of connections between economic stress and crime for African Americans. The first is the same problem raised earlier for overall postwar economic trends, namely, that economic conditions for African Americans seemed to be generally improving at the same time that their crime rates were dramatically rising. And second, the gap between African American and white average income was either holding stable or declining at the same time that African American crime rates were rapidly increasing. Admittedly, these were not enormous economic improvements for African Americans. Nevertheless, Figure 7.4 shows that in 1948 the average income of black men was 54 percent of comparable white male income whereas in 1995 it had increased to 67 percent.

When my colleague Kriss Drass and I compared other absolute measures of income for African Americans and whites, we discovered similar relationships.[64] Thus, measures of median family income, median income of men in the year-round workforce, and proportion of families below the poverty line all generally show postwar improvements for African Americans both in general terms and in relationship to whites. In fact, we found strong correlations between trends for all of these income measures

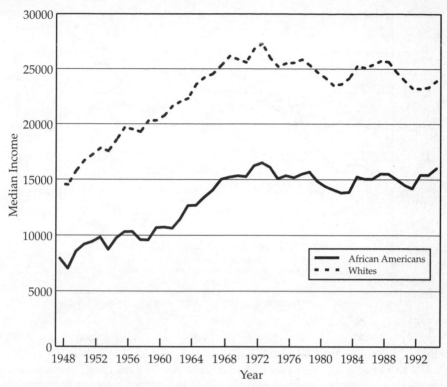

FIGURE 7.4 Trends in Median Income of African American and White Males, 1948–1995 (in 1995 Dollars)
NOTES: Males 15 years and over beginning in 1980 and males 14 and over for previous years. Data are for African Americans and other minorities before 1967.
SOURCE: U.S. Bureau of the Census, "Money Income in the United States: 1995," *Current Population Reports,* Series P-60, No. 193 (Washington, DC: Government Printing Office, 1996), pp. B-13, B-14.

as well as measures of unemployment and proportion of adult males not in the labor force. And in every case, the middle postwar years were a period in which rapidly accelerating crime rates for African Americans were associated with seemingly favorable economic conditions, both in absolute terms and in comparison to whites.

But as with overall economic trends, these seeming anomalies are more understandable if we instead examine relative measures of economic stress. Figure 7.5 compares African Americans and whites on one such measure: the interquartile range of family income inequality. Figure 7.5 shows that for both groups inequality of family income increased during much of the middle postwar years. The increase was especially steep for African Americans from 1962 to 1972.

FIGURE 7.5   Race and Family Income Inequality, 1957–1990 (in 1990 Dollars)
NOTE: Data before 1967 are for African Americans and other minorities.
SOURCE: Gary LaFree and Kriss A. Drass, "The Effect of Changes in Intraracial
Income Inequality and Educational Attainment on Changes in Arrest Rates for
African Americans and Whites, 1957 to 1990," *American Sociological Review* (1996)
61:614–634. Reprinted with permission.

In our analysis of homicide, robbery, and burglary rates, 1957 to 1990,
Kriss Drass and I found that measures of income inequality such as the
one shown in Figure 7.5 were associated with increasing crime rates during the postwar years for both African Americans and whites. In contrast,
absolute measures of economic stress such as median male income had
no connection to black crime trends and a less consistent connection to
white crime trends.[65] Thus, although African Americans as a group made
economic progress during the postwar period, both in absolute terms and
in comparison to whites, this progress was offset by growing intraracial
income inequality.

African Americans, Crime, and Migration

Migration has often been suggested as a critical factor in explaining both
the economic stress and high street crime rates associated with African

Americans during the postwar period.[66] As we have already seen, migration is also a logical explanation because it has been a key variable in explaining the economic status and criminal behavior of waves of earlier immigrants in U.S. history.[67] And in fact, a major migration of African Americans from the rural South to inner-city urban areas of the North occurred during the postwar years. From 1940 to 1970, the percentage of African Americans living in the South dropped from 80 to 53 percent.[68] In only one generation, the black population shifted from being predominantly rural to becoming more urbanized than the white population.[69]

The economist Frank Levy points out that this migration was quite understandable in economic terms.[70] The southeastern part of the United States lagged behind all other areas of the country in average salary and number of manufacturing jobs. Many African Americans left jobs as tenant farmers in the rural South for better-paying manufacturing jobs in the North.

Given the size of these changes, migration would seem to be an obvious candidate for explaining high inner-city African American crime rates as well as other social problems.[71] In a review of the impact of migration on African Americans, the journalist Nicholas Lemann concludes, "Every aspect of the underclass culture in the ghettos is directly traceable to roots in the South—and not the South of slavery but the South of a generation ago."[72] But the connections between African American migration and African American urban social problems during the postwar years are in fact complex.

To begin, much of the migration of rural, southern African Americans to the urban North occurred in the 1940s and 1950s.[73] In the decade of the 1950s alone, the proportion of all African Americans living in central cities jumped from 41 to 51 percent.[74] African American migration rates from the South peaked in 1960.[75] By the 1970s and 1980s, the Southeast actually had substantial amounts of African American in-migration.[76] In short, some of the largest increases in African American migration to the North happened at the same time that African American crime rates were at historically low levels.

Moreover, contemporary inner-city areas with extremely high crime rates are not generally composed of recent migrants from the rural South. The sociologist William Julius Wilson shows that of the northern metropolitan areas that have been among the top ten in African American population in 1960, 1970, or 1980, only two (Newark, New Jersey; and Detroit, Michigan) gained African American population through migration between 1970 and 1980, and even for these two cities the gains were modest.[77] The large U.S. cities that captured the public imagination for their crime problems in the late postwar period—New York, Chicago, Philadelphia, Detroit—gained little or no African American population through migration during this period. In fact, these northern cities generally lost more African Americans through out-migration than they gained through in-migration.[78]

Wilson also argues that African Americans who have migrated from the South to the urban North have generally fared better economically than African Americans born in the urban North.[79] Wilson shows that compared to northern-born African Americans, southern-born African Americans who have migrated to the North have higher earnings, higher labor force participation rates, and lower unemployment and are less likely to be receiving welfare.[80]

But despite the fact that the relationship between African American migration from the rural South to the urban North does not appear to be related to African American crime trends in any straightforward way, African American crime trends may nevertheless have been affected by migration. William Julius Wilson's theory of the urban underclass claims that the exodus of middle- and working-class families from inner-city neighborhoods during the postwar period has resulted in "concentration effects," whereby a disproportionate number of the most disadvantaged segments of the urban African American population have been left behind.[81]

Indeed, one of the most important migration movements of the postwar period has been the flight of both African Americans and whites from inner cities to suburbs.[82] During the 1960s, central cities as a group had net out-migration of 345,000 persons per year.[83] During the 1970s, central cities' net out-migration averaged 1.3 million persons per year. By the 1990s, more Americans lived in the suburban fringe around central cities than in central cities themselves.[84] Wilson argues that much of this out-migration from central cities for African Americans is the result of racial desegregation, which has allowed middle- and upper-class blacks to leave behind troubled inner-city neighborhoods.[85] By contrast, the demographer Douglas Massey and his colleagues argue that the major explanation for the concentration of African American disadvantage in inner-city neighborhoods has been public policies and private practices such as "redlining" by banks and "blockbusting" tactics of real estate agents[86] that have encouraged residential segregation based on race.[87]

Regardless of the precise forces at work, the people who have left cities have had higher incomes than the people who have stayed.[88] In constant dollars, the income gap between central city and suburban families in 1959 was $2,100, or 11 percent.[89] By 1983, it had widened to 24 percent—$23,300 in central cities versus $30,600 in suburbs.[90] And as we shall see in the next chapter, these differences are in turn closely related to changes in families.

Conclusions: Crime and the Postwar Economy

In this chapter, I explored the possibility that postwar U.S. crime trends are explained in part by the varying stresses imposed on Americans by their economic institutions. In general, the idea that economic conditions produced the crime trends that we have observed for postwar America works best for the early postwar period—when economic conditions were generally strong and crime rates were low and flat—and for the late postwar period—when economic conditions were generally weak and crime rates were high and flat. The middle postwar years—from 1961 to 1973—are hardest to explain by referencing economic conditions. This is because most absolute measures of economic well-being were in fact improving during the period when crime rates skyrocketed.

Economic stress arguments for the middle postwar years are more convincing when we turn to a consideration of trends in relative measures of economic stress. In particular, economic inequality and inflation began to increase consistently in the 1960s and continued to increase into the early 1990s. During the mid-1990s, inflation increased more slowly, and economic inequality actually declined in 1994 and 1995. It appears that relative measures of economic stress, such as inequality and inflation, rather than absolute measures, such as income and unemployment, are more closely linked to the crime boom of the 1960s and early 1970s.

Compared to the linkage between absolute measures of economic stress and crime for whites, the linkage for African Americans is even more problematic. In particular, African Americans had relatively low crime rates during the 1940s and 1950s, when they were severely disadvantaged on all major economic indicators, but record high crime rates during the 1960s and 1970s, a period of major economic gains. Still, there is strong evidence that economic trends in the postwar period were related to African American crime trends. Just as the economic position of African Americans has been consistently worse than that of whites throughout the postwar period, black crime trends are likewise consistently higher than white crime trends throughout the postwar years. Moreover, aggregate economic gains made during the postwar period by African Americans were offset by a widening gap between rich and poor blacks.

The early postwar period was a golden age for mainstream American criminology. The strong economy and correspondingly low crime rates made it look as if social problems such as crime could be solved with a bit of fine-tuning rather than through wholesale changes. Low crime rates were both a cause and a product of the feeling that the United States was in a unique position compared to other nations of the world.

The crime boom of the 1960s severely challenged this self-satisfaction. Especially vexing for liberal policymakers was the fact that crime rates were increasing at the same time that economic conditions seemed to be relatively favorable. Some policymakers and researchers in the 1960s tried to skirt these issues by arguing that increases in street crime were illusory because of the hopelessly flawed nature of official UCR crime data. But later analysis would show that the crime trends picked up by the UCR were, in fact, generally accurate. A more effective liberal approach would have been to emphasize relative measures of economic well-being. Although absolute measures of economic conditions were strong during the middle postwar years, relative measures were much weaker.

Somewhat paradoxically, the declining economy during much of the late postwar period has again brought mainstream criminology theory into closer alignment with economic reality. In this case, a weaker national economy facing increasingly intense global competition more closely matches the historically high levels of crime being recorded. Perhaps these conditions explain in part the resurging interest within the criminology research community after the 1970s in theories of why people commit crime.[91] If policymakers could look to low crime rates in the early postwar period as evidence that a strong economy produced a smoothly running society, policymakers have used high crime rates in the late postwar period to justify major changes in public policy aimed at deterring and incapacitating offenders.

As this book was being prepared, street crime rates were showing signs of not just remaining in place but actually beginning to decline. Interestingly, these changes correspond to an economy that seems to be gaining strength, in both relative and absolute terms.

•   •   •

In the next chapter, I turn to trends in a third major institution with important implications for crime: the family. The American family has undergone enormous changes during the postwar period. In Chapter 8, I examine the connections between these changes and crime rates.

eight

Crime and Changes in the American Family

There is a perennial invasion of barbarians who must somehow be civilized and turned into contributors to fulfillment of the various functions requisite to societal survival.

—Norman B. Ryder[1]

Little kids are . . . nasty little bastards.

—John Wayne[2]

The appeal of the family as an explanation for crime and delinquency is easy to understand. Unlike political or economic institutions, which are intentionally constructed by human actors, family institutions depend directly on relationships developed through birth and blood.[3] This has given family institutions a special role in socializing human beings and regulating their conduct. Families typically have control over individuals earliest, longest, and most intensively.

Family-related variables also seem promising as an explanation for the crime trends I have described previously, because family structure, like crime, changed enormously in America during the postwar years. The sociologists Frances Goldscheider and Linda Waite argue that the American family in the second half of the twentieth century simultaneously underwent two revolutionary changes, one inside and one outside.[4] The inside change was in economic relationships between men and women. The industrial economy in which women were effectively limited to low-level jobs in caretaking, clerical, and retail areas is gradually giving way to a postindustrial economy based on knowledge, information, and service skills in which women are increasingly filling positions at all economic levels.[5] The outside change with major implications for family institutions was the extraordinary postwar rise in the proportion of people living outside of families, including unmarried young, divorced, and widowed adults.[6]

Connections between families and crime also seem promising for explaining postwar differences between African Americans and whites. On any common measure of family organization, African Americans began the postwar period with greater variation in family structure and gathered increasing heterogeneity faster than whites. Compared to white women, black women had more children outside of marriage, were more likely to head their own families, and were less likely to marry and remarry; compared to white children, black children were less likely to live with both biological parents.[7] Hence, differences between black family organization and white family organization are logical possibilities for explaining some of the observed dissimilarity between black crime rates and white crime rates during the postwar years.

Family Organization and Legitimacy

How Do Family Institutions Regulate Crime?

Before going further, it would be useful to consider more specifically the mechanisms by which family institutions regulate crime rates. The literature on these connections is voluminous, but most arguments emphasize the family's role in reducing criminal motivation and providing social control and protection. The family has the most obvious impact on the motivation of individuals to commit crime through its role as the primary agent for passing institutional rules from one generation to the next.[8] As discussed in Chapter 5, because humans have underdeveloped instincts they are dependent on socialization for ensuring that children learn social rules. With few exceptions, human societies give children more frequent and longer contacts with family members than with others, family contacts are generally prior to other contacts, and family contacts are usually more emotionally intense than any other social contacts. Throughout human history, the family has been the major institution for teaching children right from wrong, instilling moral values, and emphasizing appropriate long-term goals.

Families also control crime and deviance by directly regulating the behavior of their members. In particular, families can reduce the incidence of crime by restricting the activities of their children, by maintaining physical surveillance over them, and by knowing their whereabouts when they are out of sight.[9] It is important to recognize that these social control functions of families operate on an extremely broad spectrum. Families can reduce the criminal behavior of their children through direct physical surveillance of their activities, but perhaps even more important, families can control the social behavior of their children by simply commanding their love and respect. A good deal of research confirms that children who care about their family are more likely to avoid behavior that they know may result in shame, embarrassment, or inconvenience for family members.[10]

Although these social control functions are most obvious when applied to children, families also regulate the behavior of adult family members. In a reanalysis of Sheldon and Eleanor Glueck's mid-century study of 500 delinquents and 500 nondelinquents from childhood to adulthood, the sociologists Robert Sampson and John Laub show that the strength of family attachments during youth continues to explain participation in crime, independent of prior criminal behavior, far into adulthood.[11]

And finally, the family often serves as a crime-reducing agent through the guardianship it provides its members. Families may diminish the criminal victimization of their members by protecting them from property crimes such as burglary and theft, as well as by shielding them from the attacks of would-be molesters, muggers, and rapists.[12]

Family Legitimacy and Crime

The legitimacy of family institutions is related to their success in regulating crime in at least four ways. First, societies in which family institutions are accorded greater legitimacy are likely to be more effective as socializing agents because they are able to present a more ubiquitous and congruent picture of acceptable and unacceptable behavior to family members. Socialization messages given by highly legitimated families are more likely to be reinforced and upheld by all family members, as well as by members of other institutions with which family members have contact. Research shows that the more children receive similar, consistent messages from a wide variety of sources, the greater the likelihood that such messages will eventually be internalized.[13]

Second, societies in which family institutions have greater legitimacy are also likely to be more successful in regulating the immediate behavior of their members. As the sociologist Travis Hirschi points out, "Parental supervision may be essential to proper socialization, but it is effective in preventing delinquency even when it has no long-term impact on behavior."[14] That is, even if families do not succeed in convincing their children of the rightness of particular behavior, they may nevertheless serve important social control roles by simply restricting their children's activities, keeping an eye on them as much as possible, and knowing what they are doing when they are out of sight. Parents in families with greater legitimacy are likely to receive more consistent support from other family members and the community in monitoring the behavior of their children. Such families are likely to be more effective at attending to their children's activities, enforcing curfews, and requiring their children to provide information on where they are going and with whom when they are out of sight.

Third, societies in which family institutions enjoy high levels of legitimacy are also likely to be more effective in reducing further criminal behavior even when family members nevertheless break the law.[15] It is well known in criminology that family members often serve as advocates for their children in interactions with the criminal justice system, in essence acting as unofficial probation officers willing to guarantee their children's good conduct.[16] In their influential study of confrontations between juvenile gang members and police officers, Carl Werthman and Irving Piliavin found that one of the main variables associated with the police decision to arrest juveniles was the officer's assessment of whether parents would be able to control the behavior of their children in the absence of an arrest.[17] Family institutions with greater legitimacy are more likely than other families to have the internal organization necessary to serve as effective advocates for their children and to command the respect of those working in legal and social service agencies in order to win more favorable treatment of their children.

Finally, societies in which family institutions have high legitimacy are also likely to be more effective than other societies in protecting their members from the criminal behavior of others. Again, greater family legitimacy improves the effectiveness of guardianship by strengthening the family's internal organization and also by providing the family with greater authority in its dealings with other individuals and institutions. As the sociologists Lawrence Cohen and Marcus Felson observe, a major predictor of property crimes in an area is simply the proportion of homes occupied during the day.[18] Families with lots of household-centered activity generally have lower burglary rates. Furthermore, societies in which family institutions have high legitimacy are likely to be more successful in protecting their members from assault, violence, and physical harm.[19] In short, compared to other families, strongly legitimated families are likely to be more effective in socializing, controlling, and protecting their members.

My argument here is that the declining legitimacy of traditional family institutions in postwar America contributed to the crime wave of the 1960s and 1970s. Moreover, I argue that, compared to white families, the legitimacy of black family institutions started lower and declined more rapidly during the postwar years. But as the speed of change in family institutions slowed in the late postwar years and society began to institutionalize emerging alternatives to the nuclear family formed with two biological parents, levels of family legitimacy have begun to stabilize somewhat.

I should hasten to add here that I am not arguing that there is anything intrinsically crime reducing about the family model with two biological parents, a male breadwinner, and a female housewife that dominated American society at the beginning of the postwar period. Obviously, a wide range of other family forms have historically resulted in low and stable crime rates.[20] Rather, my argument is that American families became less successful at preventing crime during the middle postwar years because, on average, traditional forms of the family lost legitimacy and were not immediately replaced by equally effective new forms. In fact, exceptions to these general trends are telling.

In her careful study of an inner-city black neighborhood during the middle postwar period, the anthropologist Carol Stack shows how community and kin networks were able to maintain relatively stable social systems with few two-parent nuclear families.[21] Similarly, Frank Furstenberg's more recent study of Garrison Heights, a poor white neighborhood in Philadelphia, shows how single parents were aided in child rearing by a community in which "neighborhood kids represent the whole neighborhood" and "everyone assumes a stake in their behavior."[22] To the extent that these communities were able to effectively regulate the behavior of their children, it is because they had developed highly legitimated social alternatives to traditional family forms.

Research on Crime and Family Legitimacy

As I argued in Chapter 5, legitimacy can be conceptualized as how successful institutions are in keeping human behavior within widely accepted, institutionally prescribed channels. Thus, we can gauge changes in the legitimacy of the traditional family by studying alternatives to the ideal type. There have been few longitudinal time-series studies of the links between alternatives to traditional family forms and crime. Cohen and Felson, however, created a longitudinal measure they call a "household activity ratio" by adding the number of married households with women in the paid labor force to the total number of non–husband-and-wife households.[23] They use this measure to estimate changes in the amount of activity engaged in away from households. But note that it is also a measure of the amount of time individuals spend outside of traditional nuclear families. In their longitudinal analysis of homicide, rape, aggravated assault, robbery, and burglary from 1947 to 1974, Cohen and Felson confirm that increases in the proportion of time individuals spend away from traditional families are consistently associated with increases in all of these street crimes. The same results were largely confirmed in a later longitudinal study of murder, robbery, and burglary in the United States from 1948 to 1985.[24]

In contrast to the paucity of time-series studies, there is an extensive cross-sectional literature on the relationship between alternatives to traditional family organization and crime. Measures of family disruption, including divorce rates, percentage of female-headed households, and number of children born outside marriage have all been associated in prior research with higher rates of juvenile delinquency and crime.[25] In their classic 1950 study, Sheldon and Eleanor Glueck compared the family experiences of 500 boys who had been convicted of delinquency with a matched sample of 500 boys who had not been convicted. The Gluecks found that more than 60 percent of the delinquent sample were from broken homes, compared to 32 percent of the nondelinquent sample. The Gluecks concluded that they could predict juvenile delinquency from an early age by examining just five family background variables: discipline of the boy by the father, supervision of the boy by the mother, affection of the father for the boy, affection of the mother for the boy, and cohesiveness of the family.[26]

More recently, in a study of robbery and homicide rates in 150 U.S. cities, Robert Sampson found that rates of divorce and female-headed households were more closely related to urban crime rates than a wide variety of other variables, including poverty, age structure, and urbanization.[27] Similarly, in a study of crime in London, the criminologist David Farrington concludes that separation of juveniles from their parents before the age of ten predicts both juvenile and adult criminal conviction rates and can continue having measurable effects on conviction rates up until offenders reach middle age.[28]

We might also expect levels of family legitimacy to show up in parenting styles. In particular, compared to other families, highly legitimated families should be more successful at providing consistent supervision and support of their children. In an extensive review of the linkage between parenting-related variables and juvenile delinquency, the researchers Rolf Loeber and Magda Stouthamer-Loeber analyzed dozens of prior studies.[29] Among the cross-sectional research reviewed, the authors found that the most important predictors of juvenile delinquency were the amount of discipline and supervision children received from parents, the level of parental involvement with children, and whether parents had rejected their children. Similarly, among the studies that measured the behavior of children over time, the best predictors of juvenile delinquency were parental supervision, parental rejection of their children, and parental involvement with their children.[30]

Family Change and Crime Trends

By now, the general contours of postwar crime trends should be clear. The key question here is how well do changes in the legitimacy of the traditional American family during the postwar period match the street crime trends described earlier? And as in previous chapters, I also consider how differences between white experiences and black experiences might provide additional insights into crime trends.

The impact of declining family institutions on crime in postwar American was undoubtedly amplified by the long-term trend to focus increasing responsibility for raising children on the two-parent family. Social historians point out that in the early part of the twentieth century parents were much more likely than they were at the end of the century to share child-rearing responsibilities with church groups, extended kin networks, and other members of the community.[31] As the family became more private and specialized during the twentieth century, individual parents were increasingly forced to become "solo practitioners" in rearing their children.[32] In fact, this increasing isolation of housewives from other community support networks was one of the major criticisms of traditional families raised by feminists in the 1960s.[33] In other words, at the same time that the traditional nuclear family was becoming especially important for raising children the structure of the traditional family began to unravel.

In the next two sections, I consider two major challenges to the legitimacy of the traditional American family during the postwar period. The first challenge was ideological and aimed directly at the traditional family as a male-dominated institution. This challenge quickly resulted in a much greater diversity of family forms. The second major challenge, related in complex ways to the first, was largely economic. Economic changes had profound effects on the total amount of time most individuals spent in families in the postwar United States.

New Families and No Families

The postwar years have witnessed landmark changes in the forms that families and households take in America. The main development here has been a proliferation of alternatives to the form of the family with two biological parents, the husband as breadwinner and the wife as household manager, that dominated the immediate postwar years. Challenges to the legitimacy of the traditional family became especially important in the middle postwar years. Perhaps the most effective of these challenges came from the feminist movement beginning in the 1960s.

The defining aspect of the feminist critique of the traditional family was its rejection of the undisputed dominance of the husband and father. Kate Millet, in an influential statement of feminist ideology first published in 1969, claims that patriarchy rests on two straightforward principles: "male shall dominate female, elder male shall dominate younger."[34] Although Millet claims that patriarchal organization is evident in all major social institutions, she concludes that "patriarchy's chief institution is the family."[35]

Millet agrees with other theorists that the major role of family institutions is in teaching young people appropriate social rules and values, but she points out that this socialization includes the propagation of a patriarchal system in which "the status of both child and mother is primarily or ultimately dependent upon the male."[36] This critique strikes directly at the kind of postwar family serialized in *Ozzie and Harriet*, the popular sitcom of the 1950s. Here, we have two biological parents with two children, the husband working outside the home and the wife an unpaid household manager. Millet concludes that this "modern nuclear family, with its unchanged and traditional division of roles, necessitates male supremacy by preserving specifically human endeavor for the male alone, while confining the female to menial labor and compulsory child care. Differences in status according to sex follow inevitably."[37]

In addition to the feminist critique of the postwar nuclear family, the traditional family form also conflicted in many ways with the growing emphasis on individualism during the postwar period.[38] The social commentator Francis Fukuyama argues that rights-based individualism has long been deeply embedded in American society but that it grew especially during the second half of the twentieth century.[39] The legal scholar Lawrence Friedman claims that changes in family law during the postwar period reflect the increasing influence of this individualism.[40]

Friedman points out that because marriage had long enjoyed a special moral and religious status in the United States and because divorce was frequently considered immoral, formal laws made divorce difficult to obtain. Thus, individual freedom to choose a particular lifestyle was subjugated to the sanctity of the traditional family form. Even though laws had begun to relax somewhat by the end of World War II, divorce was still only available to "innocent victims"—mostly those who had experienced absent, adulterous, or habitually drunken mates.[41] But when California enacted the first "no fault" divorce laws in the United States in 1970, it encouraged a major metamorphosis in the forms that families took. One of the most basic of these transformations was a rapid increase in nonfamily living.

Nonfamily households are those in which none of the individuals residing together are related by birth, marriage, or adoption.[42] In 1950, less than 11 percent of American households contained individuals living together without family connections. By 1995, the total had nearly tripled to 30 percent of American households.[43] Between 1970 and 1980 alone, the total percentage of American nonfamily households jumped from under 19 percent to over 26 percent.[44] Thus, although the total number of nonfamily households during this period increased by 73 percent, the total number of all family households increased by only 13 percent. There were two main sources for the increases in nonfamily households. The smaller of the two was an increase in the number of widowed persons choosing (or being forced) to live alone. Before 1950, the majority of widows and widowers over 65 lived with their married children; by 1980, barely one-quarter did so.[45]

The other change, and the one that is probably more consequential for crime rates, was an explosion in nonfamily living among young adults. Prior to World War II, almost all unmarried Americans lived with their parents, their married children (if they had them), or their married siblings.[46] Most of those who did not have access to the homes of family members boarded with other families. But beginning in the 1960s, this situation changed dramatically. For example, the percentage of unmarried men age eighteen to twenty-four living alone or with nonrelatives jumped from 1 percent in 1950 to over 13 percent in 1980.[47] As the sociologists Frances Goldscheider and Linda Waite observe, these changes meant that for the first time in American history, the "privacy, independence, and authority of having one's own place" no longer required marriage.[48]

In fact, the explosion in nonfamily living coincided with rapid increases in the total proportion of unmarried men and women. Between 1960 and 1985, the proportion of women in their twenties who were unmarried more than doubled from 28 to 58 percent.[49] Among those in their mid-to-late twenties, the proportion never married rose from 10 to 26 percent.[50] And although virtually all of these single people—90 percent or more—would marry eventually,[51] their marriages would be much less stable than those of their predecessors.

Rapid increases in divorce rates also greatly changed the structure of families. Figure 8.1 shows divorce rates per 1,000 married American women from 1946 to 1994. I again include robbery rates to allow easy comparison. Dislocations caused by World War II led to a relatively high ratio of divorced to married women in 1946. The proportion declined rapidly after the war, reaching a postwar low in 1958. Divorce rates then began to accelerate in the mid-1960s. From 1964 to 1975 alone, divorce rates more than doubled, increasing from 10 percent to over 20 percent. After reaching a postwar peak in 1979, divorce rates remained relatively high but stable for the rest of the century. About two out of every three first marriages now end in divorce or separation.[52] And increasingly, divorced persons are not remarrying, choosing instead to cohabit.[53]

The close relationship between divorce rates and robbery rates in Figure 8.1 is striking. Both rates declined following World War II, reaching postwar lows in the 1950s. Both rates climbed precipitously in the 1960s and 1970s—although divorce rates reached a peak a few years after robbery rates. Both robbery and divorce rates were at relatively high yet stable levels in the 1990s.

Changes in the form of families in the postwar period have had profound implications for how children are raised. The sociologist Sandra

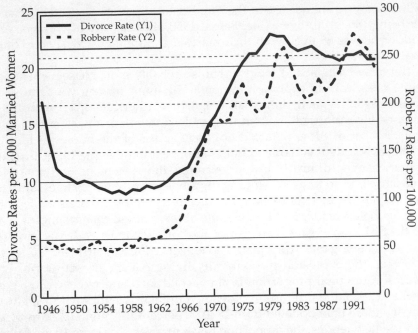

FIGURE 8.1   Divorce and Robbery Rates, 1946–1994
NOTE: Divorce rates for women 15 years old and over.
SOURCES: U.S. Bureau of the Census, *Statistical Abstract of the United States* (Washington, DC: Government Printing Office, 1996), p. 104; U.S. Bureau of the Census, *Historical Statistics of the United States: Colonial Times to 1970* (Washington, DC: Government Printing Office, 1975), p. 64.

Hofferth points out that although 84 percent of children born during the first half of the 1950s were, by the age of fourteen, living with both biological parents, only one-third of all children born in the early 1980s were still living with both biological parents when they reached the same age.[54] Another quarter of these children were living with a stepparent. In fact, by the end of the twentieth century stepparents were part of nearly half of all two-parent families. Coupled with the decline of remarriage and the rise of out-of-wedlock parenthood, the largest percentage of American children (more than 40 percent) from the 1990s birth cohort will be raised in one-parent families.

The Depopulation of the American Home

Changes in the legitimacy of the American family during the postwar years were not all produced by ideological challenges to its male-dominated form. Fundamental economic changes during the postwar period also had major implications for the legitimacy and organization of family institutions. In fact, the revolution in twentieth-century family living was preceded by a nineteenth-century revolution in urbanization and industrialization that took the production of many goods and services out of the home as men left farms to work in factories and offices.[55] These trends, and those that followed, were obviously not unique to the United States, but occurred in virtually all societies of the world.[56] Taken together, economic changes during the postwar period encouraged a "depopulation" of the American family.

Perhaps the most effective way to demonstrate the importance of these economic developments is to consider how the daily activities of family members have increasingly shifted away from the household during the postwar period. These shifts are in turn related to major changes in institutionalized roles for men, women, and children. Although a comprehensive examination of this topic would fill volumes, I concentrate here on three of the most consequential of the economic changes: The movement of men from agricultural to nonagricultural labor; the shift of women from household managers to members of the paid labor force; and the increasing levels of educational participation by children, adolescents, and young adults.

Following the industrial revolution, American men, like men in other Western nations, steadily moved from employment at home in agriculture to paid labor outside the household. As recently as 1900, nearly 40 percent of all employed men in the American labor force worked in agricultural jobs.[57] By 1947, the percentage of all males working in agriculture had already dropped to only 13 percent.[58] But agricultural employment for men continued to decline methodically in the postwar period. The proportion dropped below 10 percent in the 1950s, below 5 percent in the late 1960s, and below 3 percent in the 1980s. By 1995, less than 2 percent of employed American men worked in agricultural occupations.[59] These changes represent about an 85 percent drop in male agricultural employment from 1947 to 1995.

As men moved steadily from farm employment to jobs in the nonagricultural labor force, women's connections to family and work underwent even more dramatic changes. In 1940, less than 25 percent of all women age sixteen and older were in the paid labor force.[60] By 1995, the percentage had more than doubled to 59 percent.[61] Growth was especially rapid in the 1960s and 1970s. From 1965 to 1980 alone, female labor force participation increased by nearly 31 percent. Only recently has growth begun to slow somewhat, increasing by about 1.5 percent from 1990 to 1995.

It is difficult to overstate the importance of these changes for the American family. By the 1990s, over two-thirds of women in the prime working ages of twenty-four to fifty-four were in the paid labor force.[62] Even among women historically least likely to work for pay—mothers with children under one year of age—participation in the paid labor force was over 50 percent. In the space of a generation, paid employment became the most common option for the majority of working-aged American women.[63]

Another development that accelerated the depopulation of the American household during the postwar period was the tremendous expansion of schooling. This happened in two main ways. First, a progressively higher proportion of all children attended school during the prime school attendance ages of six to seventeen years. And second, schooling gradually expanded beyond the traditional school attendance ages to include increasingly younger children and older adolescents and young adults.

In the 1900–1901 school year, 78 percent of American children age five to seventeen were enrolled in school.[64] By the end of World War II, this percentage had increased to 91 percent.[65] School enrollments continued to increase systematically throughout the postwar period. By 1995, school enrollments for children five or six years old had reached 96 percent, for seven- to thirteen-year-olds enrollments reached 99 percent, and for fourteen- to seventeen-year-olds they stood at 96 percent.

Even greater changes in postwar educational attendance occurred for children and young adults outside the traditional school attendance ages of six through seventeen years. As recently as 1965, less than 11 percent of American children three or four years old were enrolled in school.[66] By 1995, the percentage had nearly quintupled to 49 percent. Similarly, in 1945, only about 21 percent of Americans age eighteen or nineteen were enrolled in school. By 1995, enrollment among this group had nearly tripled to over 59 percent. And school attendance continues to include a higher proportion of adults. In 1995, 45 percent of adults age twenty or twenty-one; 23 percent of adults age twenty-two to twenty-four; 12 percent of adults age twenty-five to twenty-nine; and 6 percent of adults age thirty to thirty-four were enrolled in school.[67]

Changes in the extent of male agricultural employment, female labor force participation, and schooling totally restructured the American family. No matter how we look at it, the average American male, female, and child spent considerably less time in a household that contained other family members at the end of the postwar years than at their beginning. Although families—sometimes heroically—were often able to maintain strong organization despite these fundamental changes, it is clear that the strength of the traditional family with two parents, husband as breadwinner, and wife as household manager greatly declined during the postwar period.

African American Families and White Families

Given my arguments, I am looking here for evidence that black family institutions have had less legitimacy throughout the postwar period and lost legitimacy more rapidly than white families during the high crime increase decades of the 1960s and 1970s. To the extent that legitimacy can be measured by the strength of traditional family forms, the first of these assertions is indisputably true. Regardless of the specific measure used, African Americans have been less likely than whites to adhere to the traditional form of the postwar family. Compared to whites, blacks have higher divorce rates, higher rates of children born to unmarried mothers, and lower marriage rates.[68] Moreover, there is evidence that these patterns extend well beyond the postwar period.

The sociologist Steven Ruggles shows that from 1880 through 1960 the proportion of black children under the age of fifteen who were living with both biological parents remained fairly constant at about 70 percent.[69] By contrast, for the same period about 90 percent of white children lived with both biological parents. Ruggles concludes that in every census year he examined (1880–1980) the percentage of black children under age fifteen living without one or both biological parents was at least twice as high as the corresponding percentage among white children. Other measures of family structure tell much the same story. Compared to whites, African Americans had higher divorce rates, lower marriage rates, and lower remarriage rates throughout the postwar period.

As we have already seen, changes in the traditional form of the family were especially rapid in the 1960s and 1970s. But there is evidence that the changes began earlier and were faster for black families than white families. These patterns are clear in comparisons of the proportion of black households and white households headed by women. Figure 8.2 shows the percentage of female-headed households for the two groups, 1957 to 1995.[70]

Figure 8.2 shows that black female-headed households were more than twice as common as white female-headed households in the late 1950s. Rates for both groups accelerated in the 1960s and 1970s. But acceleration was far more rapid for black women than white women. From 1960 to 1980, the proportion of female-headed black households nearly doubled—from 21 percent to more than 40 percent. For whites, during the same period rates grew more modestly, from 8 percent to 12 percent.

Differences between black families and white families with regard to the proportion of children born to unmarried women are equally dramatic. The proportion of black children born to unwed mothers rose somewhat in the early years after World War II—changing from 17 percent in 1946 to 22 percent in 1960.[71] But after the 1960s, the increases were much more rapid. The proportion of live births to unwed mothers among black women first exceeded 30 percent in 1968, 40 percent in 1971, 50 percent in 1976, and 60 percent in 1985. By the early 1990s, it had reached 68 percent. During the high crime increase years of 1963 to 1975, the proportion of live births to unmarried black women more than doubled.

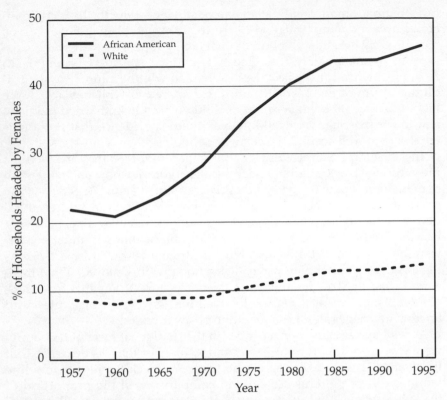

FIGURE 8.2   Proportion of Female-Headed Households by Race, 1957–1995
SOURCE: U.S. Bureau of the Census, *Statistical Abstract of the United States,*
1990–1996 (Washington, DC: Government Printing Office, individual years,
1990–1996).

Although the proportion of births to unwed white women lags far behind the rates for black women, it too has increased rapidly during the
postwar years. The proportion of births to unwed white women fell to a
postwar low of 1.6 percent in 1952 and 1953. In 1960, it was still just above
2 percent. But starting in the 1960s, the proportion began to increase
rapidly, reaching 4 percent in 1966, 8 percent in 1977, and 16 percent in
1987.

As with the changes in political and economic institutions discussed
previously, changes in family institutions might explain in part why
African Americans have consistently higher crime rates than other groups
during the postwar years. There is evidence that African Americans have
long been less likely than whites to be part of traditional families. There is
also evidence that, compared to whites, the proportion of African Ameri-

cans living in traditional families declined more rapidly during the high crime growth decades of the 1960s and 1970s.

Connections Between the Family and Other Institutions

Of course, family institutions do not exist in a social vacuum but are related in complex ways to other institutions. For example, attitudes toward political institutions are most likely shaped first and foremost by the family.[72] Through early childhood socialization, families can be expected to pass on and reinforce beliefs about political institutions, including their legitimacy and fairness. Families continue to shape the attitudes of their children toward political institutions as children mature.

Families are also related in complex ways to economic institutions. The declining legitimacy of economic institutions can have profound effects on family stability and functioning. At the same time, there is considerable evidence that strong family institutions can serve as a buffer against the tensions and stress generated by economic change.[73]

Connections between family institutions and other institutions may also help explain the extraordinarily high rates of offending among men, and particularly African American men, during the postwar period. As men became increasingly alienated from political and economic institutions in the 1960s, rapid changes in the traditional family may have been especially threatening. After all, in the early postwar period men who were marginal to political and economic institutions could still rely on their superior position with regard to women and children in families.[74] But as the legitimacy of the traditional, male-dominated family also began to decline during the middle postwar period, many men were left with few institutional sources of power.[75]

This reasoning may be particularly relevant to African American men during the postwar years. The sociologist Karen Heimer points out that in negotiating gender identity young minority men may be especially vulnerable because, compared to white men, they receive more negative messages about their identity from school and the workplace.[76] In the late 1960s, feminists recognized the importance of this issue and began criticizing liberals for assuming that racial equality required that African American men be restored as the principal authority figure within their family.[77] Because compared to white men the attachments of black men to political and economic institutions probably deteriorated more completely during the postwar period, African American men might have been especially threatened by the declining legitimacy of the patriarchal nuclear family. In this context, African American men may have been more likely to display the kind of male posturing and machismo that all too frequently results in street crime.

The changes in families described in this chapter were of course taken quite seriously by social policy makers. As changes in the American family accelerated during the postwar years, there was considerable effort to use other social institutions to support functions previously performed by the family. The most obvious example here is education. Researchers have long noted the close connection between family and educational institutions.[78] Like families, schools are generally responsible for transmitting basic cultural standards to children and, to a lesser extent, for controlling the behavior of children and protecting them from victimization. As the legitimacy of traditional families declined during the postwar period, American society looked increasingly to schools to perform functions previously performed exclusively by families.

Although the connections are not as obvious, the United States has also relied increasingly on criminal justice and welfare institutions to replace family functions. Like families, criminal justice institutions are directly responsible for regulating the criminal behavior of juveniles and also for protecting juveniles from victimization. Increasingly, educational programs administered by criminal justice systems—such as the Drug Resistance Education Program (DARE) and various antigang education programs (e.g., Gang Resistance Education and Training, or GREAT)—have been aimed at buttressing the traditional family role of proper socialization.[79] Welfare programs, most notably Aid to Families with Dependent Children (AFDC), have also been intended in part to reduce the economic stresses on single-parent families.

These relationships between family institutions and other institutions make it difficult to interpret the independent effects of changes in the family on crime trends. In general, I would expect that greater economic inequality and distrust in political institutions renders family institutions less successful in reducing crime. On the other hand, greater investments in education, criminal justice, and welfare institutions generally helps families to be more successful in reducing crime.

Conclusions and Implications

There is considerable support for the conclusion that postwar American crime rates increased along with the declining legitimacy of the traditional family. The most serious threats to the traditional family were ideological assaults on its patriarchal form and sweeping economic changes. Ideological challenges greatly increased alternatives to family living. Economic changes encouraged substantial declines in the amount of time individuals spent in households as men continued to abandon agricultural employment, women joined the paid labor force in record numbers, and children and young adults pursued ever more schooling. Taken together, these processes have meant that Americans at the end of the twentieth century spent a far greater proportion of their time outside the supervision and protection of their family than they did following World War II.

Interestingly, a stabilization of family structure might also help explain the modest downturn in crime rates beginning in the 1990s. Divorce rates per 1,000 married women peaked in 1979 and declined slightly into the 1990s.[80] The proportion of births to unwed mothers was still increasing in the 1990s, but more slowly than it was in earlier decades.[81] Several economic indicators of family change also held steady or even reversed direction at the end of the twentieth century. For example, trends in female labor force participation, school enrollments, and the formation of nonfamily households were basically flat in the 1990s.[82]

Moreover, the end of the twentieth century is more than three decades after the most rapid changes in family organization began. Blended, dual-career, male–household manager, single-parent, and even gay family forms are becoming increasingly institutionalized. As these alternatives to the traditional family become routinized, their ability to prevent crime and deviance should increase. This is the genius of institutionalization.

• • •

Now that I have considered changes in political, economic, and family institutions, I am ready to examine several of the major institutional responses to the postwar American legitimacy crisis that have direct implications for crime rates. To varying degrees, criminal justice, education, and welfare institutions were all justified during the postwar period as anticrime measures. In the next chapter, I consider how these three social institutions changed during the postwar years and how their changes were related to crime trends.

nine

Institutional Responses to the Legitimacy Crisis

Criminal Justice, Education, and Welfare

The most important single demand that any political community must meet is the demand for protection.
—Martin van Creveld, *The Transformation of War*, 1991[1]

In the sunset of dissolution, everything is illuminated by the aura of nostalgia, even the guillotine.
—Milan Kundera, *The Unbearable Lightness of Being*, 1984[2]

As the legitimacy of political, economic, and family institutions eroded during the 1960s, American policymakers increasingly turned to newer institutions to restore public confidence in the social system. To some extent, these newer responses were specific to declines in each of the three institutions reviewed previously. To shore up political institutions, American society funded major increases in criminal justice spending; to reduce the deleterious consequences of a rapidly changing economy, American society spent more on welfare; and to help support declining family institutions, American society invested heavily in education. But it would be simplistic to portray these institutional responses as narrow reactions to a single type of institutional decline. For example, welfare spending was justified not only in terms of reducing economic stress but also in terms of supporting the family and increasing trust in political institutions. Similarly, educational spending was justified not only as supporting functions previously performed by families but also as a means for improving economic opportunities and increasing confidence in political institutions.

The growing emphasis on criminal justice, education, and welfare institutions also had varying effects on crime rates. The most obvious connections are between crime and criminal justice institutions. There is evidence, however, that trends in educational and welfare institutions also affected crime rates. Welfare and educational institutions expanded most rapidly during the middle postwar years and grew more slowly in the later postwar years. In fact, plans to substantially change the size and scope of welfare institutions were being implemented while this book was in preparation. Criminal justice solutions were a popular response to crime throughout the postwar period, but the major forms of criminal justice spending on crime shifted during the postwar years. During the middle postwar period, the main emphasis of public funding was on the police and prevention whereas the late postwar period witnessed major funding increases instead aimed at prisons and other forms of punishment.

As with the three institutions examined in previous chapters, the relationship of African Americans and whites to these three emerging institutions during the postwar period differed in fundamental ways. African Americans have long been disproportionately affected by the criminal justice system. Throughout this century, African Americans were more likely than whites to be arrested, convicted, and remanded to the custody of the corrections system. But differences in criminal justice processing by race, particularly with regard to the corrections system, grew even more lopsided during the postwar period.

Likewise, African Americans began the postwar period with tremendous disadvantages in access to education. But although disadvantages no doubt remain, improvements in access to educational institutions were greater for African Americans than whites during the middle and late postwar period.[3] Finally, compared to whites, African Americans have been disproportionately likely to receive public welfare throughout the postwar period. And as welfare spending increased in the 1960s and 1970s, it had a correspondingly greater impact on African Americans than on whites.

Perhaps the most puzzling issue raised by considering separately African American connections to these three rapidly expanding social institutions is that the growth in all three institutions seems to be associated with increases rather than decreases in crime rates. Thus, compared to whites, African Americans during the postwar period increased educational attainment more rapidly, were disproportionately likely to receive public welfare, and were far more likely to be subject to the authority of the criminal justice system. If these three institutions were effective in reducing crime, why did African Americans nevertheless have such high crime rates?

The explanation for this seeming paradox is that education, welfare, and criminal justice institutions bear a fundamentally different relationship to crime trends than the political, economic, and family institutions discussed in earlier chapters. Although declines in the legitimacy of the latter three institutions led to the crime boom of the 1960s and 1970s, growth in education, welfare, and criminal justice institutions were largely societal responses to this declining legitimacy. As I argued in Chapter 5, the relationship between crime trends and these six social institutions are temporally patterned. First came declines in the legitimacy of political, economic, and family institutions. Next came major increases in crime rates. And finally, American society responded to declining legitimacy and increasing crime by strengthening support for education, welfare, and criminal justice institutions.

Postwar Trends in Criminal Justice, Education, and Welfare

In this chapter, I examine postwar trends in criminal justice, educational, and welfare institutions and the ways in which these trends were related to crime rates. I begin by considering general relationships between these three institutions and crime and then consider the timing of changes in each institution.

Criminal Justice Institutions

Although volumes have been written about the relationship between legal institutions and crime, at base there are four main ways that formal criminal justice institutions can reduce crime: prevention, deterrence, rehabilitation, or incapacitation. Prevention includes programs aimed at averting crime before it happens, including some aspects of policing and drug and alcohol treatment programs. Deterrence reduces crime by increasing the costs of criminal behavior to offenders or would-be offenders through punishment or the threat of punishment. Rehabilitation includes programs that seek to reduce crime by offering some form of training or treatment to offenders. Incapacitation reduces crime by simply keeping offenders incarcerated and out of public circulation.

When most people think of responding to street crime, they think first of legal institutions—especially police, courts, and corrections. Clearly, political promises to control crime are most often based on the assumption that changes in the formal legal apparatus will bring down crime rates. Indeed, governments have enormous resources that can be directed at preventing and deterring crime and at apprehending, treating, or incarcerating convicted offenders. These resources can make a difference when they are focused on crime control.

But despite the obvious power of criminal justice institutions, it is painfully clear that criminal justice sanctions alone are likely to be only marginally successful in situations of strong offender motivation to commit crime and weak informal social controls. In short, the formal criminal justice system is most effective when buttressed by social institutions that first socialize people to obey laws and then enmesh them in informal social control networks that keep them law abiding. From beginning to end, effective criminal justice systems depend on the informal support of citizens.

This reliance starts with citizen-police relationships. Research tells us that the vast majority of all crimes initially come to the attention of the criminal justice system through citizen reports.[4] If citizens fail to report crimes to the police, in most cases no legal processing occurs. Once a crime has been reported, citizens become critical to police investigation by providing eyewitness accounts, evidence, and information. Police are likely to be ineffective in communities that oppose or halfheartedly support investigative efforts.

The importance of citizen participation follows cases into the courts. Prosecutors depend heavily on witnesses to cooperate and can do little without strong witness support. In the United States, the jury system is perhaps the most obvious link between citizens and legal decision–making. Decisions of juries are final and unreviewable. In extreme cases, juries can "nullify" the law by refusing to apply it in particular cases.[5]

The importance of the community extends into the corrections system. Research suggests that for punishment to be most effective in permanently changing behavior, it needs to have the clear support of the community.[6] Punishment is less likely to have an impact on the future behavior of either the punished offender or other community members in societies in which political and legal institutions have little legitimacy. From start to finish, to operate effectively, the legal system depends on the trust and support of the citizens it regulates. Without citizen confidence in the legal system, police are less effective, courts are less likely to convict, and corrections are less likely to rehabilitate or deter.

Educational Institutions

The idea that increasing educational opportunity can reduce crime rates has been a cornerstone of U.S. policy throughout most of the postwar period.[7] In contrast to legal systems, schools are less obviously connected to formal social control but are more directly connected to the socialization and informal social control of children; juveniles; and, increasingly, young adults. As children, juveniles, and young adults in the United States spend a growing proportion of their time away from families in schools, American society has come to depend increasingly on schools to properly socialize them. And there is evidence that schools perform important socialization roles. Juveniles who accept the legitimacy of education and who have high educational aspirations and long-term educational goals are less likely to engage in delinquency.[8] More generally, research consistently shows a strong tendency for offenders to be drawn from those with low levels of educational attainment.[9]

As with families, the potential social control functions of schools are broad gauged. Schools can reduce crime by effectively monitoring and supervising the behavior of children under their custody.[10] Even more important, schools can reduce delinquency by creating environments in which children are strongly committed to education and care about their school performance. Research evidence confirms that children who are weakly attached to school or actively dislike it are more likely to engage in delinquency.[11] Similarly, there is near-universal support for an association between poor school performance and delinquency.[12] Finally, in theory at least, schools, like families, may serve a guardianship function, protecting children from the criminal behavior of others.[13]

The effects of educational attainment on crime are likely to be complex, however. The very fact that education can improve the life chances of individuals who successfully pursue it means that it can also decrease the life chances of those who do not. This is because educational attainment is relative up and down the education hierarchy.[14] Thus, although expanding educational attainment may improve the prospects for graduates, it may also lower the prospects for nongraduates. Subjectively, this might be expected to increase the very feelings of deprivation or frustration identified by criminologists as contributing to increased crime.[15] Objectively, educational attainment can actually worsen the economic well-being of nonstudents and unsuccessful students by producing educational "inflation": As educational attainment rises, jobs are increasingly filled by those with more advanced credentials. Thus, by itself, "expanded education does not expand opportunities; it simply replaces previously less-educated occupants with more-educated ones."[16]

In fact, there is evidence that these processes were especially important in American inner cities during the postwar period. The sociologist William Julius Wilson shows that from 1970 to 1984 all major northern cities he examined had consistent job losses in industries that depended on workers with less than a high school degree, whereas there was consistent employment growth in industries that depended on those with some education beyond high school. These changes may have been especially devastating for inner-city African Americans. The sociologist John Kasarda has concluded that the decline in stable employment opportunities for inner-city minority residents with less than a college education resulted in "a serious mismatch" between educational levels and jobs during the postwar years.[17]

More generally, the relativity of educational attainment means that its ability to create a more egalitarian society ultimately depends on the economy. In an analysis of the landmark *Brown v. Board of Education* decision, the legal scholar James Liebman points out that the philosophy of educational mobility embodied in the 1954 decision was "simultaneously simple, optimistic and naive," but he notes that perhaps it was understandable, "given the period's flush economic conditions."[18] But of course, rapid increases in educational attainment in the postwar period were not always met by a "flush" economy. In fact, much of the improvement in access to education during the postwar years coincided with periods of growing economic inequality and stress. The ability of expanding educational opportunity to reduce crime may be severely limited in the context of increasing economic inequality or a stagnant economy.

Welfare Institutions

Connections between welfare institutions and crime are even more indirect. The most obvious association is with regard to welfare's presumed ability to ameliorate economic stress and thereby reduce the motivation of potential offenders to commit crime and, more generally, to improve the effectiveness of informal social control mechanisms. These connections would presumably apply most directly to crimes with immediate economic benefits such as robbery and burglary. In one of the most comprehensive longitudinal studies of the impact of welfare spending on crime to date, the sociologist Joel Devine and his colleagues found that total spending on AFDC and other public relief was consistently associated with declining burglary rates and marginally associated with declining robbery rates during the postwar period.[19] Spending on welfare had no effect on homicide rates in the United States. Several cross-national studies support the conclusion that countries that spend more on public assistance have lower rates of child homicide victimization.[20]

The Shifting Impact of New Institutional Responses

Although I am considering the effects of criminal justice, education, and welfare institutions on crime in the same chapter, the timing of their greatest influence has varied during the postwar period. These changes can be seen most clearly by considering the relative importance of each institution during the early (1946–1960), middle (1961–1973), and late (1974–present) postwar years.

In terms of institutional responses to crime, we could call the early postwar period "the age of Ozzie and Harriet." The major weekly dilemmas faced by this suburban couple were rarely more serious than whether their cleanly scrubbed children should be allowed to visit the local malt shop after school. Of course, in the 1950s there was no African American television equivalent of the Nelson family. Moreover, subsequent developments would make it clear that not all American "Harriets" were equally enamored with the position being assigned to them within the traditional nuclear family. Nevertheless, with strong families, a booming economy, and high levels of trust in political institutions, there was little in the American experience to justify major new spending on social institutions. Total spending on criminal justice, education, and welfare institutions during this period, adjusted for inflation, was at a lower level than it would ever be again during the rest of the century.

But as the legitimacy of social institutions began to decline during the middle postwar period, triggering a major crime boom, this complacency quickly evaporated. Social policy experts began advocating both "carrot" and "stick" approaches to declining institutional legitimacy and rising crime rates. Strengthening educational opportunity and increasing welfare support were the two main carrot approaches. As I pointed out in Chapter 1, the connections between educational and welfare institutions and crime were stated clearly in the 1967 report of President Lyndon Johnson's Commission on Law Enforcement and the Administration of Justice, which concluded, "Warring on poverty, inadequate housing and unemployment, is warring on crime" and "Money for schools is money against crime."[21] The main stick approach was increased spending on criminal justice, especially prisons and corrections-based supervision.

In general, liberals during the postwar period have supported carrot approaches and conservatives, stick approaches. The success of proponents of these two views at influencing the national agenda changed over time. Carrot approaches were generally dominant at first, beginning with the legitimacy crisis of the 1960s. By contrast, stick approaches, especially imprisonment, were most influential later, in the 1980s and 1990s.

Although it is difficult to prove conclusively, it seems likely that the civil rights movement played a major role in the timing of carrot and stick approaches to crime in America. Given differences in offending rates, it was clear to anyone paying attention that African Americans were going to be disproportionately affected by just about any crime control strategy adopted. As the civil rights movement began to convincingly communicate the pervasive injustices of racial segregation, solutions to crime based primarily on stick approaches seemed increasingly unfair.[22] Although spending on criminal justice did grow substantially during the middle postwar years, it was aimed more at the police (whose main job is to prevent crime and protect the public) than at prisons and corrections. In fact, during the middle postwar period many academic criminologists went so far as to argue that convicted offenders were really "political prisoners."[23] But as spending on social reforms continued into the 1970s without declines in crime rates, stick-oriented solutions gradually gained ground both among the general public and among policymakers and researchers

In the next section, I consider how the growing American emphasis on educational and welfare institutions was related to crime rates during the postwar period. As in earlier chapters, I also examine how differing experiences of African Americans and whites might help us better understand the underlying dynamics.

Education, Welfare, and Crime

I have already described in general terms the rapid increases in educational participation that characterized the United States during the postwar period. At the end of World War II, the only age group with nearly universal school attendance was from seven to thirteen years of age (98 percent attendance).[24] By 1995, in addition to seven- to thirteen-year-olds, educational attendance had become nearly universal for five- and six-year-olds (96 percent) and fourteen- to seventeen-year-olds (96 percent). Educational participation had also become an important fact of life for increasing proportions of younger children and older juveniles and young adults. Thus, by 1995, 49 percent of all children age three and four, 59 percent of young adults age eighteen and nineteen, and 32 percent of young adults age twenty to twenty-four were enrolled in schools.

Given that school attendance was already nearly universal for children age five to seventeen before the crime wave of the 1960s began, it is perhaps more telling to examine school expansion for very young children, who were not typically in schools at the beginning of the postwar period. Younger children are also an interesting group for those who claim that early childhood socialization is especially critical for preventing later criminal behavior.[25] Figure 9.1 shows annual school attendance percentages for American children age three or four years, from 1965 to 1993.[26] I include robbery rates to allow comparisons.

As shown in Figure 9.1, the proportion of very young children in schools increased dramatically throughout the 1960s and into the 1970s. The total percentage enrolled first passes 20 percent in 1970, 30 percent in 1975, and 40 percent in 1990. Increases were especially rapid in the 1970s. Increases have been more gradual since the early 1980s.

The first point to notice about Figure 9.1 is that increases in school attendance are clearly correlated with robbery rates. Let me hasten to add here that I am not arguing that a rise in the proportion of three- and four-year-olds in the nation's schools set off the postwar street crime wave! Rather, my argument is that declining legitimacy of social institutions, powerfully symbolized by rising crime rates, provided an important justification for increased spending on education. As the institutional legiti-

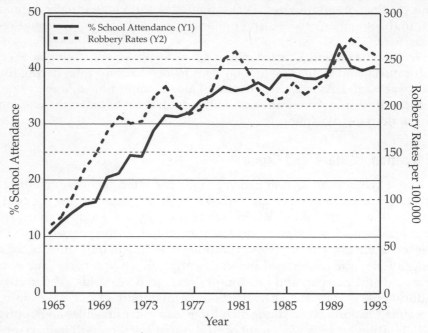

FIGURE 9.1　School Attendance of Three- and Four-Year-Olds and Robbery Rates, 1965–1993
SOURCE: U.S. Department of Education, National Center for Education Statistics, *Digest of Education Statistics, 1996* (Washington, DC: Government Printing Office, 1996), p. 15.

macy crisis deepened, American society responded by greatly expanding access to education. By the 1980s, increases in educational institutions were outpacing crime increases.

Willingness to invest money is another measure of a society's commitment to its institutions. Total spending on education (at the federal, state, and local levels) increased in the United States as soon as World War II was over—with total per capita spending in inflation-adjusted dollars nearly doubling from 1948 to 1956 alone.[27] Spending on education continued to increase annually throughout the postwar period with two exceptions: a two-year decline in 1973 and 1974, and a nine-year decline from 1977 to 1986. By 1992, the United States was annually spending $1,484 dollars per capita on education.

As with rates of educational participation, spending on education was paced by crime trends. When crime rates increased rapidly in the 1960s and early 1970s, educational spending too began rapid increases. From 1963 to 1976 alone, per capita educational spending more than doubled—from an annual rate of $576 to an annual rate of $1,253. After the mid-

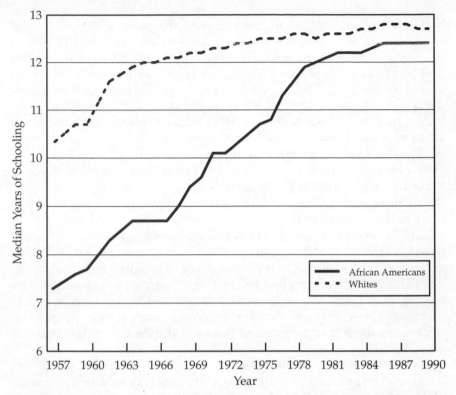

FIGURE 9.2 Median Years of Schooling for African American Males and White Males, 1957–1990
SOURCES: U.S. Bureau of the Census, "Educational Attainment in the United States, March 1990 and 1991," *Current Population Reports,* Series P-20, No. 462 (Washington, DC: Government Printing Office, 1991); U.S. Bureau of the Census, *Statistical Abstract of the United States, 1989* (Washington, DC: Government Printing Office, 1989).

1970s, educational spending rates were relatively flat, until beginning an upward climb again in the mid-1980s.

African Americans and Education

One of the legacies of slavery in the United States has been persistent differences in levels of education attained by African Americans and whites. As recently as 1958, the median years of school completed for black males stood at 7.4—a full 3 years less than the median for white males.[28] This gap narrowed substantially during the postwar years, however. Figure 9.2 compares median years of education obtained by black males and white males, 1957 to 1990.[29]

Figure 9.2 shows that although educational attainment increased for both whites and African Americans during the postwar period, overall changes were more than twice as great for African Americans as whites: Average educational attainment increased by about 2.5 years for whites and by about 5.5 years for African Americans during the 34 years included in Figure 9.2. The average black male in 1960 had less than a middle school education whereas the average black male in 1990 had more than a high school education. By 1990, median years of schooling for white males was less than one-half of a year greater than the median for black males. One remarkable indication of these changes is the fact that in 1995 a higher percentage of African Americans than whites age three to thirty-four were enrolled in U.S. schools.[30]

Of course, convergence in total enrollments by race is not the same thing as convergence in the quality of education. The sociologist William Julius Wilson argues that as whites and middle-class blacks increasingly deserted central cities during the postwar period, they left behind "low-achieving" schools.[31] Wilson reports a study of racially segregated inner-city Chicago high schools that found that 42 percent of graduates were reading at or below the junior level.[32] Similarly, Charles Murray argues that inner-city schools serving the most economically disadvantaged students were those that deteriorated the most during the middle postwar years.[33]

Measuring changes in the aggregate quality of education for African Americans and whites is a challenging task. There is evidence that quality of education is not a simple function of the amount spent on education, however. U.S. Department of Education statistics for 1979 show that per capita spending on elementary and secondary schools in twenty of the largest cities in the United States was actually above per capita spending for the nation as a whole.[34] In fact, per capita spending on elementary and secondary schools was more than 25 percent *higher* than the national average in several cities routinely associated with serious street crime problems, including New York; Washington, D.C.; Chicago; Cleveland; Milwaukee; Philadelphia; and St. Louis. Moreover, the quality of educational experiences are no doubt closely related to the legitimacy of the social institutions reviewed in earlier chapters. I would expect educational institutions to be less effective for students from backgrounds with high levels of political distrust, high levels of economic inequality, and high levels of family disorganization compared to other students.

Public Welfare and Crime

Figure 9.3 shows the relationship between total government spending on welfare and robbery rates for the postwar period.[35] In 1948, total welfare

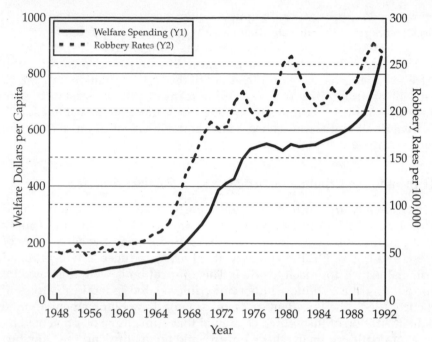

FIGURE 9.3   Government Spending on Welfare and Robbery Rates, 1948–1992 (in 1995 Dollars)
SOURCES: U.S. Bureau of the Census, *Government Finances: 1984–1992*, Series GF/92-5 (Washington, DC: Government Printing Office, 1996), p. 1; U.S. Bureau of the Census, *Historical Statistics on Governmental Finance and Employment* (Washington, DC: Government Printing Office, 1985), pp. 26–28.

spending amounted to about $83 per capita. Spending rates increased only slightly during the early postwar period, reaching $116 per capita in 1960. But in the 1960s and early 1970s, changes were rapid. From 1964 to 1978, total per capita welfare spending more than quadrupled—from $121 per year to $551 dollars per year.

In an influential book published in the mid-1980s, the political scientist Charles Murray examined similar data to suggest that welfare spending in the postwar United States has actually had the effect of increasing social problems such as crime.[36] Indeed, Figure 9.3 shows a clear positive relationship between welfare spending and robbery rates. But look carefully at the time ordering of changes in robbery and changes in welfare spending. Robbery rates began their rapid ascent in the early 1960s. Welfare spending began to increase rapidly about five years later—toward the end of the 1960s. These relationships underscore my argument that welfare spending, like educational and criminal justice spending, was not a cause of crime—as Professor Murray implies—but rather it was part of an institutional response to crime rates that had already begun to accelerate.

And as with increases in educational spending, increased spending on welfare had a disproportionate effect on African Americans. Although African Americans make up 12 percent of the U.S. population, in 1994, 38 percent of all families receiving some form of public assistance were African American.[37] Similarly, in 1994 black mothers accounted for 39 percent of all mothers receiving AFDC and 36 percent of those receiving food stamps.[38]

Crime and the Criminal Justice System in Postwar America

I have already argued that the middle postwar years were characterized more by carrot than stick approaches to crime. But I do not want to imply that criminal justice institutions were ignored during the early years of the crime boom. On the contrary, the 1960s produced a two-pronged criminal justice approach to crime. This bifurcation is well illustrated by considering the two most important crime-related federal initiatives of the late 1960s: the President's Commission on Law Enforcement and the Administration of Justice, which argued that crime must be prevented by programmatic efforts to relieve poverty and inequality, and the Omnibus Crime Control and Safe Streets Act, which sought to strengthen traditional law enforcement.[39] Moreover, the civil unrest of the 1960s was used as a justification for creating a huge federal crime-fighting bureaucracy that has remained in place ever since.[40]

But although spending on criminal justice institutions increased during both the middle and late postwar periods, the nature of these increases changed between the two periods. To understand these changes, it is useful to distinguish between "back-end" and "front-end" criminal justice approaches to crime.[41] Back-end approaches focus on events at the conclusion of the criminal justice process, emphasizing punishment for its own sake or for its deterrent or incapacitation effects. Back-enders generally favor the death penalty, long prison terms, and limited discretion for judges and parole boards who might reduce prison sentences. By contrast, front-enders seek results at the early stages of the criminal justice system, emphasizing such measures as preventative policing, gun control, drug treatment, and alternatives to prison. In general, back-enders want to punish offenders severely for committing crime, front-enders want to work at preventing crime in the first place.

In the postwar United States, corrections systems have been the primary back-end criminal justice response to crime. By contrast, although police play a critical role in back-end strategies (without arrests, convictions and sentences are impossible), the preventative role of police is central to front-end philosophies. The criminal justice emphasis during the middle postwar period was at best half-hearted with regard to back-end approaches to crime. By contrast, criminal justice policy during the late postwar period tilted heavily toward back-end strategies.

The reticence to use back-end strategies during the middle postwar period is especially important in light of the fact that the United States was experiencing a true crime boom. Despite this boom, back-end strategies were secondary in the overall criminal justice response to crime during the middle postwar years. Consider executions, the highest-profile back-end response to crime. From 1961 to 1973, there were a total of only 135 legal executions in the United States.[42] And eighty-nine of these (66 percent) occurred at the very beginning of the middle postwar period, in 1961 and 1962. Following the Supreme Court decision in *Furman v. Georgia*, there were no legal executions in the United States from 1968 to 1976.[43] The same reticence to use back-end approaches to meet rising crime rates was evident in prison policies. Despite dramatic increases in crime, imprisonment rates per 100,000 Americans actually dropped from 1960 to 1973, reaching a postwar low in 1972.[44]

And although criminal justice spending increased substantially during the middle postwar years, budgets for the police (associated with front-end approaches) outpaced spending on corrections. From 1961 to 1973, total per capita spending on police grew by 2.3 times, but total per capita spending on corrections increased by only 1.9 times.[45]

But as crime rates remained persistently high into the late postwar years, back-end views of criminal justice gained ground. They undoubtedly received their greatest postwar champion with the election in 1980 of President Ronald Reagan. Every type of back-end strategy increased dramatically under Reagan. From 1980 through 1988, the number of death row inmates more than tripled—from 691 to 2,124.[46] In the mid-1970s, the United States admitted about 50,000 new inmates to federal and state prisons each year—a decade later this rate had quadrupled to 200,000 new inmates a year. By the end of Reagan's second term in 1988, the United States had one of the highest incarceration rates in the world.[47] Many of the nation's most populous states, notably, California, Florida, and Texas, undertook massive, multibillion-dollar prison construction projects. But despite immense state and federal prison construction programs, 35 states and the U.S. Federal Bureau of Prisons were at more than 100 percent of their rated capacity in 1995.[48] In fact, the average state and federal prison in 1995 had 15 percent more inmates than it was designed to incarcerate.

By 1995, an estimated 5.4 million Americans were under correctional supervision, including 1.1 million in prisons, 499,000 in jails, 700,000 on parole, and 3.1 million on probation.[49] This amounted to 4.7 percent of the

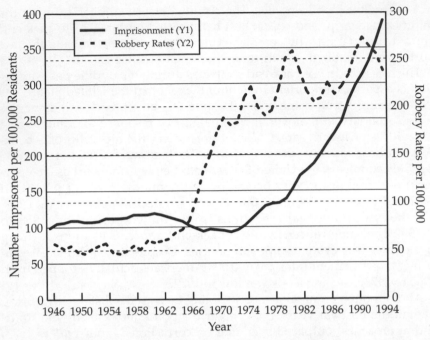

FIGURE 9.4   Imprisonment and Robbery Rates, 1946–1994
SOURCE: U.S. Bureau of Justice Statistics, *Sourcebook of Criminal Justice Statistics, 1995* (Washington, DC: Government Printing Office, 1996), p. 556.

total adult male population of the United States.[50] The economist Richard Freeman provides the startling conclusion that by 1995 the number of American men under the supervision of corrections had surpassed the total number of unemployed men.[51] And the rates are much higher for young men. Among young men age eighteen to thirty-four, the number under correctional supervision amounted to 11 percent of the total workforce.

Punishment trends are perhaps most clearly illustrated by examining postwar imprisonment rates—shown in Figure 9.4 along with robbery rates. As appears in Figure 9.4, from the end of World War II until the mid-1970s imprisonment rates in the United States hovered around 100 prisoners per 100,000 residents. In fact, imprisonment rates in 1973 were about the same as they had been in 1946. But these rates began to change rapidly thereafter, reaching 150 per 100,000 in 1981, 250 per 100,000 in 1989, and 350 per 100,000 in 1993. Overall, U.S. imprisonment rates more than tripled from 1974 until 1994. By the end of 1996, the U.S. rate of incarceration had reached 427—a new high for the twentieth century.[52]

Note again the relationship between imprisonment and robbery rates shown in Figure 9.4. Although robbery rates began to increase rapidly in the 1960s, imprisonment rates did not begin their large increases until the 1980s. The big buildup in criminal justice institutions—like those for education and welfare—happened after crime rates had already escalated. In fact, the back-end philosophy of imprisonment represents the most recent institutional response to a legitimacy and crime problem that really got under way more than thirty years earlier.

The shift toward back-end criminal justice strategies is also illustrated by examining relative spending on police and corrections during the late postwar period. From 1974 to 1992, per capita spending on police increased by one and one-half times. By contrast, per capita spending on corrections during the same period more than tripled.[53]

African Americans and Punishment

The increasing emphasis on back-end strategies during the late postwar period has had an especially grave effect on African Americans. Available evidence suggests that African Americans have been overrepresented in the nation's prisons throughout the twentieth century. For example, the U.S. Bureau of Justice Statistics researcher Patrick Langan reports that in 1926 African Americans made up 21 percent of the 44,328 inmates admitted to state and federal prisons.[54] But the proportion of African American prisoners became much more lopsided during the middle and late postwar years. In particular, as the prison boom of the late 1970s began, the proportion of new admissions that were African American skyrocketed. The African American proportion of new inmates first topped 35 percent in 1970, 40 percent in 1978, and 50 percent in 1989. By 1993, a racial minority constituting 12 percent of the total U.S. population made up 52 percent of new admissions to state and federal prisons. U.S. Bureau of Justice Statistics researchers estimate that African American men born in the United States in the mid-1990s faced a nearly 29 percent risk of going to prison at some point during their lifetime—and these estimates do not include jail or probation time.[55]

These troubling statistics are not limited to prison admissions. Regardless of the specific type of criminal justice punishment examined, African Americans are considerably more likely to receive it. The imbalance begins with the most serious of all criminal justice sanctions, executions. Of the 4,116 persons legally executed in the United States from 1930 to 1994, 53 percent were African American.[56] Even looking at the most recent years for which data are available, 1990 through 1994, 36 percent of 137 legal executions were of African Americans.

Similar differences are found in jail, probation, and parole sentences. In the late twentieth century, African Americans made up 47 percent of all persons serving time in local jails,[57] 46 percent of adults on parole,[58] and 33 percent of adults on probation.[59] Combining probation and parole statistics with incarceration rates produces the startling conclusion that nearly 25 percent of all African American men age twenty to twenty-nine are under the authority of the corrections system on any given day.[60] The economist Richard Freeman estimates that by the 1990s, 37 percent of the labor force of African American men age eighteen to thirty-four was under the authority of the corrections system.[61]

Evaluating the Impact of Criminal Justice Institutions on Crime

Have the increases in spending on corrections during the late postwar period resulted in lower crime rates? Although this issue is highly contentious, the balance of research suggests that they have—at least when examined longitudinally for the entire United States.[62] The researchers Thomas Marvell and Carlisle Moody examined the relationship between changes in imprisonment rates and U.S. rates of homicides, robberies, and assaults from 1930 to 1994.[63] The authors found that a 10 percent increase in prison population was associated with about 13 percent fewer homicides during this period. Imprisonment rates also led to significant declines in robberies and assaults. Other longitudinal studies of the United States have reached similar conclusions.[64]

The controversy involving the effect of imprisonment on street crime rates has probably been stoked in part by self-report survey evidence on crimes committed by inmates. For example, in the late 1980s the Department of Justice researcher Edward Zedlewski published results of a survey in which he asked prisoners about the total number of crimes they had committed—including those for which they were never apprehended.[65] Zedlewski used the results to estimate that the imprisonment of each inmate in his survey had averted 187 additional nondrug street crimes per year. But a major problem with Zedlewski's method was that a handful of prisoners who claim to have committed an enormous number of crimes (sometimes more than one per day) had a tremendous impact on the resulting averages.

In response to this criticism, several researchers using self-report methods have either truncated extreme responses or used median scores.[66] These methods produce estimates of annual offending per inmate of about one-tenth of those originally estimated by Zedlewski. Nevertheless, using these more conservative methods still results in sizeable effects. In a book by the former drug czar William Bennett and his colleagues, the authors conclude that, on average, each inmate in prison had committed twelve property or violent crimes, excluding drug offenses, before his or her imprisonment.[67]

Some simple extrapolation from these estimates produces fairly impressive results. In 1994, there were 541,000 new admissions to federal and state prisons in the United States.[68] Based on the estimates by Bennett and his coauthors , and even assuming some misreporting and exaggeration in the self-reports, these 541,000 new admissions in 1994 should have averted more than 5 million serious nondrug crimes.

Given the size of estimates such as these, the actual reduction in crime rates since the 1980s must be regarded as surprisingly modest. Rather than asking whether imprisonment has led to reduced crime rates in the United States, the more relevant question may be, "Why haven't the massive changes in punishment had more of an effect?"

Part of the reason has to do with the size of gaps in the criminal justice "net." We know that about 40 percent of all serious street crimes are reported to police.[69] Of these, about one-fifth result in an arrest.[70] About a third of those result in a conviction, and a much smaller percentage of persons convicted end up in a state or federal prisons.[71] Taken together then, the 20 million serious crimes committed annually in America produce about 550,000 incarcerations a year—about a third of which are for nonviolent drug offenses and drunk driving.[72] This means that the link between committing a crime and being imprisoned for it is extremely weak. Since the 1960s, research has consistently shown that deterrence is likely to be effective only when the perceived certainty of punishment is high.[73] Incapacitation processes may still be effective, but even if each convicted felon is responsible for many more than one crime, incarcerating such a small fraction of all serious offenders means that the effect on total crime will be relatively modest.

The other main reason why substantial increases in punishment have had less of a payoff than we might otherwise expect may have to do with the general ineffectiveness of formal social control systems to change behavior in an environment in which social institutions have little legitimacy. Nearly a century ago, the French sociologist Emile Durkheim observed, "To punish is not to make others suffer in body or soul; it is to affirm, in the face of an offense, the rule that the offense would deny."[74] The declining legitimacy of social institutions during the postwar years, especially among African Americans, meant that not only was it more difficult to apprehend, convict, and punish offenders, but also punishment was likely to have less effect on deterring either their future criminal behavior or the future criminal behavior of other community members.

A growing body of evidence from diverse sources underscores the conclusion that formal criminal justice punishment may have little effect—or even a counterproductive effect—when coupled with low levels of institutional legitimacy. The criminologist John Braithwaite argues that criminal sanctions can be delivered in either "reintegrative" or "stigmatizing" ways, the former by drawing social shame to the act and the latter by shaming and rejecting the actor.[75] Braithwaite argues that reintegrative shaming controls crime whereas stigmatic shaming increases it. Similarly, the psychologist Tom Tyler distinguishes between sanctions citizens perceive as fair or unfair.[76] Tyler argues that fair sanctions increase compliance with the law by affirming the legitimacy of law enforcement, but unfair sanctions reduce compliance by reducing legitimacy. Finally, the criminologist Larry Sherman's "defiance" theory argues that the perceived legitimacy of punishment is essential for deterrence.[77] Sherman argues that although punishment perceived as just may reduce future crime, punishment perceived as unjust may actually increase it.

Again, African Americans provide the clearest example of how these processes might work. Perhaps the unprecedented levels of formal punishment experienced by African Americans during the postwar period have had modest effects on African American crime rates because of the historically low levels of legitimacy African Americans have felt for political, economic, and family institutions.

Although evidence for such a process is sparse, a few recent studies are suggestive. The sociologist Anthony Harris studied 234 black prison inmates and white prison inmates and found that although whites suffered major decreases in self-esteem when they were caught for crimes, as a group African Americans did not.[78] Perhaps most disturbing, Harris found that for the African American prisoners in his study a greater commitment to criminal behavior actually raised self-esteem.[79] Although Harris's study was limited to prison inmates, at least one study of a noninstitutionalized population produced related results. The criminologists Susan Ageton and Delbert Elliott found that black high school students with no prior police contact nevertheless had more strongly delinquent self-conceptions than comparable white students.[80]

Compared to whites, African Americans entered the late twentieth century with greater distrust of political institutions, more economic inequality, and higher levels of family disorganization. If the arguments I am making are correct, these developments generally increased the motivation of African Americans to commit crime; reduced the effectiveness of informal social controls aimed at preventing their criminal behavior; and, at least for family institutions, reduced the effectiveness of guardianship. An institutional response based only on formal punishment is bound to have some effect on behavior, but when coupled with the low legitimacy of these other institutions, formal punishment by itself will have far less effect than would otherwise be the case. In fact, some research suggests that under the right circumstances, formal punishment might actually lead to increases in future criminal behavior.

The New Interest in Front-End Strategies

As American prison populations continued to swell in the 1990s, there was renewed interest in front-end approaches to crime. The most tangible evidence of this interest has been the recent adoption—or revival—of policing styles variously called "community policing" or "community-oriented policing."[81] The other main development supporting a renewed interest in front-end strategies for street crime has been the move by policy experts to define violent crime as a public health problem.[82] The best publicized example thus far of the new front-end thinking applied to street crime has been taking place in New York City.

In the early 1990s, New York City expanded its police force from just over 25,000 to more than 32,000 officers.[83] Then, under the New York City Police Commissioner William Bratton, the police were reorganized to concentrate more on specific community problems. Police officers at the precinct level were called on to provide regular information about their neighborhoods and develop methods for targeting these problems. The police also began a citywide campaign against "quality of life" offenses—drinking in public, urinating in the streets, making excessive noise, and other forms of incivility.[84] Police often targeted aggressive young toughs who were especially threatening to neighborhoods.

The results have been widely heralded. Only 985 homicides occurred in New York City in 1996—a 57 percent decline from the peak number of 2,262 in 1990.[85] Similar stories are now coming in from Boston, Baltimore, Dallas, Houston, San Diego, San Francisco, and Seattle.[86] Nevertheless, the former New York City Police Commissioner Raymond Kelly recently scoffed that giving credit to Police Commissioner Bratton for these crime reductions was "like trying to take credit for an eclipse."[87] And although a growing emphasis on community-oriented policing appears for now to be a promising strategy, we still need to explain why crime rates in the late twentieth century declined for the nation as a whole, including many cities that had not implemented community policing. If the arguments being made in this book are correct, the success of policies like community policing ultimately depends on the fundamental legitimacy of social institutions within the communities implementing them. My hunch is that declines in crime in New York City and elsewhere in the mid-1990s had more to do with the increasing legitimacy of social institutions than community policing per se.

Summary and Conclusions

Like an organism battling infection, American society fought back against declining legitimacy and increasing crime rates in the postwar years by generating a variety of institutional "antibodies." Educational and welfare institutions were expanded to counteract rising distrust of government, to mitigate growing economic inequality, and to offset major changes in the structure of families. Criminal justice institutions were also substantially bolstered. In the middle postwar years, criminal justice spending emphasized the police. But as crime rates remained high into the late postwar period, more punitive back-end approaches took center stage.

It is difficult to disentangle the impact of these new institutional responses on crime. Their general effect resembles a cannonball being shot into a large net—the net expands to slow down the force of the ball for a time, but eventually (if the net is strong enough) it halts the ball's forward momentum. As this book was being prepared at the end of the twentieth century, there were signs that the crime boom that began in the 1960s was finally slowing down. As I argued previously, this is likely due to a combination of institutional changes: stabilization in levels of trust in government, improvement in indicators of economic inequality, and a slowing in the rapidity of family change coupled with growing institutionalization of new family forms. Without these changes, it is difficult to say what impact education, welfare, and criminal justice would be having on crime rates. Still, this much seems certain: Without a growing commitment to education, welfare, and criminal justice institutions during the postwar period, crime rates would have increased faster and remained higher longer than they have.

● ● ●

I have now reviewed the relationship between postwar crime trends, three social institutions that have traditionally been closely related to crime, and three postwar institutional responses to declining legitimacy and rising crime rates. In the final chapter, I sum up the arguments being made and consider some of the implications of the findings for research and policy.

ten

Crime and Institutional Legitimacy in Postwar America

The apparent indeterminacy of the future is merely a result of our ignorance.

—Bertrand Russell, *Our Knowledge of the External World as a Field for Scientific Method in Philosophy*, 1914[1]

. . . all existence in society carries with it an element of bad faith.

—Peter L. Berger, *Invitation to Sociology: A Humanistic Perspective*, 1963[2]

Because as you get deeper into the search, you unify. You understand more and more specimens by fewer and fewer formulae.

—Walker Percy, *The Moviegoer*, 1960[3]

I begin this chapter with an evaluation of the evidence I have presented for connections between crime and institutional legitimacy in postwar America. Because I have concentrated on links between crime and individual institutions, I also consider in this chapter the relationships between the institutions I have reviewed. Following these explorations, I consider strategies that might be useful in reducing crime through strengthening the legitimacy of institutions. I then explore the implications of postwar trends in crime and institutional legitimacy for further research and social policy. I conclude with a few general observations about crime, institutions, and social change.

My strategy in this book has been to first describe changes in postwar crime rates and then evaluate, one by one, plausible explanations for these changes. The success of this strategy depends not only on the accuracy of the information presented but also on the validity of the crime explanation I have offered.

To summarize, I have argued that the United States began the postwar period with low street crime rates, high levels of trust in political institutions, low levels of economic inequality, and strong family organization. Spending for criminal justice, education, and welfare institutions was at historically low levels. By contrast, I have argued that the United States ended the postwar period with high street crime rates, low levels of trust in political institutions, high economic inequality, and high levels of family disorganization. Support for criminal justice, education, and welfare institutions in the late postwar period has been at historically high levels. I have also argued that the rise in street crime rates and the decline in the legitimacy of traditional social institutions accelerated rapidly beginning in the early 1960s. How good is the evidence to support these arguments?

The evidence is quite good that street crime rates were at their lowest postwar levels in the 1940s and 1950s, that these rates were at their highest postwar levels in the 1980s and 1990s, and that a substantial crime wave connected these two periods. These were not minor fluctuations. Total street crime rates increased about eightfold during the second half of the twentieth century. The conclusion that trends for a wide variety of street crimes were highly correlated during this period is also well supported by the available evidence.

What about evidence for the measures of institutional change? The legitimacy of political institutions is a complex concept to measure, but both attitudinal and behavioral measures of trust in government show clear declines during the high crime increase decades of the 1960s and 1970s. Although the United States today is facing no organized protest of the scope or magnitude of the civil rights movement or the Vietnam War protests, the measures reviewed here suggest that levels of trust remain far below the levels recorded in the mid-1940s. The evidence supporting an association between growing political distrust and street crime rates beginning in the early 1960s is strong. Also, the high but stable levels of distrust in political institutions today resemble the high but stable street crime rates.

Absolute measures of economic stress like poverty and unemployment do not fare that well in explaining postwar crime rates, especially the crime wave of the 1960s. Relative measures of inequality and inflation, however, are consistent. The evidence is strong for a postwar connection in the United States between high street crime rates, high inflation, and high economic inequality. Moreover, modest declines in economic inequality and inflation in the 1990s are consistent with the recent crime downturn.

In many ways, connections between family legitimacy and crime are especially difficult to measure. Because of the family's role in socialization and social control, the full effect of family change on crime may not be clear for many years after changes begin. What we do know is that the traditional American family has gone through a revolutionary transformation during the past fifty years. In the early postwar period, the family with two parents, husband as breadwinner, and wife as household manager was both the norm and the goal for most Americans. By the end of the postwar period, this was no longer the case. The explosion of alternative family forms and the rise of nonfamily living was especially pronounced during the postwar crime boom.

Most researchers have treated support for criminal justice, education, and welfare institutions in the same way that they have treated other potential crime determinants, such as poverty or divorce rates. My argument here is that the timing of these newer institutional responses make them different. The evidence clearly shows that the biggest increases in criminal justice spending and, to a large extent, education and welfare spending came after crime rates had already started to boom. This supports my contention that criminal justice, education, and welfare spending are best interpreted as reactions to crime rather than causes of it.

I have argued throughout this book that a consideration of African American postwar crime experiences provides valuable additional information about the nature of crime trends. Given the tragedies of African American history, an objective view here is especially important. The following facts seem well supported: Compared to other racial groups, African Americans have experienced higher rates of street crime, lower levels of political trust, more economic inequality, and more rapid change in family forms throughout the postwar period. The evidence supports the conclusion that changes in African American connections to social institutions were especially rapid during the postwar crime boom. Unsurprisingly, African Americans have also been disproportionately affected by institutional responses to crime: Compared to members of other racial groups, African Americans have been more likely to be arrested, convicted, and imprisoned; have changed more dramatically in terms of educational attainment; and have received a disproportionate amount of welfare support.

Undoubtedly, factors outside of the six social institutions on which I have concentrated also contributed to postwar U.S. crime trends. I have endeavored to evaluate some of the most important of these. The rapidity of postwar crime changes rules out many of the most popular explanations. Crime trends simply moved too fast for common biological and psychological explanations. Although some recent biological and psychological explanations may still be relevant in that they posit direct connections to more rapidly changing social variables, they nevertheless depend on these social variables for their viability. Crime changes were also too rapid for many slow-moving social changes that have been argued for, such as the popular notion that crime rates are produced by deeply entrenched cultural values passed between generations.

The timing of postwar crime trends also reduces the plausibility of many common crime explanations. The fact that the boom coincided in large part with low poverty and unemployment rates and rising personal and family income makes explanations based on absolute economic measures problematic. Likewise, the fact that crime rates were low at a period of openly discriminatory race relations and low rates of imprisonment and other types of punishment calls into question common explanations based on discrimination or deterrence.

The simple fact that an especially large cohort of young people reached early adulthood at the time of the postwar crime boom surely deserves a place in any explanation of postwar crime trends. The importance of age in explaining the American postwar crime boom, however, is frequently exaggerated. Moreover, even if age is an important variable in explaining crime, we still have to explain what it is about age that makes it so. The institutional argument that I have advanced is quite compatible with the conclusion that, compared to older people, younger people have higher crime rates. To a far lesser extent, part of the postwar crime wave can also be attributed to the growing criminality of women. But again, the idea that, compared to the behavior of men, the behavior of women is more constrained by social institutions and that these constraints lessened somewhat during the postwar period is generally consistent with the institutional arguments I have presented.

Because I have examined the effects of political, economic, and family institutions separately, I have not spent much time reviewing connections between these institutions. In the next section, I examine the relationships between these three institutions and consider whether a case can be made for arguing that any one of the three should have priority in crime explanations.

Connections Among the Three Institutions

In considering the relative effects of political, economic, and family institutions on crime, the most common argument has probably been that economic institutions determine the development of the other two. This argument can be traced most directly to Karl Marx and researchers who have used Marx to explain crime.[4] Similar arguments are also evident in contemporary anomie and strain theories. In an attempt to explain high crime rates in the United States, the sociologists Steven Messner and Richard Rosenfeld argue that economic goals have increasingly displaced other institutional goals in American society.[5] They claim that the dominance of economic institutions in America is demonstrated by the devaluation of noneconomic institutional functions and roles, the accommodation of other institutions to economic requirements, and the penetration of economic norms into other institutional domains.[6] Thus, economic policies in the United States have been supported even when they have had the effect of destroying families and communities; educational attainment is frequently considered valuable only as a means to attaining more wealth; and American politicians are judged increasingly only by their ability to facilitate individual economic prosperity.[7]

A good case can be made for the impact of economic institutions on both political and family institutions. Clearly, increasing economic inequality and stress are likely to be associated with rising political distrust.[8] Likewise, many of the extraordinary changes in the American family during the postwar period were directly linked to changing economic requirements, in particular, the rise of female labor force participation, the decline in male participation in agricultural employment, and the major increases in schooling requirements.

But arguments about the primacy of economic explanations for predicting crime in the postwar United States are not as straightforward when viewed longitudinally. In terms of economic inequality and inflation, the two economic measures that are most consistently related to postwar crime rates, changes do not seem to have clearly preceded political and family effects on crime. Instead, both economic inequality (Figure 7.2) and inflation (Figure 7.3) began their most rapid expansion after the Vietnam War was heating up in the middle 1960s—a time when measures of political distrust (Figure 6.1) and family change (Figure 8.1) were already trending sharply upward.

In addition, there is some evidence that changing political and family institutions also affected the economy. Growing political distrust generally increases the cost of doing business in a society. As the commentator Francis Fukuyama observes, declining trust imposes a kind of tax on economic transactions by making it necessary to take more elaborate precautions to get things done.[9] Also, to some extent at least, declining trust in political institutions probably spills over into distrust of economic institutions. In fact, many of the concerns expressed about big government in the United States during the 1960s and 1970s were also directed at big business.[10]

Changes in family structure also had an enormous impact on economic conditions during the postwar period, particularly on economic inequality. This is because income distributions vary greatly by family arrangement. Most important here has been the explosion of single-parent, usually female-headed families. Based on income averages from the mid-1980s, the economist Frank Levy estimates that husband-wife families, with spouses age forty-five to fifty-four and both working, had an average income that was more than eight times higher than the average income of families headed by single women age twenty-five or under.[11]

The family also directly affects the economy in its role as the major institution for raising new generations of labor force participants. Although a good deal of national attention is devoted to the creation of more and better jobs, it is easy to overlook the fact that it is primarily the family that prepares workers for these jobs. As the economist Shirley Burggraf points out, creating good jobs doesn't benefit an economy unless society also produces good workers to fill them.[12]

Changes in political and family institutions during the postwar may also have been related in important ways. As we have already seen, a growing distrust of political institutions in the 1960s quickly overlapped with rising misgivings about the traditional, patriarchal family. In many cases, arguments made about the injustices of political institutions were very similar to those made about injustices of male-dominated households.[13] Conversely, given its central role in socialization and social control processes, the family is in turn directly related to the perceived legitimacy of political and economic institutions. After all, it is in the family that attitudes toward both institutions are most likely to be developed and reinforced.[14]

The historical intersection of growing political distrust, rising economic inequality, and increasingly insistent challenges to the traditional family coalesced in the 1960s to produce the postwar American crime wave. As we have seen, these three institutions differ enormously in their organization, scope, and history. Yet, declining legitimacy in all three had similar implications for crime: Rising political distrust meant that people were less likely to respect the polity and to work to enforce its rules; growing economic inequality meant that people were less likely to view the economy as deserving of their lawful behavior and the lawful behavior of others; the declining legitimacy of traditional family institutions meant that the motivation and the ability of families to teach their children the importance of adhering to rules, monitoring this adherence, and protecting children from the criminality of others were all greatly reduced. In Robert Merton's descriptive words, the rules governing conduct in these three major institutions lost much of "their savor and their force."[15]

What Can Be Done to Reduce Crime?

At one level, the implications of this research for reducing crime are straightforward—either strengthen traditional crime control institutions or spend more on newer institutional responses to crime or pursue some combination of both strategies. Strengthening traditional institutions would include increasing trust in political institutions, reducing economic inequality and stress, and renewing families. Given differences in street crime rates, increasing the legitimacy of institutions for African Americans is especially urgent. Of course, as the postwar period amply demonstrates, building institutional legitimacy is not straightforward. In this section, I consider some of the directions that such efforts might take for each of the major institutions reviewed in the book.

Political Institutions

The problem of increasing the legitimacy of political institutions in a society can be conceptualized more generally in terms of social capital. I argued previously that social capital accumulates in relationships of trust between individuals in a society. Societies with greater trust in their political institutions have greater stores of social capital, which makes it easier for them to reach common goals. The social upheavals that occurred in the United States during the postwar period severely reduced social capital. As first the civil rights movement and, later, other rights-based movements gained momentum, levels of trust in political institutions declined substantially.

There is evident irony here. After all, to the extent that civil rights movements increased equality between groups, they might be expected to have increased rather than to have reduced social capital. But as we have seen, attempts to build legitimacy by imposing rules from outside on resisting or unwilling individuals are likely to be less effective than legitimacy that develops organically from within communities. One of the lessons of the postwar period may be that we cannot take institutional legitimacy for granted. Especially during the middle postwar period, liberal policymakers frequently used law to mandate equality without considering the impact of these mandates on the cohesiveness of communities.[16]

William Julius Wilson's work illustrates some of the unintended consequences of desegregation on urban African American communities.[17] To the extent that Wilson's thesis is correct, the easing of segregation in the United States allowed more prosperous black individuals and families to flee inner-city neighborhoods, leaving behind a seriously disadvantaged, predominately black underclass. The dilemma is also well illustrated by Frank Furstenberg's research on Garrison Heights, a predominately white, poor neighborhood in Philadelphia that despite great disadvantages has nevertheless maintained low crime rates.[18]

Furstenberg shows how Garrison Heights has managed to maintain social capital and offer a remarkable amount of support to its children. This is accomplished in large part by a collective sharing of child-rearing responsibilities. But at the same time, Furstenberg shows that this very cohesiveness is firmly rooted in a "fierce racism" that provides community solidarity in the face of constant infighting and friction.[19] The general problem this case study raises is how to rid communities of racial segregation and racism without destroying the institutional fabric that binds these communities together.

But although we can fault liberals for failing to foresee the impact that campaigns to guarantee equality would have on community cohesiveness, with regard to the civil rights movement at least, the choices were limited. The irony of fighting a world war to end tyranny and injustice but simultaneously relegating racial minorities to second-class status was eventually too obvious to ignore.

If liberals during the middle postwar period erred in underestimating the toll that legislating equality would have on community cohesiveness, conservatives in the late postwar period may be erring by overestimating the strength of civil society to solve problems without help from the state. As this book was being prepared, the elimination of the AFDC program was beginning to be felt by people with too few family and community resources to provide even minimal living standards in the absence of state support. It is far too early to assess the eventual impact of these changes on crime rates. Moreover, changes in welfare support in the late 1990s are happening in tandem with a relatively strong economy. Their impact during an economic downturn remains to be seen.

Given the disproportionate importance of street crime committed by African Americans, building political trust in the African American community is especially critical. There is growing evidence that punishment, even draconian punishment, is likely to have far less impact on groups who do not trust in the basic fairness of the political system. John Braithwaite's emphasis on "reintegrative shaming," Tom Tyler's discussion of the perceived fairness of criminal sanctions, and Lawrence Sherman's recent development of "defiance" theory are all consistent with the idea that legal responses to crime that are not buttressed by a widespread belief in the legitimacy of political institutions may actually increase rather than reduce future criminal behavior. Until African Americans believe in the justice of political institutions, the legal system is likely to go on exacting a frightening toll on the African American community and still not achieve the public safety demanded by the supporters of these measures.[20] In fact, there is much evidence for a large and maybe even widening chasm between African Americans and whites with regard to political distrust. Following the O. J. Simpson murder trial, a national poll found that just 13 percent of African Americans thought Simpson was guilty, compared to 48 percent of whites.[21] A 1990 survey of 1,000 black church members in five cities found that more than one-third believed that the AIDS virus was produced in a germ warfare laboratory as a form of genocide against blacks.[22] Another one-third said they were unsure whether AIDS was created to kill blacks. The findings held firm even among more highly educated respondents. Similar attitudes have led some black leaders in major U.S. cities to oppose needle exchange programs for intravenous drug users, who are disproportionately likely to be black. Thus, the former New York City councilman Hilton B. Clark of Harlem called needle distribution in his city genocide and argued that the architect of New York City's needle exchange program "should be arrested for murder and drug distribution."[23]

On the other hand, recent national polls also show that African Americans and whites are concerned about many of the same social problems: crime, poor education, the breakdown of the family.[24] Moreover, a strong majority of both groups in one recent poll agreed that the United States has made a great deal of progress in easing black-white tensions in the past ten years and that racial integration has been good for society.[25] It remains to be seen what impact, if any, the movement during the last few years of the twentieth century to turn back affirmative action programs will have on African American trust in political institutions.

Economic Institutions

More than a century ago, the French sociologist Emile Durkheim argued that the occupational structure will only produce solidarity if labor is divided in such a way that "social inequalities exactly express natural inequalities."[26] In other words, solidarity in a society is based in part on allowing economic inequality to be no greater than is warranted by differences in individual talent. There is evidence to suggest that the distribution of economic rewards in the United States is becoming increasingly removed from Durkheim's guidelines for a well-ordered society. For example, a 1997 survey of the top executives of 350 of the largest corporations in the United States showed that the median compensation for these administrators was $2.4 million—about sixty times greater than the median U.S. family income of $40,000.[27] Multimillion-dollar salaries have become commonplace in professional sports and the entertainment industry in America. *Forbes* magazine reports that over a five-year period the heavyweight fighter Evander Holyfield earned $177.8 million, Arnold Palmer $82.4 million, Shaquille O'Neal $78.2 million, Andre Agassi $74.8 million, and Jack Nicklaus $74.6 million. In two years, Steven Spielberg earned $150 million, the Beatles $130 million, Michael Jackson $90 million, the Rolling Stones $77 million, Arnold Schwarzenegger $74 million, and Jim Carrey $63 million.[28]

As the social commentator Charles Handy observes, "Capitalism depends on the fundamental principal of inequality."[29] And in fact, most citizens of Western-style democracies accept some amount of economic inequality as fair. The Australian sociologists Jonathan Kelley and M.D.R. Evans studied attitudes toward economic inequality among respondents from the United States and eight other developed nations and found that few of the respondents believed in complete economic equality or anything close to it.[30] There was also widespread consensus on which occupations should be more highly paid and which less. Respondents from the nine countries differed substantially, however, in how much inequality was viewed as justifiable. Unsurprisingly, citizens of the former Soviet bloc (Hungary, Poland) favored less inequality than citizens of capitalist nations. Among the latter, Austrian citizens favored the most inequality; the United States, Britain, Germany, the Netherlands, and Switzerland were similar; and Australians favored the least inequality.

Thus, although most citizens accept the legitimacy of some inequality, the question of a fair level of inequality is an ongoing concern. It seems a safe bet to conclude that the proportion of Americans who would argue that the amount of economic inequality in the United States is too high grew substantially during the middle and late postwar years. Moreover, individuals are only likely to accept an unequal system when opportunities for achievement in that system are perceived to be equally distributed. In Charles Handy's words, inequality will only be accepted when "most people have an equal chance to aspire to that inequality."[31] And as with levels of political trust, the issue of a just level of economic inequality and fair opportunities to aspire to it is particularly critical for African Americans.

Family Institutions

At the end of World War II, the core organizing feature of most American families was what economists call "a double coincidence model."[32] Because the socially constructed desires of men and women substantially coincided, it was possible to maintain sex role specialization and a division of responsibilities within the family without paying women for their labor. But this traditional arrangement was forcefully challenged in the middle postwar years. These challenges were magnified by fundamental changes in the nature of work.

Judging from some of the recent political debates on the American family, it seems that many commentators believe that the way to solve the problems created by these changes is to move toward a restoration of the family form that was dominant at the end of World War II.[33] However appealing this view may appear to some, it seems no more likely at the end of the twentieth century to expect that women will leave the paid labor force in large numbers than it was at the end of the nineteenth century to expect men to abandon jobs in the paid labor force and return to farming.

Moreover, although divorce rates and rates at which children are born out of wedlock fluctuate a great deal over time, there is little evidence to suggest that a wholesale reduction in rates is on the horizon. In fact, one interesting feature of changes in the family during the postwar period is that divorce and illegitimacy rates kept climbing methodically through both good economic times and bad.

Many of the changes in the family are clearly here to stay and are likely to produce living arrangements in the twenty-first century that are even further removed from the traditional postwar family form that dominated the early postwar years. So, with regard to controlling crime, the challenge for society seems to be how to best shore up the socialization, social control, and guardianship functions formerly performed almost exclusively by the traditional nuclear family. A variety of recent research provides some promising leads.

One important potential reform involves reconsidering the economic structure of the contemporary family. While families were undergoing revolutionary changes in the postwar period, much of the economic debate centered on the logic of extending equal opportunities to women. In general, conservatives fought a rearguard action by arguing in favor of keeping women out of the paid labor force altogether. Liberals more commonly argued in favor of ensuring women equal access to occupational positions and rewards.[34] The conservative view is problematic because it appears certain that women in the United States as well as all other Western democracies are in the paid labor force to stay. The liberal view is not so much unimportant as incomplete. It has undoubtedly benefited professional women in their efforts to penetrate traditional employment barriers. But equality of employment does little to soften the impact of the changing structure of the family and employment conditions on children.

In short, the economic system has not adjusted to the rapid flight of women into the paid labor force. As the economist Shirley Burggraf puts it, "An economic system that says someone is worth $200 an hour as a lawyer but worth nothing as a parent . . . is not a whole economic system."[35] Parents offered a choice between paid employment in the labor force and no pay in the home have no real choice at all. If society puts a high value on properly raising its children, it must be willing to pay for this child rearing. We need to redesign the economic system to enable families to compete with the paid labor force for the resources they need to do their job.[36] This could involve a wide variety of policy changes, including tax incentives for people rearing children, more generous family leave policies, higher wages for child care providers, and greater investment in work-related child care.

Beyond these mostly economic changes are a host of programs for shoring up family efforts to socialize and educate their children. The range of these programs is far too broad to summarize adequately here.

Among the most relevant of these programs for present purposes are those aimed at reducing chronic juvenile delinquency and antisocial behavior. A review article by Hiro Yoshikawa evaluates many of the best-known initiatives.[37] In particular, Yoshikawa identifies four programs that offered both social support for families and extensive early education programs for very young children. The Perry Preschool project targeted low-income African American families, the Houston Parent-Child Development Center focused on low-income Mexican American families with one child, the Syracuse University Family Development Research Project examined low-income mothers with less than a high school education, and the Yale Child Welfare Project studied low-income mothers with one child. Although sample sizes and experimental treatments for these four projects varied greatly, all included home visits by professional personnel trained to provide assistance to both children and parents. In addition, three of the four programs provided emotional support, three provided parenting advice, and the Yale project provided medical assistance.

A two-year follow-up evaluation of the Perry Preschool project found that children in the experimental group had significantly higher IQ scores than those in the control group.[38] A fourteen-year follow-up (when the subjects were seventeen to nineteen years old) found that 17 percent of the control group children but only 7 percent of the experimental group children had committed five or more criminal offenses. In addition, compared to the control group, the experimental group had 20 percent fewer school dropouts, half the teenage pregnancy rate, and twice the employment rate.

At its conclusion, the Houston parenting study found that, compared to mothers in the control group, those in the experimental group were more affectionate and responsive and less punishing with their children.[39] At a one-year follow-up, the children in the experimental group had higher cognitive scores. At a five- to eight-year follow-up, the children in the experimental group were rated by their teachers as less likely to engage in fighting and other disruptive, impulsive, or restless behavior.

Three years after the conclusion of the Syracuse study, compared to children in the control group, children in the experimental group had higher cognitive and social-emotional ratings.[40] After ten years, 22 percent of the children in the control group but only 6 percent of the children in the experimental group had juvenile records. After the completion of the Yale project, children in the experimental group had significantly higher scores on verbal ability and the Yale project families were more likely to have gotten off welfare, to have delayed having a second child, and to include mothers who had furthered their education during the project.[41] Studies like these offer valuable insights into how today's beleaguered families could be provided with the support they need to keep a higher proportion of their members from engaging in crime.

Criminal Justice, Education, and Welfare Institutions

I argued in earlier chapters that the three main institutional responses to declining legitimacy and rising crime rates in postwar America have been criminal justice, education, and welfare. These three approaches are loosely linked to political orientation, with conservatives generally favoring criminal justice approaches and liberals generally favoring education and welfare approaches. When the liberal agenda had the upper hand in the 1960s and 1970s, conservatives argued forcefully that crime rates were soaring because of the failure of liberal policymakers to invest in criminal justice and, particularly, to support harsher punishments for crime. Similarly, after the prison boom demanded by conservatives began in the late postwar years, liberal policymakers severely criticized the vengeful spirit of programs aimed at simply "warehousing" offenders.[42] In the next three sections, I briefly consider how spending on criminal justice, education, and welfare institutions might affect crime rates in the years ahead.

Criminal Justice and Punishment. The debate on the impact of rising rates of imprisonment on crime in the 1990s has been especially acrimonious. On one side of this controversy are researchers who argue that recent increases in imprisonment have had an important impact on reducing crime, especially for African Americans, and that, if anything, even more prisons are needed.[43] On the other side are researchers who argue that imprisonment has had little or no effect on crime and that it siphons off resources from programs aimed at rehabilitating offenders or strengthening families, schools, and communities.[44] Critics of the rapid increase in imprisonment argue that it has had a disproportionately negative impact on African Americans.

Perhaps a way around this impasse is to concentrate not on whether imprisonment reduces crime but rather on whether it is the most desirable way to reduce crime, for the individuals being processed, for crime victims, and for the nation as a whole. The weight of prior research suggests that imprisonment has reduced crime in America. But at what cost? Clearly, both conservatives and liberals should be nervous about a social policy that now ensnares nearly 25 percent of young male members of the nation's largest racial minority group. Moreover, researchers and policymakers on both sides of the current debate must concede that even when amply justified prison is an extremely expensive resource that should be used prudently. Finally, both sides must agree that back-end strategies like prisons can do nothing to erase the criminal victimization that has already occurred.

Education. The difficulty with marketing education as a crime-reduction measure is that compared to investing in police or prisons its effects on crime are likely to be far more indirect and long term. As summarized previously, however, a growing number of studies show that providing at-risk children with access to early education and support can produce impressive long-term payoffs. Unfortunately, thus far these programs have been small pilot projects with a very limited number of participants. Head Start remains the only nationwide early intervention program in America.[45] And as many researchers have observed, the family support component of Head Start has been severely hampered by the fact that family service social workers frequently have caseloads that are twice as high as those recommended.[46]

Just as we find a lag in an economic system that encourages women to compete equally with men in the paid labor force but provides few compensatory systems for raising children, so too we find educational institutions that seem resistant to the growing demands being placed on them by a society that increasingly spends less time in families. Even though the vast majority of American children between the ages of three and nineteen are now enrolled in public, parochial, or private schools, educational institutions continue to define their responsibilities for these children in extremely limited terms.[47] In fairness, the school was originally constructed as a narrow-purpose organization with specific tasks that were far less extensive than those fulfilled by the family.[48] This view of schools is increasingly out of step with reality, however. Clearly, more flexible thinking about the role of schools as day care providers and community support centers is sorely needed by many families with parents in the paid labor force.

But expanding the role of schools and teachers has obvious economic implications. Moreover, the costs of hiring more and better teachers is being compounded by the same labor market dynamics that have increasingly pulled women out of households: The best and brightest women in the past were often forced into teaching because they were effectively blocked from other male-dominated professions, but as these professions have begun to open up to women, education faces its own "brain drain."[49] The economist Shirley Burggraf's solution to this problem is similar to her advice for restoring the importance society places on properly raising its children—to give educational careers more economic value. Obviously, as long as women or men can make ten times more as lawyers or doctors than as teachers, there is going to be a tendency for the best and the brightest to avoid teaching careers.

Welfare Systems.   Of the three major institutional responses to postwar crime, criminal justice, education, and welfare, the future of public welfare in America is clearly the most precarious. Apart from the income tax, by the 1990s, AFDC had become America's least popular government program,[50] encouraging Congress to substantially overhaul it in 1996. In that year, the Temporary Assistance for Needy Families (TANF) plan replaced AFDC and several other long-established welfare programs with a system of block grants to the states. The new law mandates that federal funding for TANF programs be capped at $16.4 billion annually through the year 2002 and stipulates that recipients can only receive TANF benefits for a maximum of five years. The law mandates that unmarried teen parents must live at home or in another adult-supervised setting and attend school to be eligible for TANF benefits. It is too early to tell how much of an impact (if any) these changes will have on future crime trends. But by 1997, national welfare caseloads were down by 23 percent from their peak level in 1994.[51]

Although the recent changes in welfare have received the most media attention, efforts to make welfare less economically attractive actually started in the mid-1970s, as political conservatives gained ground in the federal government. Between 1976 and 1988, the typical welfare recipient's purchasing power fell about 16 percent.[52]

In a thoughtful essay on reforming welfare, Kathryn Edin and Christopher Jencks conclude that a major defect of AFDC was the fact that it had no moral legitimacy in the eyes of its recipients.[53] Edin and Jencks discovered that mothers on AFDC in their Chicago-area study could not live on their AFDC payments and that they therefore supplemented these payments from other sources and lied about it to AFDC caseworkers. The researchers also concluded that welfare dependency was not produced by psychological or cultural characteristics but by simple economic expediency: Although welfare paid badly, low-wage jobs paid even worse.[54] Edin and Jencks argue that the U.S. welfare system should be replaced with a system that focuses on all workers in low-wage jobs who are trying to support children. They suggest providing earned income tax credits, tax credits for child care expenses, subsidized Medicaid coverage, tax credits for housing expenses, and mortgage subsidies for the working poor.[55]

Shirley Burggraf notes that the most basic reform needed in the welfare system is simply to begin recognizing the substantial contributions child rearing makes to the economy.[56] Burggraff points out that even for those in the bottom one-third of the income distribution, it costs a small fortune to raise a child.[57] Burggraf's point is that aid to poor families who are trying their best to produce productive future citizens should be seen not as charity, but as investment.[58] A major challenge for policymakers is to design support systems that provide real incentives to families to do their jobs well.

Part of the problem could be solved by reversing postwar trends in tax laws that have become increasingly unfavorable to families. Burggraf points out that income tax deductions for family dependents have shrunk about 30 percent in real dollars since 1960.[59] At the same time, the tax system has relentlessly eliminated deductions for family dependents and created a substantial tax penalty for married couples. Burggraf estimates that the Social Security system is now taking over $300 billion per year away from families and expects to transfer over $16 trillion out of families (an amount approximately equal to the total tangible wealth of the U.S. economy) during the lifetimes of people currently in the system.[60]

Implications for Research, Theory, and Social Policy

The Importance of Longitudinal Research

One of the themes with which I began this book was the importance of longitudinal information for understanding postwar trends in crime rates. The indispensable advantage of longitudinal approaches is that they allow us to sort out the causal ordering between variables in a way that is difficult or impossible with cross-sectional data. The sociologist Stanley Lieberson states categorically, "All causal propositions have consequences for longitudinal change."[61] In other words, whenever we argue that some variable X causes some outcome Y, we are implicitly arguing that changes over time in X cause changes over time in Y.

This observation often has important implications. For example, cross-sectional studies of the relationship between welfare payments and crime rates in the postwar United States are likely to show that crime rates are higher in cities or states with higher welfare payments. But concluding on the basis of such cross-sectional evidence that increases in welfare payments cause crime to increase would be erroneous. As I have shown, major increases in welfare spending in the United States occurred in large part after the crime wave had already begun. Despite the importance of longitudinal analysis, the vast majority of studies in the behavioral sciences are still based on cross-sectional data.[62]

Implications for Other Countries

There is a long tradition among social observers both in and outside the United States of regarding the United States as an exceptional society—for better or worse. Perhaps the most famous example of this is the observations made more than 150 years ago by the French aristocrat, Alexis de Tocqueville, who came to the United States to determine why efforts at establishing a democracy had worked out more successfully in the United States than in France and other European nations.[63] But these observations are by no means limited to the past. In a 1996 book titled *Amer-*

ican Exceptionalism, the sociologist Seymour Martin Lipset chronicles many of the distinctive features of American society that seem to separate it from other Western democracies.[64]

As we have seen previously, the United States is frequently regarded by both policymakers and researchers as exceptional with regard to its high crime rates. Although it is easy to exaggerate the differences, crime rates in the contemporary United States are exceptional with regard to violent crimes—especially those committed with firearms.[65] There are also important differences between the United States and other industrialized democracies with regard to the social institutions I have considered in previous chapters. In general, compared to other industrialized nations, the United States is characterized by low levels of trust in political institutions and authority in general,[66] high levels of economic inequality,[67] and high levels of family disintegration.[68] In terms of the major institutional responses to crime, the contemporary United States is characterized by high per capita spending for criminal justice, especially prisons,[69] high spending on education,[70] and low spending on social welfare programs.[71]

But despite these obvious differences, there is some evidence that the postwar experiences of the United States might have important implications for other industrialized democracies. The most intriguing possibility is that the United States is not so much exceptional with regard to trends in crime and fundamental social institutions as precocious. As we have seen, the rapid increase in street crimes in the United States began in the early 1960s but had peaked by the 1980s. By contrast, much of the increase in street crime rates for other developed nations has occurred after the early 1970s.[72] Moreover, although street crime rates have stabilized and even declined in the United States in recent years, such declines are not yet evident in other Western-style democracies. It may be that the United States was simply early in experiencing a postwar street crime surge.

Another interesting point of convergence between the United States and other developed nations is found in parallels between race, ethnicity, immigration, and crime issues. In a recent review, Michael Tonry concludes categorically that for every Western country he examined there was at least one racial, ethnic, or national-origin minority group that was disproportionately likely to be arrested, convicted, and imprisoned for violent, property, and drug crimes.[73] In support, Roland Chilton and his associates found that compared to German citizens, non-German residents from other countries living in Germany had substantially higher rates of robbery and assault as well as larceny.[74] Similarly, Pamela Irving Jackson concludes that recent immigrants to France, particularly those from North Africa and Turkey, had crime rates that far exceeded those of nonimmigrants.[75] Compared to their respective nonminority national populations, crime rates are generally higher for North African immigrants to

Italy, Afro-Caribbean immigrants to Canada and England, East European immigrants to Germany, Finnish immigrants to Sweden, aborigines in Australia, and Koreans in Japan.[76]

Connections between social institutions and crime are also relevant worldwide. Particularly interesting in other Western democracies is the potential effect on crime rates of recent reductions in social welfare spending. It seems likely that in the past many Western nations have been able to blunt challenges to institutional legitimacy by providing a comprehensive social welfare net for the less fortunate. As international pressures build to reduce spending on social welfare, these changes may well translate into rising crime rates.

Although compared to the problems of collecting national crime data the difficulties of gathering cross-national crime data are even more daunting, such data sources are clearly improving.[77] International crime statistics are now compiled annually by Interpol; the United Nations; and, for homicide only, the World Health Organization. In addition, beginning in 1988, scholars from several nations have collaborated to collect international victimization data.[78] It would be useful in future research to determine the extent to which the rapid changes in crime rates I have identified for the postwar United States are beginning to occur in other nations and to determine the extent to which these changes are linked to the legitimacy of social institutions.

Effects of Global Processes

Although I have focused almost entirely in this book on trends for the United States, many of the processes that shaped postwar social institutions in the United States are no doubt directly related to broader, global developments. This is perhaps most obvious with regard to economic institutions. The increasing role of transnational flows of goods and capital has been a universal feature of postwar economic growth for all countries that participate in the capitalist world system.[79] This fact is well illustrated in an essay by the journalist Eric Schlosser, who describes the migrant farm labor camps that have sprung up in southern California in response to the increasingly lucrative strawberry market.[80] Schlosser points out that the low wages, lack of benefits, and poor working and living conditions of these laborers are increasingly being set not by rational planning but by global laws of supply and demand: "The market will drive wages down like water, until they reach the lowest possible level. Today that level is being set not in Washington or New York or Sacramento but in the fields of Baja California and the mountain villages of Oaxaca." [81]

But the United States is both being shaped by and shaping these economic developments. The sociologist Saskia Sassen argues that during the early postwar period the United States led the world in developing the idea of a "family wage."[82] To support viable families, the United States developed mass production to the highest level in history and encouraged suburbanization as a mechanism for ever-increasing family consumption. But the idea of the family wage and the implied compact between labor and employers has been severely eroded in the United States during the late postwar period by a tremendous increase in part-time workers, temporary workers, workers without seniority protection, and workers without pension and health benefits. Sassen argues that these changes are producing a new global alignment the edges of which are seen most clearly in large U.S. cities. The hallmark of these changes is jarring inequality: a rapid expansion of high-income workers juxtaposed with extreme urban poverty.[83]

Although changes in economic institutions provide the most obvious example of how global processes are increasingly affecting social changes within societies, there is evidence that many of the institutions reviewed in this book are increasingly being affected by transnational trends. For example, there are growing similarities between nations with regard to the structure and interpretation of political, educational, and welfare institutions.[84]

Institutions, Crime, and Social Change

A common plotline in science fiction literature involves a group of explorers who uncover some seemingly ancient space craft only to learn later in the story that the craft has in fact been created by a previous civilization on earth and then lost to recorded history. In a way, humans continually face a similar problem with regard to the social institutions they create. We build economic and political structures and then somehow lose sight of the fact that we have built them. Of course, the power of institutions stems from their ability to appear to be transparent, outside of human creation, objective, and apart. Peter Berger and Thomas Luckmann use the term "reification" to refer to the process by which individuals come to perceive humanly created phenomena in nonhuman or suprahuman terms.[85] Like misguided space explorers, humans continue to treat as alien the social institutions that they and their ancestors have created. Berger and Luckmann refer to this paradoxical feature of humanity as the capability of "creating a reality that denies us as creators."[86]

Robert Bellah and his colleagues have these processes in mind when they note, "The idea that institutions are objective mechanisms that are essentially separate from the lives of the individuals who inhabit them is an ideology that exacts a high moral and political price."[87] But paradoxically, one of the most encouraging aspects of the rapid changes observed in postwar American social institutions is the very fact that institutions are capable of such change. Just as researchers are getting more proficient at understanding genetic processes to override certain instincts in animals, researchers and policymakers can also get more proficient at studying our institutions and making them do what we want them to do. When we read that crime rates have increased rapidly, that thousands of people are homeless, or that millions of children are living in poverty, it is not true that there is nothing to be done. We created these social conditions and we can change them.

In fact, we must not lose sight of the fact that this ability of humanly created institutions to change is often a positive trait. It is easy to forget that the landmark changes in social institutions in postwar America that encouraged a major crime wave were often the same changes that brought about developments that are widely embraced today as improvements. Before we get too nostalgic for the low-crime days of the early postwar period, we should recall that this was also a period that institutionalized the most blatant forms of racial discrimination, that locked women (and often men) into roles that many of them actively disliked and were often not very good at, and that greatly curtailed the freedom and rights of many individuals whose only transgression was being different from the norm. Our ability to change the institutions that govern our lives has its advantages.

● ● ●

In an influential book about crime and social policy published in the early 1990s, the sociologist Christopher Jencks observes that crime rates went up twenty-five years ago for some "unknown reason" and concludes that they might just as well come down again, "even though criminologists cannot currently offer any reliable advice about how to make this happen."[88] The preceding chapters should make it clear that I do not regard the ability of criminology to provide insights into why crime rates change quite as pessimistically as Jencks does. On the contrary, I think we know a great deal about what made crime rates go up in the middle postwar period and why they are finally coming down a bit in the late postwar years.

Americans entered the postwar period with unprecedented levels of trust in their political institutions, historically low levels of economic inequality, and strong families. These three conditions have all been linked to low crime rates, both in the United States and in other societies. The postwar crime wave followed pervasive, even revolutionary changes in political, economic, and family institutions. Policymakers and the public, sensing the depth of the crisis, threw their support behind social policy strategies based first on strengthening educational and welfare institutions and later on expanding more punitive criminal justice institutions. Through a combination of these new institutional responses and a tapering off and even reversal of negative trends in the legitimacy of political, economic, and family institutions, street crimes began to show signs of stabilization by the 1980s and declines by the mid-1990s.

In a very real sense, science is the history of making the invisible visible. Charles Darwin's theory of natural selection made visible intricate biological processes that were previously thought to be divinely created. Albert Einstein's theory of relativity made visible the invisible behavior of matter. Watson and Crick's theory of DNA made visible the genetic structure of cells. With increasing momentum over the past century, similar processes have been at work in the social sciences. Thus, Emile Durkheim's insistence that societies are as real as physical objects made visible a previously invisible construct. We cannot see, smell, hear, touch, or feel social institutions. Yet, they are as real as species, matter, or DNA strands. We have barely begun to understand the invisible social institutions that shape our lives. Yet, they are perhaps the most important and powerful of all human creations.

Notes

Chapter One

1. Milan Kundera, *The Unbearable Lightness of Being* (New York: Harper & Row, 1984), p. 223.

2. John Updike, *Rabbit at Rest* (New York: Alfred A. Knopf, 1990), p. 44.

3. U.S. Federal Bureau of Investigation, *Uniform Crime Reports for the United States, 1994* (Washington, DC: Government Printing Office, 1995).

4. Wesley G. Skogan, *Disorder and Decline: Crime and the Spiral of Decay in American Neighborhoods* (New York: Free Press, 1991); Research and Forecasts, Incorporated, *America Afraid: How Fear of Crime Changes the Way We Live* (New York: New American Library, 1983).

5. Following popular usage, I use the term "wave" to refer to the rapid increase in U.S. crime rates that began in the early 1960s and began to taper off (depending on crime type) in the early 1980s. Some researchers might instead refer to this relatively short time frame as a "cycle." See David Hackett Fischer, *The Great Wave: Price Revolutions and the Rhythm of History* (New York: Oxford University Press, 1996), Appendix E.

6. Daniel Glaser, *Crime in Our Changing Society* (New York: Holt, 1978), p. 6.

7. Eric Hobsbawm, *The Age of Extremes: A History of the World, 1914–1991* (New York: Pantheon, 1994), p. 3.

8. See, for example, Richard Sennett, "The New Censorship," *Contemporary Sociology* (1994) 23:487–491; Seymour Martin Lipset, *American Exceptionalism: A Double-Edged Sword* (New York: W. W. Norton, 1996).

9. Douglas Eckberg, "Estimates of Early Twentieth-Century U.S. Homicide Rates: An Econometric Forecasting Approach," *Demography* (1995) 32:1–16.

10. Paul A. Gilje, *The Road to Mobocracy: Popular Disorder in New York City, 1763–1834* (Chapel Hill: University of North Carolina Press, 1987); see arguments in James F. Short, Jr., *Poverty, Ethnicity, and Violent Crime* (Boulder: Westview, 1997), pp. 4–9.

11. Roger Lane, "On the Social Meaning of Homicide Trends in America," in T. R. Gurr, ed., *Violence in America: The History of Crime*, Volume 1 (Newbury Park, CA: Sage, 1989), pp. 72–73.

12. U.S. Bureau of the Census, 1990 Census of Population and Housing, Summary Tape File 3C.

13. U.S. Federal Bureau of Investigation, *Uniform Crime Reports for the United States, 1995* (Washington, DC: Government Printing Office 1996), p. 226.

14. Alfred Blumstein and Elizabeth Graddy, "Prevalence and Recidivism in Index Arrests: A Feedback Model," *Law and Society Review* (1981–1982) 16:265–290, 280.

15. Mark Mauer, *Young Black Men and the Criminal Justice System* (Washington, DC: Sentencing Institute, 1990).

16. Mauer (1990).

17. M. McCord and H. Freeman, "Excess Mortality in Harlem," *New England Journal of Medicine* (1990) 322:173–175.

18. U.S. Bureau of Justice Statistics, "The Risk of Violent Crime," U.S. Department of Justice Special Report (Washington, DC: Government Printing Office, 1985), p. 8.

19. William Julius Wilson, "The Urban Underclass," in L. Dunbar, ed., *Minority Report* (New York: Pantheon, 1984).

20. As examples, Wilson cites scholars such as Daniel Moynihan, *The Negro Family: The Case for National Action* (Office of Planning and Research: U.S. Department of Labor, 1965); and Lee Rainwater, *Behind Ghetto Walls: Black Families in a Federal Slum* (Chicago: Aldine Publishing, 1970).

21. Robert N. Bellah, Richard Madsen, William M. Sullivan, Ann Swidler, and Steven M. Tipton, *The Good Society* (New York: Alfred A. Knopf, 1991), p. 4; Peter L. Berger and Thomas Luckmann, *The Social Construction of Reality* (Garden City, NY: Anchor Books, 1967), ch. 2.

22. Max Weber, *The Theory of Social and Economic Organizations* (New York: Oxford, 1947), pp. 324–363.

23. Peter Berger, *Invitation to Sociology: A Humanistic Perspective* (New York: Doubleday, 1963), p. 87.

24. Berger and Luckmann (1967), ch. 2.

25. For this aspect of institutions, see the discussion in Robert D. Putnam, *Making Democracy Work: Civic Traditions in Modern Italy* (Princeton: Princeton University Press, 1993), p. 8.

26. President's Commission on Law Enforcement and the Administration of Justice, *The Challenge of Crime in a Free Society* (Washington, DC: Government Printing Office, 1967), p. 66.

Chapter Two

1. Lambert Quetelet, *A Treatise on Man and the Development of His Faculties*, reproduction of the English translation of 1842, introduction by S. Diamond (Gainesville, FL: Scholar's Facsimiles and Reprints, 1969).

2. Josiah Stamp, *Some Economic Factors in Modern Life* (London: King, 1929), pp. 158–159.

3. The most important attempt to modify the reporting procedures of the Uniform Crime Report system during the past sixty years is known as the National Incident-Based Reporting System (NIBRS). NIBRS grew out of recommendations for improving the UCR contained in a 1985 report prepared by Abt Associates (*Blueprint for the Future of the Uniform Crime Reporting Program*). Compared to cur-

rent UCR data, NIBRS data are far more complete. But the implementation of NIBRS has been slow and uncertain. The FBI only began accepting NIBRS data from participating states in 1989. In 1994, only nine states supplied data in the NI-BRS format. Many other states and agencies, however, are experimenting with NI-BRS (U.S. Federal Bureau of Investigation, *National Incident-Based Reporting System, Volume 1, Data Collection Guidelines* [Washington, DC: Government Printing Office, 1996]).

4. By act of Congress, arson was added to the crime index of Part I offenses in 1979 and some agencies began reporting arson rates in the mid-1980s.

5. U.S. Federal Bureau of Investigation, "Crime in the United States," *Uniform Crime Reports 1990* (Washington, DC: Government Printing Office, 1991).

6. See, for example, A. L. Porterfield, *Youth in Trouble* (Austin, TX: Leo Potishman Foundation, 1946); A. Wallerstein and C. J. Wyle, "Our Law Abiding Law Breakers," *Federal Probation* (1947) 25:107–112.

7. James F. Short, Jr., and F. Ivan Nye, "Extent of Unrecorded Delinquency, Tentative Conclusions," *Journal of Criminal Law, Criminology and Police Science* (1958) 49:296–302.

8. Michael Hindelang, Travis Hirschi, and Joseph G. Weis, *Measuring Delinquency* (Beverly Hills, CA: Sage, 1981), p. 23.

9. For example, Robert A. Dentler and Lawrence J. Monroe, "Social Correlates of Early Adolescent Theft," *American Sociological Review* (1961) 26:733–743; Maynard L. Erickson and Lamar T. Empey, "Court Records, Undetected Delinquency and Decision-Making," *Journal of Criminal Law, Criminology and Police Science* (1963) 54:456–469; Ronald L. Akers, "Socioeconomic Status and Delinquent Behavior: A Retest," *Journal of Research on Crime and Delinquency* (1964) 1:38–46.

10. Robert H. Hardt and George E. Bodine, *Development of Self-Report Instruments in Delinquency Research: A Conference Report* (Syracuse, NY: Syracuse University Youth Development Center, 1965).

11. Travis Hirschi, *Causes of Delinquency* (Berkeley: University of California Press, 1969).

12. Preben Wolf and Roger Hauge, "Criminal Violence in Three Scandinavian Countries," *Scandinavian Studies in Criminology*, Volume 5 (London: Tavistock, 1975).

13. Richard Sparks, "Surveys of Victimization: An Optimistic Assessment," *Crime and Justice: An Annual Review of Research*, Volume 3 (Chicago: University of Chicago Press, 1981), p. 2.

14. A. D. Biderman, L. A. Johnson, J. McIntyre, and A. W. Weir, *Report of a Pilot Study in the District of Columbia on Victimization and Attitudes Toward Law Enforcement*, President's Commission on Law Enforcement and the Administration of Justice, Field Survey I (Washington, DC: Government Printing Office, 1967).

15. Albert Reiss, *Studies in Crime and Law Enforcement in Major Metropolitan Areas*, President's Commission on Law Enforcement and Administration of Justice, Field Survey III, Volume 1 (Washington, DC: Government Printing Office, 1967).

16. Philip H. Ennis, *Criminal Victimization in the U.S.: Report of a National Survey*, President's Commission on Law Enforcement and Administration of Justice, Field Survey II (Washington, DC: Government Printing Office, 1967).

17. See generally, Albert D. Biderman, *An Inventory of Surveys of the Public on Crime, Justice and Related Topics* (Washington, DC: Government Printing Office, 1972); Robert M. O'Brien, *Crime and Victimization Data* (Beverly Hills, CA: Sage, 1985).

18. President's Commission on Law Enforcement and Administration of Justice, *The Challenge of Crime in a Free Society* (Washington, DC: Government Printing Office, 1967).

19. Ennis (1967), p. 9.

20. President's Commission on Law Enforcement and Administration of Justice (1967), p. 40.

21. Sparks (1981), p. 15.

22. Sparks (1981), p. 15.

23. Michael R. Rand, James P. Lynch, and David Cantor, "Criminal Victimization, 1973–95," U.S. Bureau of Justice Statistics, National Crime Victimization Survey (Washington, DC: Government Printing Office, April 1997).

24. For convenience, I refer to the entire series of victimization surveys collected by the U.S. Bureau of Justice Statistics as the "National Crime Victimization Survey" throughout the remainder of this book.

25. For example, President's Commission on Law Enforcement and Administration of Justice (1967); Walter R. Gove, Michael Hughes, and Michael Geerken, "Are Uniform Crime Reports a Valid Indicator of the Index Crimes? An Affirmative Answer with Minor Qualifications," *Criminology* (1985) 23:451–501; Robert O'Brien, "Police Productivity and Crime Rates: 1973–1992," *Criminology* (1996) 34:183–208.

26. U.S. Bureau of Justice Statistics, *Sourcebook of Criminal Justice Statistics—1991* (Washington, DC: U.S. Government Printing Office, 1992), p. 266.

27. Hindelang, Hirschi, and Weis (1981).

28. Delbert S. Elliott and Susan S. Ageton, "Reconciling Race and Class Differences in Self-Reported and Official Estimates of Delinquency," *American Sociological Review* (1980) 45:91–110.

29. Elliott and Ageton (1980), p. 107.

30. See definitions in U.S. Federal Bureau of Investigation, Uniform Crime Reports, *Crime in the United States 1994* (Washington, DC: Government Printing Office, 1995), pp. 383–384.

31. Although many states have rewritten their rape statutes to exclude assumptions about the gender of offenders and victims, the UCR still defines rape only in terms of female victims (see U.S. Federal Bureau of Investigation, Uniform Crime Reports, *Crime in the United States 1994* [Washington, DC: Government Printing Office, 1994], p. 383).

32. Thanks to a concerted FBI effort, the percentage of police departments reporting crimes to the UCR also increased substantially in 1960.

33. See, for example, Frederick S. Yang, "Crime: Two Ways of Handling a Hot Campaign Issue," *Campaigns and Elections* (1994) 15:30–32.

34. For completed crimes, victims reported 62.7 percent of rapes, 67.7 percent of robberies (with injuries), and 71.1 percent of assaults (with injuries) to police in 1990 (U.S. Bureau of Justice Statistics, *Sourcebook of Criminal Justice Statistics 1991* [Washington, DC: Government Printing Office, 1992], p. 266).

35. O'Brien (1996).

36. U.S. Bureau of Justice Statistics, *Sourcebook of Criminal Justice Statistics 1991* (Washington, DC: Government Printing Office, 1992), p. 266.

37. Lawrence E. Cohen and Marcus Felson, "Social Change and Crime Rate Trends: A Routine Activity Approach," *American Sociological Review* (1979) 44:588–607.

38. For a discussion of the complex relationship between actual crime rates and public perceptions of crime, see Katherine Beckett, *Making Crime Pay: Law and Order in Contemporary American Politics* (New York: Oxford University Press, 1997).

39. Pearson correlation coefficients for an analysis of annual rates, 1946 to 1995, ranged from a low of .83 (murder and aggravated assault) to a high of .98 (rape and aggravated assault); all were statistically significant. I also estimated correlation coefficients after "detrending" the data—that is, controlling for the fact that all of the crime trends were generally moving upward during much of the postwar period. Correlations after detrending (first difference) were greatly reduced but still statistically significant in all contrasts but two: larceny and rape and larceny and aggravated assault ($p < .07$). Detrended correlations were highest for robbery and burglary (.81), robbery and murder (.81), aggravated assault and murder (.69), and motor vehicle theft and murder (.67). For a description of the logic of detrending in time-series analysis, see David A. Dickey, William R. Bell, and Robert B. Miller, "Unit Roots in Time-Series Models: Tests and Implications," *The American Statistician* (1986) 40:12–26.

40. Ted R. Gurr, "Historical Trends in Violent Crimes: A Critical Review of the Evidence," *Crime and Justice: An Annual Review of Research*, Volume 3 (Chicago: University of Chicago Press, 1981).

41. Douglas Eckberg, "Estimates of Early Twentieth-Century U.S. Homicide Rates: An Econometric Forecasting Approach," *Demography* (1995) 32:1–16.

42. Louise Shelley, *Crime and Modernization: The Impact of Industrialization and Modernization on Crime* (Carbondale: Southern Illinois University Press, 1981), p. 76.

43. Quoted in Kenneth F. Ferraro, *Fear of Crime: Interpreting Victimization Risk* (Albany: State University of New York Press, 1995), p. 118.

44. James Lynch, "Crime in International Perspective," in J. Q. Wilson and J. Petersilia, eds., *Crime* (San Francisco: Institute for Contemporary Studies Press, 1995).

45. For a review, see Gary LaFree, "Comparative Cross-National Studies of Homicide," in M. D. Smith and M. Zahn, eds., *Homicide Studies: A Sourcebook of Social Research* (Thousand Oaks, CA: Sage, 1998).

46. World Health Organization, *World Health Statistics Annual, 1994* (Geneva, Switzerland, 1995).

47. Jan J. M. van Dijk, Pat Mayhew, and Martin Killias, *Experiences of Crime Across the World: Key Findings of the 1989 International Crime Survey*, second edition (Deventer, the Netherlands: Kluwer, 1991). Other international crime surveys are being planned.

48. See also, Franklin E. Zimring and Gordon Hawkins, *Crime Is Not the Problem: Lethal Violence in America* (New York: Oxford University Press, 1997).

49. Michael R. Gottfredson and Travis Hirschi, *A General Theory of Crime* (Stanford: Stanford University Press, 1990), p. 171.

Chapter Three

1. Alexis de Tocqueville, *Democracy in America*, translated by Francis Bowen (New York: Alfred A. Knopf, 1945 [1835]).

2. Michael J. Hindelang, "Variation in Sex-Race-Age Specific Rates of Offending," *American Sociological Review* (1981) 46:461–474, 473.

3. See, for example, Gilbert Geis, "Statistics Concerning Race and Crime," in C. E. Reasons and J. L Kuykendall, eds., *Race, Crime and Justice* (Pacific Palisades, CA: Goodyear, 1972).

4. See, for example, Michael J. Hindelang, "Race and Involvement in Common Law Personal Crimes," *American Sociological Review* (1978) 43:93–109.

5. U.S. Bureau of the Census, *Statistical Abstract of the United States: 1996* (Washington, DC: Government Printing Office, 1996), p. 14.

6. U.S. Bureau of the Census (1996), p. 14.

7. U.S. Bureau of the Census (1996), p. 15.

8. Anthony Harris, "Race, Class and Crime," in J. F. Sheley, ed., *Criminology* (Belmont, CA: Wadsworth, 1991); William J. Chambliss, *Exploring Criminology* (New York: Macmillan, 1988).

9. Wesley G. Skogan, "Reporting Crimes to the Police: The Status of World Research," *Journal of Research in Crime and Delinquency* (1984) 21:113–137.

10. Hindelang (1978); Walter R. Gove, Michael Hughes, and Michael Geerken, "Are Uniform Crime Reports a Valid Indicator of Index Crimes? An Affirmative Answer with Minor Qualifications," *Criminology* (1985) 23:451–501.

11. Hindelang (1981).

12. Delbert Elliott and Susan Ageton, "Reconciling Race and Class Differences in Self-Reported and Official Estimates of Delinquency," *American Sociological Review* (1980) 45:95–110.

13. Donald Black and Albert J. Reiss, Jr., "Police Control of Juveniles," *American Sociological Review* (1970) 35:63–77; Michael Gottfredson and Don Gottfredson, *Decision Making in Criminal Justice* (Cambridge, MA: Ballinger, 1980).

14. Gove et al. (1985), p. 451.

15. The only exception is that the UCR does provide cross-classifications of arrests by gender and age, and race and age.

16. U.S. Federal Bureau of Investigation, National Incident-Based Reporting System, Volume 1, *Data Collection Guidelines* (Washington, DC: Government Printing Office, September 1996).

17. For reviews, see James Q. Wilson and Richard J. Herrnstein, *Crime and Human Nature* (New York: Simon & Schuster, 1985), pp. 104–125; John Braithwaite, *Crime, Shame and Reintegration* (Cambridge, UK: Cambridge University Press, 1989), pp. 44–45; Michael R. Gottfredson and Travis Hirschi, *A General Theory of Crime* (Stanford: Stanford University Press, 1990), pp. 144–149.

18. U.S. Federal Bureau of Investigation, *Uniform Crime Reports 1994* (Washington, DC: Government Printing Office, 1995), p. 234. I exclude gender estimates for rape in this section because the UCR collects rape data only for female victims.

19. Freda Adler, *The Incidence of Female Criminality in the Contemporary World* (New York: New York University Press, 1981).

20. U.S. Bureau of Justice Statistics, *Sourcebook of Criminal Justice Statistics 1995* (Washington, DC: Government Printing Office, 1996), pp. 309–310.

21. Hindelang (1981).

22. Rita J. Simon, *Women and Crime* (Lexington, MA: Lexington Books, 1975); Adler (1981).

23. Freda Adler, *Sisters in Crime: The Rise of the New Female Criminal* (New York: McGraw-Hill, 1975), pp. 13–14.

24. Gottfredson and Hirschi (1990), pp. 144–149.

25. Travis Hirschi and Michael Gottfredson, "Causes of White Collar Crime," *Criminology* (1987) 25:949–974.

26. Gottfredson and Hirschi (1990), p. 145.

27. Darrell Steffensmeier, "National Trends in Female Arrests, 1960–1990: Assessment and Recommendations for Research," *Journal of Quantitative Criminology* (1993) 9:411–441; Susan A. Ageton, "The Dynamics of Female Delinquency, 1976–1980," *Criminology* (1983) 21:555–584.

28. Steffensmeier (1993).

29. U.S. Federal Bureau of Investigation, *Age-Specific Arrest Rates and Race-Specific Arrest Rates for Selected Offenses, 1965–1992* (Washington, DC: Government Printing Office, 1993). These data were only available from 1965 to 1992. I again exclude gender estimates for rape because the UCR collects rape data only for female victims.

30. Steffensmeier (1993), p. 428.

31. See also A. Browne, "Violence Against Women," *Journal of the American Medical Association* (1992) 267:3184–3195.

32. For reviews, see Gottfredson and Hirschi (1990); Wilson and Herrnstein (1985).

33. D. Riley and M. Shaw, *Parental Supervision and Juvenile Delinquency*, Home Office Research Study No. 83 (London: HMSO, 1985).

34. U.S. Federal Bureau of Investigation, Uniform Crime Reports, *Crime in the United States 1994* (Washington, DC: Government Printing Office, 1995), p. 233.

35. Travis Hirschi and Michael Gottfredson, "Age and the Explanation of Crime," *American Journal of Sociology* (1983) 89:552–584.

36. "Now for the Bad News: A Teenage Time Bomb," *Time* (1996) January 15: 52–53.

37. See Theodore Ferdinand, "Demographic Shifts and Criminality," *British Journal of Criminology* (1970) 10:169–175, for the low estimate; see Larry E. Cohen and Kenneth C. Land, "Age Structure and Crime: Symmetry Versus Asymmetry and the Projection of Crime Rates through 1990," *American Sociological Review* (1987) 52:170–183, for the high estimate.

38. Thomas B. Marvell and Carlisle E. Moody, Jr., "Age Structure and Crime Rates: The Conflicting Evidence," *Journal of Quantitative Criminology* (1991) 7:237–273.

39. There is substantial variation among researchers in the precise operational definition of young people, with some studies including only juveniles and others

including young adults as old as forty-three. The age range I use here is one of the most common. See Marvell and Moody (1991).

40. U.S. Bureau of Justice Statistics, *Sourcebook of Criminal Justice Statistics 1995* (Washington, DC: Government Printing Office, 1996), p. 237.

41. U.S. Census Bureau, *Population Projections* (Washington, DC: Government Printing Office, 1996), Table G.

42. U.S. Federal Bureau of Investigation (1993).

43. These comparisons are based on multiplying the African American percentage of total annual arrests for homicide by the total homicides committed in the United States and estimating a rate per 100,000.

44. The political scientist Ted Gurr argues that most of the surge of violent crime in the United States in the 1960s was due to sharply rising African American crime rates. See "Historical Trends in Violent Crimes: A Critical Review of the Evidence," in *Crime and Justice: An Annual Review of Research,* Volume 3 (Chicago: University of Chicago Press, 1981), p. 295. Also see, Andrew Hacker, *Two Nations: Black and White, Separate, Hostile and Unequal* (New York: Scribner, 1991).

45. The U.S. estimates are based on multiplying the percentage of total murder arrests for whites in 1991 (44.3 percent) by total murders committed (24,700) and calculating a rate per 100,000 white U.S. residents. Murder data for Finland and Italy are from the World Health Organization.

46. These estimates are based on multiplying the percentage of white arrests for robbery in 1991 (38.1 percent) by total robberies for the United States (687,730) and calculating a rate per 100,000 white residents. Rates for France, Spain, and Canada are from the International Police Organization, International Crime Statistics (St. Cloud, France: Interpol, 1993).

47. I review many of these problems in "Race and Crime Trends in the United States, 1946–1990," in D. F. Hawkins, ed., *Ethnicity, Race and Crime: Perspectives Across Time and Places* (Albany: State University of New York Press, 1995).

48. K. Peak and J. Spencer, "Crime in Indian Country: Another 'Trail of Tears,'" *Journal of Criminal Justice* (1987) 15:485–494; Marjorie Zatz, Carol Chiago Lujan, and Zoann Snyder-Joy, "American Indians and Criminal Justice: Some Conceptual and Methodological Considerations," in M. J. Lynch and E. B. Patterson, eds., *Race and Criminal Justice* (New York: Harrow & Heston, 1991).

49. Rates are somewhat higher if jurisdictions that reported less than complete data are included.

50. To allow comparisons, I calculated race-specific UCR arrest rates as $R = [a/(up)] \times 100,000$, where R is the rate, a is the number of UCR arrests for whites or African Americans, u is the population of reporting UCR jurisdictions, and p is the proportion of the total U.S. resident population by race from the 1990 census.

51. The single exception to these general patterns is for Native American (30.2) and white (32.7) robbery rates.

52. For example, Robert O'Brien, *Crime and Victimization* (Beverly Hills, CA: Sage, 1985); Albert D. Biderman and James Lynch, *Understanding Crime Incidence Statistics* (New York: Springer-Verlag, 1991).

53. Gove et al. (1985); Joel Devine, Joseph Sheley, and Dwayne Smith, "Macroeconomic and Social-Control Policy Influences in Crime Rates," *American Sociological Review* (1988) 53:407–421.

54. Pearson correlations between annual African American and white crime rates, 1946 to 1995, ranged from a high of .99 (larceny) to a low of .56 (rape). All seven correlations were highly significant $(p < .01)$. I also estimated correlations after detrending the data; detrending is a process designed to control for the fact that arrests for all seven of these crimes, for both African Americans and whites, generally moved upward during much of the postwar period. Correlations for the detrended rates (first difference) ranged from a high of .66 (burglary) to a low of .40 (robbery). Again, all seven contrasts were highly significant $(p < .01)$. For an explanation of detrending, see David A. Dickey, William A. Bell, and Robert B. Miller, "Unit Roots in Time-Series Models: Tests and Implications," *The American Statistician* (1986) 40:12–26.

55. I calculated these ratios by simply dividing total African American arrest rates per 100,000 citizens covered by the UCR by total white arrest rates for the same coverage.

Chapter Four

1. Moynihan is quoted in an article that appeared in Mickey Kaus, "The Work Ethic State," *The New Republic* (1986) July 7:22–33, 23; Daniel Patrick Moynihan, *Family and Nation: The Godkin Lectures* (San Diego: Harcourt Brace Jovanovich, 1986).

2. Cesare Lombroso, *The Criminal Man* (L'uomo Delinquente), first edition (Milan, Italy: Hoepli, 1876).

3. Individual pathology perspectives have a long history in criminology and important studies number in the hundreds. Useful reviews include James Q. Wilson and Richard J. Herrnstein, *Crime and Human Nature* (New York: Simon & Schuster, 1985); Hans J. Eysenck and Gisli H. Gudjonsson, *The Causes and Cures of Criminality* (New York: Plenum, 1989); Patricia Brennan, Sarnoff Mednick, and Jan Volavka, "Biomedical Factors in Crime," in J. Q. Wilson and J. Petersilia, eds., *Crime* (San Francisco: Institute for Contemporary Studies Press, 1995).

4. Lawrence Taylor, *Born to Crime: The Genetic Causes of Criminal Behavior* (Westport, CT: Greenwood Press, 1984).

5. P. A. Jacobs, M. Brunton, M. M. Melville, R. P. Brittain, and W. F. McClemont, "Aggressive Behaviour, Mental Sub-Normality, and the XYY Male," *Nature* (1965) 208:1351–1352; Wilson and Herrnstein (1985), pp. 100–102.

6. Paul Frederic Brain, "Hormonal Aspects of Aggression and Violence," in A. Reiss, K. Miczek, and J. Roth, eds., *Biobehavioral Influences*, Volume 2 of *Understanding and Preventing Violence* (Washington, DC: National Academy Press, 1994), p. 228.

7. Klaus A. Miczek, Allan F. Mirsky, Gregory Carey, Joseph DeBold, and Adrian Raine, "An Overview of Biological Influences on Violent Behavior," in A. J. Reiss, K. A. Miczek, and J. A. Roth, eds., *Biobehavioral Influences*, Volume 2 of *Understanding and Preventing Violence* (Washington, DC: National Academy Press, 1994).

8. Martin Daly and Margo Wilson, "Evolutionary Social Psychology and Family Homicide," *Science* (1988) 242:519–524; Margo Wilson, "Marital Conflict and Homicide in Evolutionary Perspective," in R. W. Bell and N. J. Bell, eds., *Sociobiology and the Social Sciences* (Lubbock: Texas Tech University Press, 1989).

9. Alan Booth and D. Dwayne Osgood, "The Influence of Testosterone on Deviance in Adulthood: Assessing and Explaining the Relationship," *Criminology* (1993) 31:93–117.

10. Booth and Osgood (1993).

11. Martin Daly and Margo Wilson, *Homicide* (Hawthorne, NY: Aldine de Gruyter, 1988).

12. Quoted in Robert Wright, "The Biology of Violence," *The New Yorker* (1995) March 13:68–77, 72; see also, Wilson (1989).

13. Gary S. Becker, "Crime and Punishment: An Economic Approach," *Journal of Political Economy* (1968) 76:169–217; Peter Schmidt and Ann D. Witte, *An Economic Analysis of Crime and Justice* (New York: Academic Press, 1984).

14. For reviews, see Jack P. Gibbs, *Crime, Punishment and Deterrence* (New York: Elsevier, 1975); A. Blumstein, J. Cohen, and D. Nagel, eds., *Deterrence and Incapacitation: Estimating the Effects of Criminal Sanctions on Crime Rates* (Washington, DC: National Academy of Sciences, 1978).

15. Philip J. Cook, "Punishment and Crime: A Critique of Current Findings Concerning the Preventive Effect of Criminal Sanctions," *Law and Contemporary Problems* (1977) 41:164–204; Blumstein et al. (1978).

16. For example, David I. Cantor and Kenneth C. Land, "Unemployment and Crime Rates in the Post–World War II United States: A Theoretical and Empirical Analysis," *American Sociological Review* (1985) 50:317–332; Joel A. Devine, Joseph F. Sheley, and M. Dwayne Smith, "Macroeconomic and Social-Control Policy Influences on Crime Rates, 1948–1985," *American Sociological Review* (1988) 53:407–421.

17. Frances Fox Piven and Richard A. Cloward, *Regulating the Poor: The Functions of Public Welfare* (New York: Vintage, 1971).

18. James DeFronzo, "Economic Assistance to Impoverished Americans: Relationship to Incidence of Crime," *Criminology* (1983) 21:119–136.

19. Robert Fiala and Gary LaFree, "Cross-National Determinants of Child Homicide," *American Sociological Review* (1988) 53:432–445.

20. Charles R. Tittle, *Control Balance: Toward a General Theory of Deviance* (Boulder: Westview, 1995).

21. Amitai Etzioni, *The Moral Dimension: Toward a New Economics* (New York: Free Press, 1988), p. xi.

22. Michael R. Gottfredson and Travis Hirschi, *A General Theory of Crime* (Stanford: Stanford University Press, 1990), ch. 2.

23. William J. Chambliss, "Types of Deviance and the Effectiveness of Legal Sanctions," *Wisconsin Law Review* (1967) Summer:703–719; Tittle (1995), p. 41.

24. Etzioni (1988), p. xi.

25. Harold G. Grasmick and Donald E. Green, "Deterrence and the Morally Committed," *Sociological Quarterly* (1981) 22:1–14.

26. Etzioni (1988), p. xi.

27. Howard Becker, *The Outsiders: Studies in the Sociology of Deviance* (New York: Free Press, 1963), p. 9.

28. Becker (1963), p. 17.

29. Matthew T. Zingraff and Randall J. Thomson, "Differing Sentencing of Women and Men in the U.S.A.," *International Journal of the Sociology of Law* (1984)

12:401–413; W. G. Staples, "Toward a Structural Perspective on Gender Bias in the Juvenile Court," *Sociological Perspectives* (1984) 27:439–467.

30. Michael Rutter and Henri Giller, *Juvenile Delinquency: Trends and Perspectives* (New York: Guilford, 1984).

31. Emile Durkheim, *The Division of Labor in Society*, translated by George Simpson (New York: Free Press, 1947 [1893]).

32. Emile Durkheim, *Suicide*, translated by John A. Spaulding and George Simpson (New York: Free Press, 1951).

33. Robert K. Merton, "Social Structure and Anomie," *American Sociological Review* (1938) 3:672–682.

34. Merton (1938).

35. Robert K. Merton, *Social Theory and Social Structure*, second edition (New York: Free Press, 1957), p. 146.

36. Richard A. Cloward and Lloyd E. Ohlin, *Delinquency and Opportunity: A Theory of Delinquent Gangs* (New York: Free Press, 1960), p. 98.

37. Merton (1938).

38. See, for example, James Q. Wilson, *Thinking About Crime* (New York: Vintage Books, 1975).

39. Merton (1938), footnote 17.

40. Cloward and Ohlin (1960), p. 86.

41. In Albert K. Cohen, Alfred Ray Lindesmith, and Karl F. Schuessler, eds., *The Sutherland Papers* (Bloomington: Indiana University Press, 1956), p. 9.

42. William Julius Wilson, *The Truly Disadvantaged: The Inner City, the Underclass and Public Policy* (Chicago: University of Chicago Press, 1987); Christopher Jencks, *Rethinking Social Policy: Race, Poverty and the Underclass* (Cambridge, MA: Harvard University Press, 1992).

43. See, for example, Walter B. Miller, "Lower-Class Culture as a Generating Milieu of Gang Delinquency," *Journal of Social Issues* (1958) 14:5–19.

44. Travis Hirschi, *Causes of Delinquency* (Berkeley: University of California Press, 1969), p. 3.

45. Emile Durkheim (1951), p. 209.

46. Hirschi (1969).

47. See, for example, D. S. Elliott, B. A. Knowles, and R. J. Carter, *The Epidemiology of Delinquent Behavior and Drug Use* (Beverly Hills, CA: Sage, 1981); Allen E. Liska and Mark D. Reed, "Ties to Conventional Institutions and Delinquency: Estimating Reciprocal Effects," *American Sociological Review* (1985) 50:547–560.

48. For example, Robert Agnew, "A Revised Strain Theory of Delinquency," *Social Forces* (1985) 64:151–167; H. B. Kaplan and C. Robbins, "Testing a General Theory of Deviant Behavior in Longitudinal Perspective," in K. T. Van Dusen and S. A. Mednick, eds., *Prospective Studies of Crime and Delinquency* (Boston: Kluwer-Nijhoff, 1983).

49. For example, George Masnick and Mary Jo Bane, *The Nation's Families: 1960–1990* (Cambridge, MA: Joint Center for Urban Studies, 1980).

50. *The Negro Family: The Case for National Action*, Office of Planning and Research (Washington, DC: Government Printing Office, 1965), p. 4.

51. Much of the current debate about the urban underclass examines these issues. See, e.g., Wilson (1987); Jencks (1992).

52. For a review of this literature, see Christopher Birkbeck and Gary LaFree, "The Situational Analysis of Crime and Deviance," *Annual Review of Sociology* (1993) 19:113–137.

53. Lawrence Cohen and Marcus Felson, "Social Change and Crime Rate Trends: A Routine Activity Approach," *American Sociological Review* (1979) 44:588–608.

Chapter Five

1. Emile Durkheim, *Moral Education*, translated by Everett K. Wilson and Herman Schnurer (New York: Free Press, 1903), p. 61.

2. Mary Douglas, *How Institutions Think* (Syracuse, NY: Syracuse University Press, 1986), p. 124.

3. Peter L. Berger and Thomas Luckmann, *The Social Construction of Reality: A Treatise in the Sociology of Knowledge* (Garden City, NY: Anchor Books, 1967), p. 54.

4. Berger and Luckmann (1967), p. 54.

5. Berger and Luckmann (1967), p. 60.

6. Robert Bellah, Richard Madsen, William Sullivan, Ann Swindler, and Steven Tipton, *The Good Society* (New York: Alfred A. Knopf, 1991), p. 4.

7. Talcott Parsons, "The Motivation of Economic Activities," *Canadian Journal of Economics and Political Science* (1940) 6:187–203, 190.

8. Bellah et al. (1991), p. 12.

9. Francis Fukuyama, *Trust: The Social Virtues and the Creation of Prosperity* (New York: Free Press, 1995), p. 26; Diego Gambetta, "Can We Trust Trust?" in D. Gambetta, ed., *Trust: Making and Breaking Cooperative Relations* (Oxford, UK: Blackwell, 1988), p. 217.

10. David H. Bayley, *Forces of Order: Police Behavior in Japan and the United States* (Berkeley: University of California Press, 1975); Setsuo Miyazawa, *Policing in Japan: A Study on Making Crime*, translated by Frank Bennett, Jr., with John Haley (Albany: State University of New York Press, 1992); Fukuyama (1995), ch. 15.

11. See Pierre Bourdieu, "The Forms of Capital," in J. G. Richardson, ed., *Handbook of Theory and Research for the Sociology of Education* (New York: Greenwood Press, 1985). For a thoughtful review of current applications of the social capital concept in sociology, see Alejandro Portes, "Social Capital: Its Origins and Applications in Modern Society," *Annual Review of Sociology* (forthcoming).

12. James S. Coleman, *Foundations of Social Theory* (Cambridge, MA: Harvard, 1990), p. 305.

13. James S. Coleman, "Social Capital in the Creation of Human Capital," *American Journal of Sociology* (1988) S95–S120, S100.

14. Fukuyama (1995), p. 26; Portes (forthcoming), p. 11.

15. Peter L. Berger, *Invitation to Sociology: A Humanistic Perspective* (Garden City, NY: Anchor Books, 1963), pp. 87–91.

16. Peter Blau, *Exchange and Power in Social Life* (New York: John Wiley, 1964), p. 277.

17. Talcott Parsons, *Essays in Sociological Theory Pure and Applied* (Glencoe, IL: Free Press, 1949), p. 35. The emphasis on institutional stability in Parson's work may be overdrawn by his critics. In the same work (p. 311), Parsons notes, "Insti-

tutional patterns are the 'backbone' of the system. But they are by no means rigid entities and certainly have no mysteriously 'substantial' nature. They are only relatively stable resultants of the process of behavior. "

18. See John W. Meyer, John Boli, and George M. Thomas, "Ontology and Rationalization in the Western Cultural Account," in G. M. Thomas, J. W. Meyer, F. O. Ramirez, and J. Boli, eds., *Institutional Structure: Constituting State, Society, and the Individual* (Newbury Park, CA: Sage, 1987).

19. Dennis Wrong, "The Oversocialized Conception of Man in Modern Sociology," *American Sociological Review* (1961) 26:183–193.

20. Interestingly, the view of Americans as "oversocialized" was probably far more defensible prior to the decade in which Wrong published this article than it was in the years immediately afterward.

21. Berger and Luckmann (1967), p. 52.

22. Mark Granovetter, "Economic Action and Social Structure: The Problem of Embeddedness," *American Journal of Sociology* (1985) 91:481–510, 487.

23. John Hagan, *Structural Criminology* (New Brunswick, NJ: Rutgers University Press, 1989), ch. 6.

24. Hagan (1989), p. 153.

25. Hagan (1989), p. 154.

26. The cat and mouse example is borrowed from Berger (1963), p. 88.

27. Max Weber, *The Theory of Social and Economic Organizations* (New York: Oxford University Press, 1947), p. 324.

28. Weber (1947), pp. 329–363.

29. Berger and Luckmann (1967), p. 93.

30. See, for example, Talcott Parsons, *The Structure of Social Action* (Glencoe, IL: Free Press, 1949), p. 669; Seymour Martin Lipset, "Political Sociology," in R. K. Merton, L. Broom, and L. S. Cottrell, Jr., eds., *Sociology Today: Problems and Prospects* (New York: Basic Books, 1959), pp. 108–110.

31. Weber (1947), pp. 126–127.

32. Berger (1963), p. 89.

33. The fact that these crimes are universally outlawed, however, does not mean that there is no disagreement about how they are defined and what types of specific behavior should be included; nor does it deny the existence of "moral entrepreneurs" who campaign for changes in criminal definitions. For example, some members of society consider the abortion of a fetus to be murder, whereas others do not; some consider the legal execution of an offender to be murder, whereas others do not. Similarly, some argue that a husband can be guilty of rape, whereas others disagree. Nevertheless, the amount of social agreement over instances of these crimes is likely to be much higher than we would find for crimes such as drug use, gambling, or prostitution.

34. Jonathan H. Turner, *The Structure of Sociological Theory* (Homewood, IL: Dorsey, 1974), p. 282.

35. Robert J. Sampson, Stephen W. Raudenbush, and Felton Earls, "Neighborhoods and Violent Crime: A Multilevel Study of Collective Efficacy," *Science* (1997) 277:918–924, 918.

36. Donald Black, *The Behavior of Law* (New York: Academic Press, 1976), p. 105.

37. Locations, types, and forms of social control have themselves generated a complex research literature. For a discussion of some of these complexities, see David H. Bayley, *Social Control and Political Change* (Princeton: Center for International Studies, 1985), ch. 2.

38. Jeremy Bentham, *An Introduction to the Principles of Morals and Legislation* (London, UK: The Athlone Press, 1970 [1789]), pp. 134–136.

39. We should keep in mind, however, that police states with extraordinarily rigid formal social control may also be able to produce relatively low crime rates. But even here, legitimacy is critical. Consider, for example, modern prisons, which typically are highly regulated but nevertheless generally have high crime rates; see U.S. Bureau of Justice Statistics, *Sourcebook of Criminal Justice Statistics 1995* (Washington, DC: U.S. Department of Justice, 1996), p. 603.

40. John Braithwaite, *Crime, Shame and Reintegration* (Cambridge, UK: Cambridge University Press, 1989), p. 8; Charles Tittle, *Sanctions and Social Deviance* (New York: Praeger, 1980).

41. Robert Putnam, *Making Democracy Work: Civic Traditions in Modern Italy* (Princeton: Princeton University Press, 1993), p. 112.

42. Putnam (1993), p. 113.

43. Putnam (1993), p. 165.

44. Fukuyama (1995), p. 27.

45. Granovetter (1985).

46. Weber (1947), p. 327.

47. See Talcott Parsons, *The Social System* (Glencoe, IL: Free Press, 1951); Leon H. Mayhew, ed., *Talcott Parsons: On Institutions and Social Evolution* (Chicago: University of Chicago Press, 1982), pp. 23–30; Blau (1964), pp. 273–282; Steven F. Messner and Richard Rosenfeld, *Crime and the American Dream* (Belmont, CA: Wadsworth, 1994), pp. 72–75.

48. See generally, Parsons (1951).

49. Blau (1964), p. 278; Messner and Rosenfeld (1994), p. 73.

50. Parsons (1951).

51. James S. Coleman, "The Rational Reconstruction of Society," *American Sociological Review* (1993) 58:1–15, 2.

52. Blau (1964), p. 278.

53. I use trust here in the usual sense of level of reliance on the equity, justice, or evenhandedness of others. See Diego Gambetta, ed., *Trust: Making and Breaking Cooperative Relations* (New York: Basil Blackwell, 1988).

54. Although I concentrate here on street crimes, there is some evidence that trust in political institutions may have a different effect on white-collar offenses. David Nelken ("Who Can You Trust? The Future of Comparative Criminology," in D. Nelken, ed., *The Futures of Criminology* [London: Sage, 1994], p. 237) points out that if trust in a society's political institutions is so great that social control mechanisms are ineffective or totally absent, white-collar offenders may actually find it easier to operate undetected. For a discussion of differences in how trust affects street and white-collar crime, see Susan P. Shapiro, "Collaring the Crime, Not the Criminal: Reconsidering the Concept of White-Collar Crime," *American Sociological Review* (1990) 55:346–365.

55. See James F. Short, Jr., and Fred. L. Strodtbeck, *Group Process and Gang Delinquency* (Chicago: University of Chicago Press, 1965); Travis Hirschi, *Causes of Delinquency* (Berkeley: University of California Press, 1969); Braithwaite (1989).

56. John D. McCarthy and Mayer N. Zald, "Resource Mobilization and Social Movements," *American Journal of Sociology* (1977) 82:1212–1241; David R. Snyder and Charles Tilly, "Hardship and Collective Violence in France, 1830–1960," *American Sociological Review* (1972) 37:520–532.

57. Most commonly, resource mobilization theorists simply consider crime along with other indicators of "personal pathology" such as suicide, alcoholism, and drug use. See Charles Tilly, Louise Tilly, and Richard Tilly, *The Rebellious Century, 1830–1930* (Cambridge, MA: Harvard University Press, 1975).

58. See Michael R. Gottfredson and Travis Hirschi, *A General Theory of Crime* (Stanford: Stanford University Press, 1990), p. 256.

59. Harold G. Grasmick and Donald E. Green, "Deterrence and the Morally Committed," *The Sociological Quarterly* (1981) 22:1–14.

60. Elijah Anderson, *A Place on the Corner* (Chicago: University of Chicago Press, 1978); Jack Katz, *Seductions of Crime* (New York: Basic Books, 1988).

61. John P. Hewitt, *Social Stratification and Deviant Behavior* (New York: Random House, 1970); Roger Hood and Richard Sparks, *Key Issues in Criminology* (New York: McGraw-Hill, 1970); John Braithwaite, *Inequality, Crime and Public Policy* (London: Routledge & Kegan Paul, 1979); but see also, Charles R. Tittle, Wayne J. Villemez, and Douglas A. Smith, "The Myth of Social Class and Criminality: An Empirical Assessment of the Empirical Evidence," *American Sociological Review* (1978) 43:643–656.

62. Robert K. Merton, *Social Theory and Social Structure* (Glencoe, IL: Free Press, 1957).

63. Albert Cohen, *Delinquent Boys: The Culture of the Gang* (New York: Free Press, 1955).

64. Richard Cloward and Lloyd Ohlin, *Delinquency and Opportunity: A Theory of Delinquent Gangs* (New York: Free Press, 1961).

65. Delbert Elliott, "Delinquency and Perceived Opportunity," *Sociological Inquiry* (1962) 32:216–222; James F. Short, Jr., "Gang Delinquency and Anomie," in M. B. Clinard, ed., *Anomie and Deviant Behavior* (New York: Free Press, 1964); J. O. Segrave and D. N. Hastad, "Evaluating Three Models of Delinquency Causation for Males and Females: Strain Theory, Subculture Theory and Control Theory," *Sociological Focus* (1985) 18:1–17.

66. Frank Levy, *Dollars and Dreams* (New York: Russell Sage, 1987), p. 197.

67. Levy (1987), p. 199.

68. William Julius Wilson, *The Truly Disadvantaged: The Inner City, the Underclass and Public Policy* (Chicago: University of Chicago Press, 1987); Levy (1987).

69. Gerald F. Seib and Joe Davidson, "Shades of Gray: Whites, Blacks Agree on Problems; the Issue Is How to Solve Them," *Wall Street Journal* (1995) November 3:1.

70. Kingsley Davis, *Human Society* (New York: Macmillan, 1948), p. 395.

71. V. Zelizer, *Pricing the Priceless Child* (New York: Basic Books, 1985); Christopher Lasch, *Haven in a Heartless World* (New York: Basic Books, 1977).

72. Travis Hirschi, "The Family," in J. Q. Wilson and J. Petersilia, eds., *Crime* (San Francisco: Institute for Contemporary Studies Press, 1995), p. 128.

73. Hirschi (1995), p. 128; Braithwaite (1989), p. 48.

74. Hirschi (1995), p. 18.

75. Frank F. Furstenberg, Jr., "How Families Manage Risk and Opportunity in Dangerous Neighborhoods," in W. J. Wilson, ed., *Sociology and the Public Agenda* (Newbury Park, CA: Sage, 1993), p. 233.

76. See, for example, David Popenoe, *Disturbing the Nest: Family Change and Decline in Modern Society* (New York: Aldine de Gruyter, 1988), p. 51.

77. Betty Friedan provides the classic statement of this view in *The Feminine Mystique* (New York: Dell, 1963); see also, Kate Millet, *Sexual Politics* (Garden City, NY: Doubleday, 1970).

78. For a discussion of stereotypical thinking about the past forms of families, see Stephanie Coontz, *The Way We Never Were: American Families and the Nostalgia Trap* (New York: Basic Books, 1992).

79. Shirley P. Burggraf, *The Feminine Economy and Economic Man: Reviving the Role of Family in the Post-Industrial Age* (Reading, MA: Addison-Wesley, 1997), p. 18.

80. Levy (1987), p. 198.

81. The suggestion that existing institutions by definition offer the most "functional" responses to particular problems, associated especially with the work of Talcott Parsons, has been strongly criticized (for a summary, see David Downes and Paul Rock, *Understanding Deviance: A Guide to the Sociology of Crime and Rule Breaking* [Oxford, UK: Clarendon Press, 1982]). I argue here only that the United States witnessed a tremendous growth in the size and scope of criminal justice, education, and welfare-related institutions during the postwar period and that this growth was justified at least in part on the grounds that it would reduce crime.

82. U.S. Bureau of the Census, *Historical Statistics on Governmental Finance and Employment* (Washington, DC: Government Printing Office, 1985), pp. 26–28; U.S. Bureau of the Census, *Government Finances: 1984–1992*, Series GF/92-5 (Washington, DC: Government Printing Office, 1996), p. 1.

83. See, for example, Frances Fox Piven and Richard A. Cloward, *Regulating the Poor: The Functions of Public Welfare* (New York: Vintage, 1971).

84. Allen E. Liska and Paul E. Bellair review some of these effects in "Violent-Crime Rates and Racial Composition: Convergence over Time," *American Journal of Sociology* (1995) 101:578–610, see especially, pp. 579–582.

85. Robert J. Sampson, "Urban Black Violence: The Effect of Male Joblessness and Family Disruption," *American Journal of Sociology* (1987) 93:348–382.

86. See, for example, Rosemary Gartner, "The Victims of Homicide: A Temporal and Cross-National Comparison," *American Sociological Review* (1990) 55:92–106; Robert Fiala and Gary LaFree, "Cross-National Determinants of Child Homicide," *American Sociological Review* (1988) 53:432–445.

87. See, for example, Rodney Stark, Lou Kent, and Daniel P. Doyle, "Religion and Delinquency: The Ecology of a 'Lost' Relationship," *Journal of Research on Crime and Delinquency* (1982) 19:4–24; Robert J. Sampson, "The Community," in J. Q. Wilson and J. Petersilia, eds., *Crime* (San Francisco: Institute for Contemporary

Studies Press, 1995); Ray Surette, *Media, Crime and Criminal Justice: Images and Realities* (Pacific Grove, CA: Brooks/Cole, 1992).

Chapter Six

1. Jerome Skolnick, *The Politics of Protest* (New York: Simon & Schuster, 1969), p. xxvii.

2. Charles Handy, *The Age of Paradox* (Boston: Harvard Business School Press, 1994), p. 40.

3. Elvin H. Powell, "Crime as a Function of Anomie," *Journal of Criminal Law, Criminology and Police Science* (1966) 57:161–171.

4. Stephen E. Ambrose, *D-Day June 6, 1944: The Climactic Battle of World War II* (New York: Simon & Schuster, 1994), pp. 187–188.

5. Ambrose (1994), pp. 24–25.

6. Ambrose (1994), pp. 24–25, 170.

7. Ambrose (1994), p. 576.

8. Studs Terkel, *The Good War* (New York: Pantheon, 1984).

9. Ambrose (1994), p. 25.

10. James C. Davies, "Toward a Theory of Revolution," *American Sociological Review* (1962) 27:5–19; Neil Smelser, *Theory of Collective Behavior* (New York: Free Press, 1962).

11. Emile Durkheim, *The Division of Labor in Society*, translated by George Simpson (Glencoe, IL: Free Press, 1947 [1893]).

12. Robert K. Merton, "Anomie, Anomia, and Social Interaction," in M. B. Clinard, ed., *Anomie and Deviant Behavior: A Discussion and Critique* (New York: Free Press, 1964), p. 226.

13. Emile Durkheim, *Suicide*, translated by John A. Spaulding and George Simpson (New York: Free Press, 1951).

14. John D. McCarthy and Mayer N. Zald, "Resource Mobilization and Social Movements," *American Journal of Sociology* (1977) 82:1212–1241; David R. Snyder and Charles Tilly, "Hardship and Collective Violence in France, 1830–1960," *American Sociological Review* (1972) 37:520–532.

15. Most commonly, resource mobilization theorists simply consider crime along with other indicators of "personal pathology" such as suicide, alcoholism, and drug use. See Charles Tilly, Louise Tilly, and Richard Tilly, *The Rebellious Century, 1830–1930* (Cambridge, MA: Harvard University Press, 1975).

16. Anthony Oberschall, "Theories of Social Conflict," in R. Turner, J. Coleman, and R. C. Fox, eds., *Annual Review of Sociology* (Palo Alto, CA: Annual Review Press, 1978), p. 302.

17. Frederic Solomon, Walter Walker, and Jacob R. Fishman, "Civil Rights Activity and Reduction in Crime Among Negroes," *Archives of General Psychiatry* (1965) 12:227–236.

18. George Rude, *The Face of the Crowd*, edited by Harvey Kaye (New York: Harvester, 1988 [1914]).

19. Donald Black, *Toward a General Theory of Social Control*, Volumes 1 and 2 (New York: Academic Press, 1984); see also, Martin Kilson, "Politics of Race and

Urban Crisis: The American Case," in J. Benyon and J. Solomos, eds., *The Roots of Urban Unrest* (Elmsford, NY: Pergamon, 1987).

20. See Joe Feagin and Harlan Hahn, *Ghetto Revolts* (New York: Macmillan, 1973); Tilly et al. (1975).

21. Karl Marx, "The Communist Manifesto," in F. L. Bender, ed., *Karl Marx: The Essential Writings* (Boulder: Westview, 1986), p. 251.

22. Michael R. Gottfredson and Travis Hirschi, *A General Theory of Crime* (Stanford: Stanford University Press, 1990), p. 256.

23. Gottfredson and Hirschi (1990), pp. 28–31.

24. Gottfredson and Hirschi (1990), p. 89.

25. Harold G. Grasmick and Donald E. Green, "Deterrence and the Morally Committed," *Sociological Quarterly* (1981) 22:1–14.

26. Black (1984), p. 1.

27. Black (1984), p. 13.

28. Black (1984), p. 11.

29. See Elijah Anderson, *A Place on the Corner* (Chicago: University of Chicago Press, 1978); John Allen, *Assault with a Deadly Weapon: The Autobiography of a Street Criminal*, edited by D. H. Kelly and P. Hegmann (New York: McGraw-Hill, 1977); Jack Katz, *Seductions of Crime* (New York: Basic Books, 1988).

30. Anderson (1978), p. 130.

31. Katz (1988).

32. See Feagin and Hahn (1973), p. 53; Anthony Oberschall, *Social Conflict and Social Movements* (Englewood Cliffs, NJ: Prentice-Hall, 1973), p. 329.

33. Margaret Abudu, Walter J. Raine, Stephen L. Burbeck, and Keith C. Davidson, "Black Ghetto Violence: A Case Study Inquiry into the Spatial Pattern of Four Los Angeles Riot Event-Types," *Social Problems* (1972) Winter:408–427, 408.

34. Abudu et al. (1972), p. 409.

35. H. L. Nieburg, *Political Violence: The Behavioral Process* (New York: St. Martin's Press, 1969), p. 137.

36. Mark Colvin, "The New Mexico Prison Riot," *Social Problems* (1982) 29:449–463; Bert Useem and Peter Kimball, *States of Siege: U.S. Prison Riots, 1971–1986* (Oxford, UK: Oxford University Press, 1989).

37. Tilly et al. (1975).

38. Abdul Qaiyum Lodhi and Charles Tilly, "Urbanization, Crime and Collective Violence in Nineteenth Century France," *American Journal of Sociology* (1973) 79:296–318.

39. Ted Robert Gurr, *Rogues, Rebels and Reformers: A Political History of Urban Crime and Conflict* (Beverly Hills, CA: Sage, 1976).

40. Joel A. Lieske, "The Conditions of Racial Violence in American Cities: A Developmental Synthesis," *American Political Science Review* (1978) 72:1324–1340.

41. For example, Robert N. Bellah, Richard Madsen, William M. Sullivan, Ann Swidler, and Steven M. Tipton make this argument in *The Good Society* (New York: Alfred A. Knopf, 1991).

42. Terkel (1984).

43. Eric Goldman, *The Crucial Decade and After: America, 1945–1960* (New York: Random House, 1960), pp. 82–83, 234–236.

44. The term "The American Century" was coined by Henry Luce in an editorial in *Life* magazine (1941) February 11:61–65.

45. Goldman (1960), p. 190.

46. J. Craig Jenkins and Craig M. Eckert, "Channelling Black Insurgency: White Patronage and Professional Social Movement Organizations in the Development of the Black Movement," *American Sociological Review* (1986) 51:812–829, 815.

47. Francis Fukuyama, *Trust: The Social Virtues and the Creation of Prosperity* (New York: Free Press, 1995), pp. 314–315.

48. Fukuyama (1995), p. 314.

49. John Morton Blum, *Years of Discord: American Politics and Society, 1961–1974* (New York: W. W. Norton, 1991), pp. 252–253.

50. Blum (1991), p. 51.

51. Blum (1991), p. 241.

52. Blum (1991), p. 241.

53. Mary C. Brennan, *Turning Right in the Sixties: The Conservative Capture of the GOP* (Chapel Hill: University of North Carolina Press, 1995), p. 128.

54. Walter Russell Mead, *Mortal Splendor: The American Empire in Transition* (Boston: Houghton Mifflin, 1987), p. 49.

55. Blum (1991), p. 278.

56. Blum (1991), pp. 256–257.

57. Blum (1991), p. 266.

58. Blum (1991), p. 449–450.

59. "Watergate Scandal Casts Long Shadow," *Albuquerque Journal* (1997) Sunday, June 15:A1, A10.

60. Blum (1991), p. 473.

61. *American National Election Studies Cumulative Data File, 1952–1996* (Ann Arbor, MI: Center for Political Studies, 1996).

62. Sample sizes for the forty years spanned by the data range from a low of 1,039 (in 1986) to a high of 2,232 (in 1972). Samples for African Americans are much smaller, averaging about 10 percent of the total sample for each year.

63. M. D. Blumenthal, R. Kahn, F. Andrews, and R. Head, *Justifying Violence: Attitudes of American Men* (Ann Arbor, MI: Institute for Social Research, 1972), pp. 36–44.

64. Robert L. Kahn, "The Justification of Violence: Social Problems and Social Solutions," *Journal of Social Issues* (1972) 28:155–175, 174.

65. John Hagan and Celesta Albonetti, "Race, Class, and the Perception of Criminal Injustice in America," *American Journal of Sociology* (1982) 88:329–355.

66. See generally, Don C. Gibbons, *The Criminological Enterprise: Theories and Perspectives* (Englewood Cliffs, NJ: Prentice Hall, 1979).

67. See, for example, Howard S. Becker, *Outsiders* (New York: Free Press, 1963); Ian Taylor, Paul Walton, and Jock Young, *The New Criminology* (London: Routledge & Kegan Paul, 1973).

68. Stanton Wheeler, "Trends and Problems in the Sociological Study of Crime," *Social Problems* (1976) 22:525–534; Jack P. Gibbs, "Review of *Crime and Human Nature*, by James Q. Wilson and Richard J. Herrnstein," *Criminology* (1985) 23:381–388.

69. James Q. Wilson, *Thinking About Crime* (New York: Basic Books, 1975).

70. Bellah et al. (1991), p. 125.

71. Bellah et al. (1991), p. 125.

72. Fukuyama (1995), p. 311.

73. Data for these comparisons were supplied by the Administrative Office of the United States Courts, Statistics Division, Analysis and Reports Branch, Washington, DC, *Annual Reports to the Director*, 1946–1995 (Washington, DC: Government Printing Office).

74. Robert F. Putnam, "Bowling Alone: America's Declining Social Capital," *Journal of Democracy* (1995) 6:65–78, 67.

75. Bellah et al. (1991), p. 132.

76. Marguerite Bryan, "Social Psychology of Riot Participation," *Research in Race and Ethnic Relations* (1979) 1:169–187; Feagin and Hahn (1973).

77. Dominic J. Capeci, Jr., and Martha Wilkerson, *Layered Violence: The Detroit Rioters of 1943* (Jackson: University of Mississippi Press, 1991); T. M. Tomlinson, "Ideological Foundations for Negro Action: A Comparative Analysis of Militant and Non-Militant Views of the Los Angeles Riot," *Journal of Social Issues* (1970) 26:93–119.

78. Abraham H. Miller, Louis Bolce, and Mark R. Haligan, "The New Urban Blacks," *Ethnicity* (1976) 3:338–367, 361; see also, Lieske (1978).

79. Robert K. Merton, "Social Structure and Anomie," *American Sociological Review* (1938) 3:672–682.

80. For related views, see Ted Robert Gurr, Peter N. Grabosky, and Richard C. Hula, *The Politics of Crime and Conflict: A Comparative History of Four Cities* (Beverly Hills, CA: Sage, 1977).

81. Research on the strengths and weaknesses of this method are given by Roberto Franzosi, "The Press as a Source of Socio-Historical Data: Issues in the Methodology of Data Collection from Newspapers," *Historical Methods* (1987) 20:5–15.

82. Data on riots, 1947–1976, were originally collected by Larry Isaac and William R. Kelly ("Racial Insurgency, the State, and Welfare Expansion: Local and National Evidence from the Postwar United States," *American Journal of Sociology* [1981] 86:1348–1386). The original series on total protests and direct actions were collected from 1955 to 1976 by Douglas McAdam (*Political Process and the Development of Black Insurgency*, Chicago: University of Chicago Press, 1982). It was later extended to 1980 by the sociologists J. Craig Jenkins and Craig Eckert (1986). Isaac, Kelly, McAdam, Jenkins, and Eckert generously provided the annualized direct action event counts from their earlier research. Kriss Drass and I extended the series to 1991; see Gary LaFree and Kriss A. Drass, "African-American Collective Action and Crime, 1955–1991, *Social Forces* (1997) 75:835–853; see *The New York Times Index* (New York: The New York Times Company, 1981–1991).

83. Based on statistics provided by the U.S. Federal Bureau of Investigation, Uniform Crime Reports, *Crime in the United States 1965, 1971* (Washington, DC: Government Printing Office, 1966, 1972); total street crime rates in 1965 equal 2,449.0 (per 100,000 population); total street crime rates in 1971 equal 4,164.7 (per 100,000 population).

84. Data for this estimate are from the U.S. Federal Bureau of Investigation, Uniform Crime Reports (1966, 1972); robbery rates in 1965 were 71.7; rates in 1971 were 188.0.

85. George Rude, *The Face of the Crowd*, edited by H. Kaye (New York: Harvester, 1988 [1910]).

86. James W. Button, *Black Violence: Political Impact of the 1960s Riots* (Princeton: Princeton University Press, 1978).

87. Robert Agnew, "The Techniques of Neutralization," *Criminology* (1994) 32:555–580; William Minor, "The Neutralization of Criminal Offense," *Criminology* (1980) 18:3–20.

88. Anderson (1978).

89. William J. Chambliss, "Crime Control and Ethnic Minorities: Legitimizing Racial Oppression by Creating Moral Panics," in D. F. Hawkins, ed., *Ethnicity, Race and Crime* (Albany: State University of New York Press, 1995).

Chapter Seven

1. Karl Marx and Frederick Engels, "Wage Labor and Capital," in *Selected Works in Two Volumes* (Moscow: Foreign Languages Publishing House, 1955), pp. 268–269.

2. This quote from Martin Luther King, Jr., appeared in "Showdown for Non-Violence," *Look* (1978) 32:23–25, ten years after King was assassinated.

3. Lynn McDonald, *The Sociology of Law and Order* (London: Faber & Faber, 1976).

4. J. Robert Lilly, Francis T. Cullen, and Richard A. Ball, *Context and Consequences: Studies in Crime, Law and Justice*, Volume 5 (Beverly Hills, CA: Sage, 1979), p. 182.

5. Denny Braun, *The Rich Get Richer: The Rise of Income Inequality in the United States and the World* (Chicago: Nelson Hall, 1991), p. 137.

6. Braun (1991), p. 137.

7. Barry Bluestone and Bennett Harrison, *The Deindustrialization of America* (New York: Basic Books, 1982).

8. Mike Davis, *Prisoners of the American Dream: Politics and Economy in the History of the U.S. Working Class* (London: Verso, 1986); Samuel Bowles, David M. Gordon, and Thomas E. Weisskopf, *After the Wasteland: A Democratic Economics for the Year 2000* (Armonk, NY: M. E. Sharpe, 1990).

9. Eamonn Fingleton, *Blindside: Why Japan Is Still on Track to Overtake the U.S. by the Year 2000* (Boston: Houghton Mifflin, 1995), ch. 2.

10. Fingleton (1995), pp. 5–6.

11. Economic Report of the President, *The Annual Report of the Council of Economic Advisors* (Washington, DC: Government Printing Office, 1996), p. 20.

12. Economic Report of the President, *The Annual Report of the Council of Economic Advisors* (Washington, DC: Government Printing Office, 1997).

13. Economic Report of the President (1997).

14. David Hackett Fischer, *The Great Wave: Price Revolutions and the Rhythm of History* (New York: Oxford University Press, 1996), p. 232.

15. Daniel Patrick Moynihan, *The Negro Family: The Case for National Action* (Washington, DC: Office of Policy Planning and Research, 1965), p. 2.

16. Bart Landry, *The New Black Middle Class* (Berkeley: University of California Press, 1987).

17. See, for example, Joel Devine, Joseph Sheley, and M. Dwayne Smith, "Macroeconomic and Social-Control Policy Influences in Crime Rates, 1948–1985." *American Sociological Review* (1988) 53:407–421; Gary LaFree and Kriss A. Drass, "The Effect of Changes in Intraracial Income Inequality and Educational Attainment on Changes in Arrest Rates for African-Americans and Whites, 1957 to 1990," *American Sociological Review* (1996) 61:614–634.

18. James Q. Wilson, *Thinking About Crime* (New York: Basic, 1975), p. 3.

19. Sharon Long and Ann Witte, "Current Economic Trends: Implications for Crime and Justice," in K. Wright, ed., *Crime and Criminal Justice in a Declining Economy* (Cambridge, MA: Oelgeschlager, Gunn & Hain, 1981), p.135.

20. See discussion in Christopher Jencks, *Rethinking Social Policy: Race, Poverty and the Underclass* (Cambridge, MA: Harvard University Press, 1992), pp. 14–20.

21. Robert Merton, "Social Structure and Anomie," *American Sociological Review* (1938) 3:672–682.

22. Robert K. Merton, "Anomie, Anomia, and Social Interaction: Contexts of Deviant Behavior," in M. B. Clinard, ed., *Anomie and Deviant Behavior: A Discussion and Critique* (New York: Free Press, 1964), p. 226.

23. Robert Merton, "Social Structure and Anomie," in L. D. Savitz and N. Johnston, eds., *Crime and Society* (New York: John Wiley, 1978), p. 120.

24. Albert Cohen, *Delinquent Boys: The Culture of the Gang* (New York: Free Press, 1955).

25. Richard Cloward and Lloyd Ohlin, *Delinquency and Opportunity: A Theory of Delinquent Gangs* (New York: Free Press, 1961).

26. Clifford Shaw and Henry McKay, *Juvenile Delinquency and Urban Areas* (Chicago: University of Chicago Press, 1942); see review of social disorganization theories by Robert Bursik, "Social Disorganization and Theories of Crime and Delinquency: Problems and Prospects," *Criminology* (1988) 26:519–551.

27. These three points are summarized in Bursik (1988), p. 521.

28. For reviews, see Long and Witte (1981); David Cantor and Kenneth C. Land, "Unemployment and Crime Rates in the Post–World War II United States: A Theoretical and Empirical Analysis," *American Sociological Review* (1985) 50:317–332; Theodore Chiricos, "Rates of Crime and Unemployment: An Analysis of Aggregate Research Evidence," *Social Problems* (1987) 34:187–212.

29. John Hagan and Ruth Peterson, eds., *Crime and Inequality* (Stanford: Stanford University Press, 1995).

30. Long and Witte (1981).

31. Marx and Engels, (1955), p. 94.

32. George B. Vold and Thomas J. Bernard, *Theoretical Criminology*, third edition (New York: Oxford University Press, 1986), p. 141; see also, Hagan and Peterson (1995).

33. Vold and Bernard (1986), p. 141.

34. Devine et al. (1988).

35. LaFree and Drass (1996), p. 626.

36. Claudia Goldin and Robert Margo, "The Great Compression: The Wage Structure in the United States at Mid-Century," *The Quarterly Journal of Economics* (1992) 107:1–34; Frank Levy, *Dollars and Dreams* (New York: Russell Sage Foundation, 1987).

37. Frank Levy, "Happiness, Affluence, and Altruism in the Postwar Period," in M. David and T. Smeeding, eds., *Horizontal Equity, Uncertainty and Economic Welfare* (Chicago: University of Chicago Press, 1985).

38. This section is drawn mostly from Levy (1985).

39. Log wage dispersion was 1.46 in 1940 and 1.06 in 1950; see Goldin and Margo (1992), p. 4.

40. Wilson (1975), p. 3.

41. Levy (1985), p. 14.

42. LaFree and Drass (1996).

43. Levy (1985), p. 14.

44. The interquartile range is a measure of dispersion that indicates the difference in incomes between those in the 25th and 75th percentiles of the income distribution.

45. See LaFree and Drass (1996), p. 619. We were unable to extend the series before 1957 or after 1990 because of changes in the way family income statistics were reported by the U.S. Census Bureau.

46. Fischer (1996, pp. 203–208) shows that the rise of inflation during the early 1960s was a global phenomenon, appearing in many nations at about the same time.

47. Levy (1985), p. 7.

48. Fischer (1996), p. 204.

49. Lester C. Thurow, *The Zero Sum Society* (New York: Basic Books, 1980), p. 43.

50. Levy (1985), p. 15.

51. Edward Denison, "The Interruption of Productivity Growth in the United States," *Economic Journal* (1983) 93:56–57.

52. I refer to average male salaries here to allow comparisons with earlier sections. I take up in the next chapter the fact that average salaries for women became increasingly important in terms of estimating economic changes as the postwar period unfolded.

53. Levy (1985), p. 15.

54. John D. Kasarda, "The Regional and Urban Redistribution of People and Jobs in the U.S." Paper prepared for the National Research Council Committee on National Urban Policy, National Academy of Sciences, Washington, DC, 1986.

55. Ronald B. Mincy, "The Underclass: Concept, Controversy, and Evidence," in S. H. Danziger, G. D. Sandefur, and D. H. Weinberg, eds., *Confronting Poverty: Prescriptions for Change* (New York: Russell Sage Foundation, 1994), p. 117.

56. Claude S. Fischer, Michael Hout, Martin Sanchez Jankowski, Samuel R. Lucas, Ann Swidler, and Kim Voss, *Inequality by Design: Cracking the Bell Curve Myth* (Princeton: Princeton University Press, 1996).

57. William W. Goldsmith and Edward J. Blakely, *Separate Societies: Poverty and Inequality in U.S. Cities* (Philadelphia: Temple University Press, 1992), p. 20.

58. Mincy (1994), p. 117.

59. Goldsmith and Blakely (1992), p. 21.

60. Goldsmith and Blakely (1992), p. 21.

61. John Bound and George Johnson, "Changes in the Structure of Wages in the 1980s: An Evaluation of Alternative Explanations," *The American Economic Review* (1992) 82:371–392, 371.

62. Robert Reich, *The Work of Nations* (New York: Alfred A. Knopf, 1991).

63. Economic Report of the President (1997).

64. LaFree and Drass (1996).

65. Mincy (1994), p. 117.

66. Stanley Lieberson, *A Piece of the Pie: Black and White Immigrants Since 1880* (Berkeley: University of California Press, 1980).

67. Paul A. Gilje, *The Road to Mobocracy: Popular Disorder in New York City, 1763–1834* (Chapel Hill: University of North Carolina Press, 1987); Eric Monkkonen, "Racial Factors in New York City Homicides, 1800–1874," in D. F. Hawkins, ed., *Ethnicity, Race and Crime: Perspectives Across Time and Place* (Albany: State University of New York Press, 1995).

68. U.S. Bureau of the Census, *Historical Statistics of the United States: Colonial Times to 1970* (Washington, DC: Government Printing Office, 1975).

69. U.S. Bureau of the Census (1975), pp. A276–A287.

70. Levy (1987), p. 105.

71. Nicholas Lemann, "The Origins of the Underclass," *The Atlantic Monthly* (1986) June:31–61.

72. Lemann (1986), p. 35.

73. Levy (1987), p. 135.

74. Levy (1987), p. 105.

75. Roger Lane, *Roots of Violence in Black Philadelphia, 1860–1890* (Cambridge, MA: Harvard University Press, 1986), p. 168.

76. Levy (1987), p. 109.

77. William Julius Wilson, *The Truly Disadvantaged: The Inner City, the Underclass and Public Policy* (Chicago: University of Chicago Press, 1987), p. 178.

78. Wilson (1987), pp. 178–179.

79. Wilson (1987), p. 55.

80. Wilson (1987), p. 55.

81. Wilson (1987), pp. 57–58.

82. Levy (1987), pp. 111–119.

83. Levy (1987), p. 117.

84. U.S. Bureau of the Census, *Statistical Abstract of the United States, 1990* (Washington, DC: U.S. Department of Commerce, 1991), table 4.

85. Wilson (1987), p. 143.

86. Gregory D. Squires, William Velez, and Karl E. Taeuber, "Insurance Redlining, Agency Location, and the Process of Urban Disinvestment," *Urban Affairs Quarterly* (1991) 26:567–588; Margery A. Turner, John G. Edwards, and Maris Mikelsons, *Housing Discrimination Study: Analyzing Racial and Ethnic Steering* (Washington, DC: U.S. Department of Housing and Urban Development, 1991).

87. Douglas S. Massey, Andrew B. Gross, and Kumiko Shibuya, "Migration, Segregation, and the Geographic Concentration of Poverty," *American Sociological Review* (1994) 59:425–445.

88. Levy (1987), p. 117.

89. Levy (1987), p. 117.

90. Larry H. Long and Donald C. Dahmann, *The City-Suburb Income Gap: Is It Being Narrowed by a Back-to-the-City Movement?* U.S. Bureau of the Census, Special Demographic Analyses, CDS-80-1 (Washington, DC: Government Printing Office, 1980).

91. For a discussion of these trends, see Jack P. Gibbs, "Review of *Crime and Human Nature*, by James Q. Wilson and Richard J. Herrnstein," *Criminology* (1985) 23:381–388.

Chapter Eight

1. Quoted in James Q. Wilson, *Thinking About Crime* (New York: Vintage, 1975), pp. 13–14.

2. The actor John Wayne was quoted in Marsden Wagner and Mary Wagner, *The Danish National Child-Care System: A Successful System as a Model for the Reconstruction of American Child Care* (Boulder: Westview Press, 1976), p. 3.

3. James S. Coleman, "The Rational Reconstruction of Society," *American Sociological Review* (1993) 58:1–15, 2.

4. Frances K. Goldscheider and Linda J. Waite, *New Families, No Families? The Transformation of the American Home* (Berkeley: University of California Press, 1991), p. 3.

5. Shirley P. Burggraf, *The Feminine Economy and Economic Man: Reviving the Role of Family in the Post Industrial Age* (Reading, MA: Addison-Wesley, 1997), p. 18.

6. Goldscheider and Waite (1991), pp. 2–18.

7. See summary in Gary LaFree, Kriss Drass, and Patrick O'Day, "Race and Crime in Postwar America: Determinants of African-American and White Rates, 1957–1988," *Criminology* (1992) 30:157–188, 163–165.

8. Kingsley Davis, *Human Society* (New York: Macmillan, 1948), p. 395.

9. Travis Hirschi, "The Family," in J. Q. Wilson and J. Petersilia, eds., *Crime* (San Francisco: Institute for Contemporary Studies Press, 1995), p. 128.

10. See Hirschi (1995), p. 128; John Braithwaite, *Crime, Shame and Reintegration* (Cambridge, UK: Cambridge University Press, 1989), p. 48.

11. Robert J. Sampson and John H. Laub, *Crime in the Making: Pathways and Turning Points Through Life* (Cambridge, MA: Harvard University Press, 1993), pp. 160–162.

12. Hirschi (1995), p. 18.

13. See generally, Rolf Loeber and Magda Stouthamer-Loeber, "Family Factors as Correlates and Predictors of Juvenile Conduct Problems and Delinquency," in M. H. Tonry and N. Morris, eds., *Crime and Justice: A Review of Research* (Chicago: University of Chicago Press, 1986); Michael R. Gottfredson and Travis Hirschi, *A General Theory of Crime* (Stanford: Stanford University Press, 1990), pp. 97–105; for a discussion of effective internalization, see Peter L. Berger and Thomas Luckmann, *The Social Construction of Reality: A Treatise in the Sociology of Knowledge* (Garden City, NY: Anchor Books, 1967), pp. 163–173;

14. Hirschi (1995), p. 128.

15. Frank F. Furstenberg, Jr., "How Families Manage Risk and Opportunity in Dangerous Neighborhoods," in W. J. Wilson, ed., *Sociology and the Public Agenda* (Newbury Park, CA: Sage, 1993).

16. Hirschi (1995), p. 129.

17. Carl Werthman and Irving Piliavin, "Gang Members and the Police," in D. Bordua, ed., *The Police: Six Sociological Essays* (New York: John Wiley, 1967).

18. Lawrence E. Cohen and Marcus Felson, "Social Change and Crime Rate Trends: A Routine Activity Approach," *American Sociological Review* (1979) 44:588–608.

19. Hirschi (1995), p. 129.

20. For a review of some of these forms, see William J. Goode, *World Revolution and Family Patterns* (New York: Free Press, 1963).

21. Carol Stack, *All Our Kin: Strategies for Survival in a Black Community* (New York: Harper & Row, 1974).

22. Furstenberg (1993), p. 246.

23. This sum was then divided by the total number of households to produce a rate; see Cohen and Felson (1979), p. 600.

24. Joel A. Devine, Joseph F. Sheley, and M. Dwayne Smith, "Macroeconomic and Social-Control Policy Influences on Crime Rate Changes, 1948–1985," *American Sociological Review* (1988) 53:407–420.

25. For reviews, see Gwynn Nettler, *Explaining Crime*, third edition (New York: McGraw-Hill, 1984), pp. 308–311; Hirschi (1995).

26. Sheldon Glueck and Eleanor Glueck, *Unravelling Juvenile Delinquency* (Cambridge, MA: Harvard University Press, 1950).

27. Robert Sampson, "Urban Black Violence: The Effect of Male Joblessness and Family Disruption," *American Journal of Sociology* (1987) 93:348–382.

28. David Farrington, *Psychological Explanations of Crime* (Aldershot, UK: Dartmouth, 1994), p. xxiii.

29. Rolf Loeber and Magda Stouthamer-Loeber, "Family Factors as Correlates and Predispositions of Juvenile Conduct Problems and Delinquency," in M. Tonry and N. Morris, eds., *Crime and Justice: An Annual Review* (Chicago: University of Chicago Press, 1986).

30. Not all researchers agree, however, about the linkage between family variables and crime rates. For example, in a review of the literature the sociologists Lawrence Rosen and Kathleen Neilson conclude, "The concept of broken homes, no matter how it is defined or measured, has little explanatory power in terms of delinquency" ("The Broken Home and Delinquency," in L. D. Savitz and N. Johnston, eds., *Crime in Society* [New York: John Wiley, 1978], p. 414). Other researchers have concluded that the effect of broken homes is limited to children from lower-class families, to certain types of delinquent behavior, or to specific types of families (see, for example, Joseph H. Rankin, "The Family Context of Delinquency," *Social Problems* [1983] 30:466–479). In fact, Hirschi (1995, p. 123) argues that many criminologists, especially during the middle postwar period, simply assumed that family structure was largely irrelevant for predicting crime rates.

31. Christopher Lasch, *Haven in a Heartless World* (New York: Basic Books, 1977); Viviana Zelizer, *Pricing the Priceless Child* (New York: Basic Books, 1985).

32. Furstenberg (1993), p. 233.

33. Betty Friedan, *The Feminine Mystique* (New York: W. W. Norton, 1963).

34. Kate Millett, *Sexual Politics* (Garden City, NY: Doubleday, 1969), p. 25.

35. Millet (1969), p. 33.

36. Millet (1969), p. 35.

37. Millet (1969), p. 159.

38. Mary Ann Glendon, *Rights Talk: The Impoverishment of Political Discourse* (New York: Free Press, 1991).

39. Francis Fukuyama, *Trust: The Social Virtues and the Creation of Prosperity* (New York: Free Press, 1995), p. 313.

40. Lawrence M. Friedman, *The Republic of Choice: Law, Authority, and Culture* (Cambridge, MA: Harvard University Press, 1990), p. 178.

41. Friedman (1990), p. 177.

42. U.S. Bureau of the Census, *Statistical Abstract of the United States, 1996* (Washington, DC: Government Printing Office, 1996), p. 6.

43. Goldscheider and Waite (1991), p. 18.

44. U.S. Bureau of the Census, "Household and Family Characteristics: March 1980," *Current Population Reports*, Series P-20, n. 366 (Washington, DC: Government Printing Office, 1980).

45. Goldscheider and Waite (1991), p. 17.

46. Goldscheider and Waite (1991), p. 2.

47. Goldscheider and Waite (1991), p. 17.

48. Goldscheider and Waite (1991), p. 2.

49. Goldscheider and Waite (1991), p. 14.

50. Charles F. Westoff, "Perspective on Nuptiality and Fertility," *Population and Development Review*, supplement to 12 (1986):155–170.

51. Robert Schoen, William Urton, Karen Woodrow, and John Baj, "Marriage and Divorce in Twentieth Century American Cohorts," *Demography* (1985) 22:101–114.

52. Theresa Castro Martin and Larry L. Bumpass, "Recent Trends in Marital Disruption," *Demography* (1989) 26:37–51.

53. Goldscheider and Waite (1991), p. 15.

54. Sandra Hofferth, "Updating Children's Life Course," *Journal of Marriage and the Family* (1985) 47:93–115.

55. Goldscheider and Waite (1991), p. 3.

56. David Popenoe, *Disturbing the Nest: Family Change and Decline in Modern Societies* (New York: Aldine de Gruyter, 1988); Goode (1963).

57. U.S. Bureau of the Census, *Historical Statistics of the United States: Colonial Times to 1970*, Part 1 (Washington, DC: Government Printing Office, 1975), p. 127.

58. U.S. Bureau of the Census (1975), p. 127.

59. U.S. Bureau of the Census, *Statistical Abstract of the United States, 1996* (Washington, DC: Government Printing Office, 1996), p. 410.

60. Pre-1971 statistics on female labor force participation are from U.S. Bureau of the Census (1975), p. 128.

61. Post-1970 statistics on female labor force participation are from U.S. Bureau of the Census (1996), p. 394.

62. Goldscheider and Waite (1991), p. 9.

63. Goldscheider and Waite (1991), p. 9, use this term.

64. U.S. Bureau of the Census (1975), p. 368.

65. U.S. Bureau of the Census (1975), p. 368.

66. U.S. Department of Education, *Digest of Education Statistics 1996* (Washington, DC: Center for Education Statistics, 1996), p. 15.

67. All of the these statistics are from U.S. Department of Education (1996), p. 15.

68. LaFree et al. (1992).

69. Steven Ruggles, "The Origins of African-American Family Structure," *American Sociological Review* (1994) 59:136–151, 141.

70. Data on female-headed households by race are from U.S. Bureau of the Census, *Statistical Abstract of the United States* (Washington, DC: Government Printing Office, individual years, 1990–1996). Separate estimates for African Americans and whites were unavailable before 1957.

71. Statistics on unwed mothers are from U.S. Department of Health and Human Services, *Vital Statistics of the United States, 1977* (Washington, DC: Government Printing Office, 1977), pp. 1–53; U.S. Bureau of the Census, *Statistical Abstract of the United States* (Washington, DC: Government Printing Office, individual years, 1978–1995). At the time this book was being prepared, 1991 data were the most recent available.

72. Lois B. DeFleur, *Delinquency in Argentina: A Study of Cordoba's Youth* (Pullman: Washington State University Press, 1970), pp. 15–18.

73. Hirschi (1995), p. 127; Robert J. Sampson, "Family Management and Child Development: Insights from Social Disorganization Theory," in J. McCord, ed., *Facts, Frameworks and Forecasts* (Brunswick, NJ: Transaction Press, 1992).

74. James W. Messerschmidt, *Capitalism, Patriarchy, and Crime: Toward a Socialist Feminist Criminology* (Totowa, NJ: Rowman & Littlefield, 1986), p. 58.

75. Karen Heimer, "Gender, Race, and the Pathways to Delinquency," in J. Hagan and R. D. Peterson, eds., *Crime and Inequality* (Stanford: Stanford University Press, 1995), p. 149.

76. Heimer (1995), p. 149.

77. Millet (1969), p. 39.

78. See, for example, Steven F. Messner and Richard Rosenfeld, *Crime and the American Dream* (Belmont, CA: Wadsworth, 1994), p. 73.

79. Rick Aniskiewicz and E. Wysong, "Evaluating DARE: Drug Education and the Multiple Meanings of Success," *Policy Studies Review* (1990) 9:727–747.

80. U.S. Bureau of the Census (1996), p. 104.

81. U.S. Bureau of the Census, *Statistical Abstract of the United States, 1995* (Washington, DC: Government Printing Office, 1995).

82. U.S. Bureau of the Census (1996), pp. 6, 157, 394.

Chapter Nine

1. Martin van Creveld, *The Transformation of War* (New York: Free Press, 1991), p. 198.

2. Milan Kundera, *The Unbearable Lightness of Being* (New York: Harper & Row, 1984), p. 4.

3. See Gary LaFree and Kriss A. Drass, "The Effect of Changes in Intraracial Income Inequality and Educational Attainment on Changes in Arrest Rates for African Americans and Whites, 1957 to 1990," *American Sociological Review* (1996) 61:614–634.

4. Wesley G. Skogan, "Citizen Reporting of Crime: Some National Panel Data," *Criminology* (1976) 13:535–549.

5. See Harry Kalven, Jr., and Hans Zeisel's classic, *The American Jury* (New York: Little, Brown, 1966), pp. 310–312.

6. See, for example, John Braithwaite's arguments about reintegrative shaming in *Crime, Shame and Reintegration* (Cambridge, UK: Cambridge University Press, 1989), ch. 5.

7. Peter Marris and Martin Rein, *Dilemmas of Social Reform* (Chicago: Aldine, 1973); National Advisory Commission on Civil Disorders, *U.S. Riot Commission Report* (New York: Bantam Books, 1968), pp. 424–456.

8. See, for example, Allen E. Liska, "Aspirations, Expectations and Delinquency: Stress and Additive Models," *Sociological Quarterly* (1971) 12:99–107; Josefina Figueira-McDonough, "Feminism and Delinquency," *British Journal of Criminology* (1984) 24:325–342.

9. Delbert S. Elliott and Harwin L. Voss, *Delinquency and Dropout* (Lexington, MA: D. C. Heath, 1974); Gary D. Gottfredson, "Schooling and Delinquency," in S. E. Martin, L. B. Sechrest, and R. Redner, eds., *New Directions in the Rehabilitation of Criminal Offenders*, Report of the Panel on Research on Rehabilitative Techniques (Washington, DC: National Academy Press, 1981).

10. Jackson Toby, "The Schools," in J. Q. Wilson and J. Petersilia, eds., *Crime* (San Francisco: Institute for Contemporary Studies Press, 1995), pp. 152–158.

11. For a review, see Braithwaite (1989), pp. 28–29.

12. See, for example, Robert Agnew, "A Revised Strain Theory of Delinquency," *Social Forces* (1985) 64:151–167; H. B. Kaplan and C. Robbins, "Testing a General Theory of Deviant Behavior in Longitudinal Perspective," in K. T. Van Dusen and S. A. Mednick, eds., *Prospective Studies of Crime and Delinquency* (Hingham, MA: Kluwer Nijhoff, 1983).

13. This last possibility must be regarded as mostly theoretical at this point because most research suggests that children who attend school actually face increased chances of being crime victims. See, for example, U. S. Department of Health, Education and Welfare, *Violent Schools—Safe Schools: The Safe School Study Report to Congress* (Washington, DC: Government Printing Office, 1978).

14. This point is made in a book edited by Martin Carnoy, *Schooling in a Corporate Society* (New York: McKay, 1972).

15. Richard Cloward and Lloyd Ohlin, *Delinquency and Opportunity: A Theory of Delinquent Gangs* (New York: Free Press, 1960).

16. John Meyer and Rick Rubinson, "Education and Political Development," *Review of Research in Education* (1975) 3:134–162, 142.

17. John Kasarda, "The Regional and Urban Redistribution of People and Jobs in the U.S.," Paper prepared for the National Research Council Committee on National Urban Policy, National Academy of Science, Washington, DC, 1986, pp. 26–27.

18. James Liebman, "Implementing *Brown* in the Nineties: Political Reconstruction, Liberal Recollection, and Litigatively Enforced Legislative Reform," *Virginia Law Review* (1990) 76:349–435, 353; see *Brown v. Board of Education of Topeka, Shawnee County, Kansas,* 347 U.S. 483 (1954).

19. Joel A. Devine, Joseph F. Sheley, and M. Dwayne Smith, "Macroeconomic and Social-Control Policy Influences in Crime Rates, 1948–1985," *American Sociological Review* (1988) 53:407–421.

20. See Robert Fiala and Gary LaFree, "Cross-National Determinants of Child Homicide," *American Sociological Review* (1988) 53:432–445; Sheila B. Kamerman, *Parenting in an Unresponsive Society: Managing Work and Family Life* (New York: Free Press, 1980).

21. President's Commission on Law Enforcement and the Administration of Justice, *The Challenge of Crime in a Free Society* (Washington, DC: Government Printing Office, 1967), p. 66.

22. Charles Murray makes a similar argument about welfare reform in the late 1950s, see *Losing Ground: American Social Policy, 1950–1980* (New York: Basic Books, 1984), pp. 20–21.

23. See, for example, Barry Krisberg, *Crime and Privilege: Toward a New Criminology* (Englewood Cliffs, NJ: Prentice-Hall, 1975); Ian Taylor, Paul Walton, and Jock Young, *The New Criminology: For a Social Theory of Deviance* (London: Routledge & Kegan Paul, 1973).

24. All statistics from this section are taken from U.S. Department of Education, National Center for Education Statistics, *Digest of Education Statistics, 1996* (Washington, DC: Government Printing Office, 1996), p. 15. Statistics include enrollment in any type of graded public, parochial, or other private school. They also include nursery schools, kindergartens, elementary schools, high schools, colleges, universities, and professional schools. Attendance may be on either a full-time or part-time basis, during the day or night. Enrollments in "special schools," such as trade schools, business colleges, or correspondence schools, are not included.

25. See, for example, Michael R. Gottfredson and Travis Hirschi, *A General Theory of Crime* (Stanford: Stanford University Press, 1990), pp. 272–273.

26. I could not locate comparable age data before 1965; after 1993, the Department of Education began using new procedures for collecting these data that greatly increased percentages reported (to 48.7 percent by 1995); see U.S. Department of Education, National Center for Education Statistics (1996), p. 15.

27. Data on total government spending on education are from U.S. Bureau of the Census, *Government Finances: 1984–1992,* Series GF/92-5 (Washington, DC: Government Printing Office, 1996), p. 1; and U.S. Bureau of the Census, *Historical Statistics on Governmental Finance and Employment* (Washington, DC: Government Printing Office, 1985), pp. 26–28. I divided total spending by total resident population and converted to constant 1995 dollars.

28. Reynolds Farley, *Blacks and Whites: Narrowing the Gap?* (Cambridge, MA: Harvard University Press, 1984), p. 17.

29. We could only locate a measure of median education level by race from 1957 through 1990. See LaFree and Drass (1996), p. 623.

30. Totals were 53.8 percent for whites and 56.3 percent for non-Hispanic blacks; see U.S. Department of Education, National Center for Education Statistics (1996), p. 16.

31. William Julius Wilson, *The Truly Disadvantaged: The Inner City, the Underclass, and Public Policy* (Chicago: University of Chicago Press, 1987), p. 58.

32. Wilson (1987), pp. 57–58.

33. Murray (1984), p. 108.

34. U.S. Department of Education, National Center for Education Statistics, *Digest of Education Statistics 1981* (Washington, DC: Government Printing Office, 1982), p. 46.

35. Data on welfare spending are from U.S. Bureau of the Census, *Government Finances* (1996), p. 1; and U.S. Bureau of the Census (1985), pp. 26–28. All welfare spending statistics are transformed to constant 1995 dollars.

36. Murray (1984), ch. 8.

37. U.S. Department of Commerce, Bureau of the Census, *Statistical Abstract of the United States, 1996* (Washington, DC: Government Printing Office, 1996), p. 370.

38. U.S. Bureau of the Census, *Statistical Abstract* (1996), p. 383.

39. U.S. Omnibus Crime Control and Safe Streets Act (Washington, DC: Government Printing Office, 1968); see also Devine et al. (1988), pp. 408–409.

40. James W. Button, *Black Violence: Political Impact of the 1960s Riots* (Princeton: Princeton University Press, 1978).

41. This distinction is made by David C. Anderson, "The Mystery of the Falling Crime Rate," *The American Prospect* (1997) 32:49–57.

42. Statistics on executions in the United States used in this section are from U.S. Bureau of Justice Statistics, *Sourcebook of Criminal Justice Statistics 1995* (Washington, DC: Government Printing Office, 1996), p. 615.

43. In *Furman v. Georgia,* 408 U.S. 238 (1972), the U.S. Supreme Court struck down on Eighth Amendment (which forbids cruel and unusual punishment) grounds state and federal capital punishment laws for permitting too much discretion in the application of the death penalty. Following *Furman,* states revised their statutes and rates of death row inmates began to climb. See U.S. Bureau of Justice Statistics, *Sourcebook* (1996), p. 615.

44. U.S. Bureau of Justice Statistics, *Sourcebook* (1996), p. 556.

45. These estimates are based on spending data from U.S. Bureau of the Census, *Government Finances* (1996), p. 1.

46. U.S. Bureau of Justice Statistics, *Sourcebook* (1996), p. 609.

47. See James Lynch, "Crime in International Perspective," in J. Q. Wilson and J. Petersilia, eds., *Crime* (San Francisco: Institute for Contemporary Studies Press, 1995).

48. Statistics on prison capacity are from U.S. Bureau of Justice Statistics, *Sourcebook* (1996), p. 94.

49. U.S. Bureau of Justice Statistics, *Correctional Populations in the United States, 1995* (Washington, DC: Government Printing Office, 1997), p. 5.

50. U.S. Bureau of Justice Statistics, *Correctional Populations in the United States, 1994* (Washington, DC: Government Printing Office, 1996), p. 6.

51. Richard B. Freeman, "The Labor Market," in J. Q. Wilson and J. Petersilia, eds., *Crime* (San Francisco: Institute for Contemporary Studies Press, 1995), p. 172.

52. U.S. Bureau of Justice Statistics, *Prisoners in 1996* (Washington, DC: U.S. Department of Justice, June 1997), p. 1.

53. U.S. Bureau of the Census, *Government Finances* (1996), p. 1; and U.S. Bureau of the Census (1985), pp. 26–28.

54. Statistics from 1926 to 1986 are from Patrick A. Langan, *Race of Prisoners Admitted to State and Federal Institutions, 1926–86* (Washington, DC: Government Printing Office, 1991), p. 5. Post-1986 statistics are from U.S. Bureau of Justice Statistics, *Correctional Populations* (1996), p. 15.

55. Thomas Bonczar and Allen J. Beck, "Lifetime Likelihood of Going to State or Federal Prison," *Bureau of Justice Statistics Special Report* (Washington, DC: Government Printing Office, March 1997).

56. Statistics on executions are from U.S. Bureau of Justice Statistics, *Sourcebook* (1996), p. 615.

57. U.S. Bureau of Justice Statistics, *Sourcebook* (1996), p. 549.

58. U.S. Bureau of Justice Statistics, *Correctional Populations* (1996), p. 106.

59. This last estimate is based on comparing total numbers of African Americans and whites on probation in 1994. See U.S. Bureau of Justice Statistics, *Correctional Populations* (1996), p. 39.

60. Marc Mauer, *Young Black Men and the Criminal Justice System: A Growing National Problem* (Washington, DC: The Sentencing Project, 1990), p. 8.

61. Freeman (1995), p. 172.

62. See, for example, Alfred Blumstein, "Making Rationality Relevant," *Criminology* (1993) 31:1–16; David P. Farrington and Patrick Langan, "Changes in Crime and Punishment in England and America in the 1980s," *Justice Quarterly* (1992) 9:5–46; Devine et al. (1988); William Bennett, John DiIulio, and John Walters, *Body Count* (New York: Simon & Schuster, 1996).

63. Thomas B. Marvell and Carlisle E. Moody, "The Impact of Prison Growth on Homicide," *Homicide Studies* (1997) 1:205–233.

64. Devine et al. (1988); Lawrence E. Cohen and Kenneth C. Land, "Age Structure and Crime: Symmetry Versus Asymmetry and the Projection of Crime Rates Through the 1990s," *American Sociological Review* (1987) 52:170–183.

65. Edward Zedlewski, *Making Confinement Decisions* (Washington, DC: U.S. Department of Justice, 1987).

66. W. Spelman, *Criminal Incapacitation* (New York: Plenum, 1994); Anne M. Piehl and John J. DiIulio, "Does Prison Pay? Revisited," *The Brookings Review* (1995) 13:21–25.

67. Bennett, DiIulio, and Walters (1996).

68. U.S. Bureau of Justice Statistics, *Sourcebook* (1996), p. 560.

69. According to the National Crime Victimization Survey, victims reported 41.2 percent of personal crimes and 33.9 percent of property crimes to police in 1994. See U.S. Bureau of Justice Statistics, *Sourcebook* (1996), p. 250.

70. For 1994, the UCR reports that 21.4 percent of index crimes were cleared by an arrest. See U.S. Bureau of Justice Statistics, *Sourcebook* (1996), p. 426.

71. Brian Forst, "Prosecution and Sentencing," in J. Q. Wilson and J. Petersilia, eds., *Crime* (San Francisco: Institute for Contemporary Studies Press, 1995), p. 364.

72. Anderson (1997), pp. 50–51.

73. Alfred Blumstein, Jacqueline Cohen, and Daniel Nagin, eds., *Deterrence and Incapacitation: Estimating the Effects of Criminal Sanctions on Crime Rates*, Panel on Research on Deterrent and Incapacitative Effects, National Research Council (Washington, DC: National Academy of Sciences, 1978); H. Laurence Ross and Gary LaFree, "Deterrence in Criminology and Social Policy," in N. J. Smelser and D. R. Gerstein, eds., *Behavioral and Social Science: Fifty Years of Discovery* (Washington, DC: National Academy Press, 1986).

74. Emile Durkheim, *Moral Education: A Study of the Theory and Application of the Sociology of Education* (New York: Free Press, 1961), p. 176.

75. Braithwaite (1989).

76. Tom R. Tyler, *Why People Obey the Law* (New Haven: Yale University Press, 1990).

77. Lawrence W. Sherman, "Defiance, Deterrence, and Irrelevance: A Theory of the Criminal Sanction," *Journal of Research in Crime and Delinquency* (1993) 30:445–473.

78. Anthony Harris, "Race, Commitment to Deviance, and Spoiled Identity," *American Sociological Review* (1976) 41:432–441, 440.

79. Harris (1976), p. 440.

80. Susan Ageton and Delbert Elliott, "The Effects of Legal Processing on Self Concept," *Social Problems* (1974) 22:87–100.

81. See George L. Kelling and Catherine M. Coles, *Fixing Broken Windows: Restoring Order and Reducing Crime in Our Communities* (New York: Free Press, 1996).

82. Jeffrey A. Roth and Mark H. Moore, "Reducing Violent Crimes and Intentional Injuries," *National Institute of Justice: Research in Action* (Washington, DC: Government Printing Office, October 1995).

83. Anderson (1997), p. 52.

84. Anderson (1997), p. 52.

85. Anderson (1997), p. 53.

86. Kelling and Coles (1996); Anderson (1997), p. 54.

87. Eric Pooley, "One Good Apple," *Time* (1996) January 15:55.

Chapter Ten

1. Bertrand Russell, "On the Notion of Cause with Application to the Free Will Problem," Lecture eight in *Our Knowledge of the External World as a Field for Scientific Method in Philosophy* (London: Allen & Unwin, 1914), p. 234.

2. Peter L. Berger, *Invitation to Sociology: A Humanistic Perspective* (Garden City, NY: Anchor, 1963), p. 90.

3. Walker Percy, *The Moviegoer* (New York: Alfred A. Knopf, 1960), p. 82.

4. For example, Willem Bonger, *Criminality and Economic Conditions* (Boston: Little, Brown, 1916); Richard Quinney, *Critique of Legal Order* (Boston: Little, Brown, 1973).

5. Steven F. Messner and Richard Rosenfeld, *Crime and the American Dream* (Belmont, CA: Wadsworth, 1994), p. 76.

6. Messner and Rosenfeld (1994), p. 78.

7. Messner and Rosenfeld (1994), pp. 78–84.

8. Jack A. Goldstone, *Revolution and Rebellion in the Early Modern World* (Berkeley: University of California Press, 1991); Ted Robert Gurr, *Why Men Rebel* (Princeton: Princeton University Press, 1970).

9. Francis Fukuyama, *Trust: The Social Virtues and the Creation of Prosperity* (New York: Free Press, 1995).

10. See the trends in Warren E. Miller, *American National Election Studies Cumulative Data File, 1952–1996* (Ann Arbor, MI: Center for Political Studies, 1996).

11. Frank Levy, *Dollars and Dreams* (New York: Russell Sage Foundation, 1987), p. 151. By contrast, Levy argues that increases in husband-wife families with both spouses working reduced aggregate economic inequality during the postwar period because the effect of more women joining their husbands in the labor force at low income levels was greater than its effect at high income levels.

12. Shirley P. Burggraf, *The Feminine Economy and Economic Man: Reviving the Role of Family in the Postindustrial Age* (Reading, MA: Addison Wesley, 1997), p. 175.

13. See, for example, Kate Millett, *Sexual Politics* (Garden City, NY: Doubleday, 1970), ch. 2.

14. See Lois DeFleur, *Delinquency in Argentina: A Study of Cordoba's Youth* (Pullman: Washington State University Press, 1970).

15. Robert K. Merton, "Anomie, Anomia, and Social Interaction: Contexts of Deviant Behavior," in M. B. Clinard, ed., *Anomie and Deviant Behavior: A Discussion and Critique* (New York: Free Press, 1964), p. 226.

16. For related arguments see Fukuyama (1995), p. 320.

17. William Julius Wilson, *The Truly Disadvantaged: The Inner City, the Underclass, and Public Policy* (Chicago: University of Chicago Press, 1987).

18. Frank F. Furstenberg, Jr., "How Families Manage Risk and Opportunity in Dangerous Neighborhoods," in W. J. Wilson, ed., *Sociology and the Public Agenda* (Newbury Park, CA: Sage, 1993), p. 245.

19. Furstenberg (1993), p. 245; See also, Roger Waldinger, *Still the Promised City? African-Americans and New Immigrants in Post-Industrial New York* (Cambridge, MA: Harvard University Press, 1996).

20. John Braithwaite, *Crime, Shame and Reintegration* (Cambridge, UK: Cambridge University Press, 1989); Tom R. Tyler, *Why People Obey the Law* (New Haven: Yale University Press, 1990); Lawrence W. Sherman, "Defiance, Deterrence, and Irrelevance: A Theory of the Criminal Sanction," *Journal of Research in Crime and Delinquency* (1993) 30:445–473.

21. Gerald F. Seib and Joe Davidson, "Whites, Blacks Agree on Problems; The Issue Is How to Solve Them," *Wall Street Journal* (1995) November 3:1.

22. David L. Kirp and Ronald Bayer, "Needles and Race," *Atlantic Monthly* (1993) July:38–42; Paul Raeburn, *Albuquerque Journal*, "Blacks See AIDS as Genocide," (1995) November 2:A9.

23. Kirp and Bayer (1993), p. 39.

24. Seib and Davidson (1995).

25. Seib and Davidson (1995).

26. Emile Durkheim, *The Division of Labor in Society*, translated by George Simpson (New York: Free Press, 1964 [1893]), p. 377.

27. "The Boss's Pay," *Wall Street Journal* (1997) April 10:R15.

28. Richard Harwood, "Inequalities in Salaries Are Common in America," *Albuquerque Journal* (1997) April 30.7.

29. Charles Handy, *The Age of Paradox* (Boston: Harvard Business School Press, 1994), pp. 40–41.

30. Jonathan Kelley and M.D.R. Evans, "The Legitimation of Inequality: Occupational Earnings in Nine Nations," *American Journal of Sociology* (1993) 99:75–125.

31. Handy (1994), p. 41.

32. Burggraf (1997), p. 17.

33. See, for example, the Family Impact Statement Act, Senate Bill 891, introduced by Senator Spencer Abraham, on June 12, 1997; William J. Bennett, John J. DiIulio, Jr., and John P. Walters, *Body Count: Moral Poverty and How to Win America's War Against Crime and Drugs* (New York: Simon & Schuster, 1996), ch. 5; Burggraf (1997), p. 181.

34. See, for example, Barbara Reskin and Irene Padavic, *Women and Men at Work* (Thousand Oaks, CA: Pine Forge Press, 1994).

35. Burggraf (1997), p. 14.

36. Burggraf (1997), p. 7.

37. Hiro Yoshikawa, "Prevention as Cumulative Protection: Effects of Early Family Support and Education on Chronic Delinquency and Its Risks," *Psychological Bulletin* (1994) 15:28–54.

38. J. R. Berrueta-Clement, L. J. Schweinhart, W. S. Barnett, A. S. Epstein, and D. P. Weikart, *Changed Lives: The Effects of the Perry Preschool Program on Youths Through Age 19* (Ypsilanti, MI: High Scope Press, 1984).

39. Dale L. Johnson and Todd Walker, "Primary Prevention of Behavior Problems in Mexican-American Children," *American Journal of Community Psychology* (1987) 15:375–385.

40. J. R. Lally, P. L. Mangiaone, and A. S. Honig, "The Syracuse University Family Development Research Project: Long-Range Impact of an Early Intervention with Low-Income Children and Their Families," in D. R. Powell, ed., *Annual Advances in Applied Developmental Psychology, Volume 3, Parent Education as Early Childhood Intervention: Emerging Directions in Theory, Research and Practice* (Norwood, NJ: Ablex, 1988).

41. V. Seitz, L. K. Rosenbaum, and N. H. Apfel, "Effects of Family Support Intervention: A Ten-Year Follow-Up," *Child Development* (1985) 56:376–391.

42. Franklin Zimring and Gordon Hawkins, "Lethal Violence and the Overreach of American Imprisonment," *National Institute of Justice Research Report* (Washington, DC: Government Printing Office, July 1997); Francis T. Cullen, "Assessing the Penal Harm Movement," *Journal of Research in Crime and Delinquency* (1995) 32:338–358; Michael Tonry, *Malign Neglect: Race, Crime, and Punishment in America* (New York: Oxford University Press, 1995).

43. Michael K. Block, "Supply Side Imprisonment Policy," *National Institute of Justice Research Report* (Washington, DC: Government Printing Office, July 1997); James Q. Wilson, "Crime and Public Policy," in J. Q. Wilson and J. Petersilia, eds., *Crime* (San Francisco: Institute for Contemporary Studies Press, 1995); John J. DiIulio, Jr., "The Question of Black Crime," *Public Interest* (1994) 117:3–32.

44. Zimring and Hawkins, "Lethal Violence" (1997); Cullen (1995); Tonry (1995).

45. Yoshikawa (1994), p. 45.

46. E. Zigler, "Head Start Falls Behind," *New York Times* (1992) June 27:23.

47. U.S. Department of Education, *Digest of Education Statistics 1996* (Washington, DC: Government Printing Office, 1996), p. 15.

48. James S. Coleman, "The Rational Reconstruction of Society: Presidential Address," *American Sociological Review* (1993) 58:1–15, 7.

49. Burggraf (1997), p. 13.

50. Christopher Jencks, *Rethinking Social Policy: Race, Poverty and the Underclass* (Cambridge, MA: Harvard University Press, 1992), p. 233.

51. Jerry Watts, "The End of Work and the End of Welfare," *Contemporary Sociology: A Journal of Reviews* (1997) 26:409–412; Elaine Rivera, "Hungry at the Feast," *Time* (1997) July 21:38; Rachel L. Swarns, "For Now, Few Are Going from Food Stamps to Soup Kitchens," *New York Times* (1997) July 6:13.

52. Jencks (1992), p. 227.

53. Kathryn Edin and Christopher Jencks, "Reforming Welfare," in C. Jencks, *Rethinking Social Policy: Race, Poverty and the Underclass* (Cambridge, MA: Harvard University Press, 1992), p. 205.

54. Edin and Jencks (1992), p. 225.

55. Edin and Jencks (1992), pp. 233–234.

56. Burggraf (1997), p. 174.

57. Burggraf (1997), p. 173.

58. Burggraf (1997), p. 174.

59. Burggraf (1997), p. 171.

60. Burggraf (1997), p. 172.

61. Stanley Lieberson, *Making It Count: The Improvement of Social Research and Theory* (Berkeley: University of California Press, 1985), p. 180.

62. Julia S. Brown and Brian G. Gilmartin, "Sociology Today: Lacunae, Emphases, and Surfeits," *American Sociologist* (1969) 4:283–291.

63. Alexis de Tocqueville, *Democracy in America*, edited by R. D. Hefner (New York: Mentor, 1963 [1835]).

64. Seymour Martin Lipset, *American Exceptionalism: A Double-Edged Sword* (New York: W. W. Norton, 1996).

65. Franklin E. Zimring and Gordon Hawkins, *Crime Is Not the Problem: Lethal Violence in America* (New York: Oxford University Press, 1997).

66. Lipset (1996), ch. 1.

67. Brigitte Buhmann, Lee Rainwater, Guenther Schmaus, and Timothy M. Smeeding, "Equivalence Scales, Well Being, Inequality, and Poverty: Sensitivity Estimates Across Ten Countries Using the Luxembourg Income Study (LIS) Database," *Review of Income and Wealth* (1988) 34:115–142.

68. David Popenoe, *Disturbing the Nest: Family Change and Decline in Modern Societies* (New York: Aldine de Gruyter, 1988).

69. Ineke Haen Marshall, "How Exceptional Is the United States?" *European Journal on Criminal Policy and Research* (1996) 4:7–35.

70. Charles Hampden-Turner and Alfons Trompenaars, *The Seven Cultures of Capitalism* (New York: Doubleday, 1993), p. 45.

71. Lipset (1996), p. 22.

72. H. Franke, "Violent Crime in the Netherlands: A Historical-Sociological Analysis," *Crime, Law and Social Change* (1994) 21:73–100; Marshall (1996).

73. Michael Tonry, ed., *Ethnicity, Crime and Immigration: Comparative and Cross-National Perspectives* (Chicago: University of Chicago Press, 1997), p. 1.

74. Roland Chilton, Raymond Teske, and Harold Arnold, "Ethnicity, Race and Crime: German and Non-German Suspects, 1960–1990," in D. F. Hawkins, ed., *Ethnicity, Race, and Crime: Perspectives Across Time and Place* (Albany: State University of New York Press, 1995).

75. Pamela Irving Jackson, "Minority Group Threat, Crime and the Mobilization of Law in France," in D. F. Hawkins, ed., *Ethnicity, Race, and Crime: Perspectives Across Time and Place* (Albany: State University of New York Press, 1995).

76. Tonry (1997).

77. For a review, see Gary LaFree, "Comparative Cross-National Studies of Homicide," in M. D. Smith and M. Zahn, eds., *Homicide: A Sourcebook of Social Research* (Thousand Oaks, CA: Sage, 1998).

78. Jan J.M. van Dijk, Pat Mayhew, and Martin Killias, *Experiences of Crime Across the World: Key Findings of the 1989 International Crime Survey*, second edition (Deventer, the Netherlands: Kluwer, 1991).

79. Peter B. Evans, "Transnational Linkages and the Economic Role of the State: An Analysis of Developing and Industrialized Nations in the Post–World War II Period," in P. B. Evans, D. Rueschemeyer, and T. Skocpol, eds., *Bringing the State Back In* (New York: Cambridge, 1984), p. 193.

80. Eric Schlosser, "In the Strawberry Fields," *Atlantic Monthly* (1995) November:80–108.

81. Schlosser (1995), p. 108.

82. Saskia Sassen, *The Global City: New York, London and Tokyo* (Princeton: Princeton University Press, 1991), p. 333.

83. Sassen (1991), p. 337.

84. John Boli and George M. Thomas, "World Culture in the World Polity: A Century of International Non-Governmental Organization," *American Sociological Review* (1997) 62:171–190; John W. Meyer, David Kamens, Aaron Benavot, Youn-Kyung Cha, and Suk-Ying Wong, *School Knowledge for the Masses* (London: Falmer Press, 1992).

85. Peter L. Berger and Thomas Luckmann, *The Social Construction of Reality: A Treatise in the Sociology of Knowledge* (Garden City, NY: Anchor, 1967), p. 89.

86. Berger and Luckmann (1967), p. 89.

87. Robert N. Bellah, Richard Madsen, William M. Sullivan, Ann Swidler, and Steven M. Tipton, *The Good Society* (New York: Alfred A. Knopf, 1991), p. 12.

88. Jencks (1992), p. 119.

Index

Abudu, Margaret, 95
Acquired Immune Deficiency
  Syndrome (AIDS), 180–181
Adler, Freda, 39–40
AFDC. See Aid to Families with
  Dependent Children
African Americans, 5–6, 15, 101, 112,
  175
  crime statistics, 4, 47, 50(table),
    53(table), 54
  and criminal justice system, 4–5,
    129(figure), 153, 158, 167–168
  desegregation, 179–180
  discrimination, 49, 62, 97–98, 176
  economic conditions, 82–83,
    116–117, 128–130, 129(figure),
    130(figure), 156
  education, 153, 161–162, 161(figure)
  families, 136, 146–149
  gender identity, 149
  inadequacy of rational choice
    theories, 59–60
  and labeling theories, 62
  migration effects, 130–132
  population statistics, 4, 36
  self-esteem, 170
  self-report data, 18
  and social control theories, 67
  and strain theories, 64–65
  suggestions for crime reduction, 180
  and Vietnam War, 99
  weakness of ties to social
    institutions, 9, 74, 102(figure),
    103(figure), 104, 146–149, 180–181
  and welfare, 153, 164

Age, 42–46, 176
  change in propensity to commit
    crimes, 44–45
  and crime reporting, 37–38
  crime statistics, 43, 45(figure), 46
  incarceration rates, 166
  income gap, 82
  population statistics, 36, 43,
    44(figure), 53(table), 54
  school enrollment, 141, 146, 159
  and strain theories, 64
  supply effect, 43
  and ties to social institutions, 74
  See also Juveniles
Ageton, Susan, 18, 38, 170
AIDS. See Acquired Immune
  Deficiency Syndrome
Aid to Families with Dependent
  Children (AFDC), 150, 180,
  186–187
Albonetti, Celesta, 104
Ambrose, Stephen, 92
Anderson, Elijah, 95, 111
Anomie theory, 63–65, 92–93, 108,
  117–119
Asian Americans, 48, 50(table)
Assault, 17, 19, 21–23, 40–41, 45–46,
  50(table), 139, 168
Australia, 29(table), 30(table)
Austria, 29(table)
Auto theft. See Motor vehicle theft

Becker, Howard, 61
Belgium, 30(table)
Bellah, Robert, 106, 191

Bennett, William, 168–169
Bentham, Jeremy, 76
Berger, Peter, 6, 71, 191
Bernard, Thomas, 120
Biological explanations for crime, 32–33, 57–58
Black, Donald, 94
Blakely, Edward, 127
Booth, Alan, 58
Bound, John, 127
Brain, Paul Frederic, 57
Braithwaite, John, 76, 170, 180
Burggraf, Shirley, 84, 178, 183, 186–187
Burglary, 20, 24–26, 24(figure)
    and age, 45–46
    and gender, 40, 41(figure)
    and inflation, 120
    international comparison, 30(table)
    and race, 50(table)
    and time spent living away from family, 139
    and welfare, 157
Bush, George, 100

Canada, 29(table), 30(table), 190
Capital punishment, 164–165, 167
Capone, Al, 118
Carmichael, Stokely, 99
Caucasians
    arrest rates, 50(table)
    attitudes toward government, 101, 102(figure), 103(figure), 180
    attitudes toward politically motivated violence, 104
    and criminal justice system, 153
    economic conditions, 128, 129(figure)
    education, 161–162
    families, 146–149
    population subgroups compared, 53(table), 54
    school enrollment, 161(figure)
    self-esteem, 170
Children. See Age; Education; Family; Juveniles
Chilton, Roland, 189

Civil justice system, 106, 107(figure)
Civil rights movement, 74, 80–81, 97–98, 106, 108–111, 158, 179–180
    See also Political activism
Clark, Hilton B., 181
Cleaver, Eldridge, 99
Clinton, Bill, 100, 112
Cloward, Richard, 64, 65, 81, 118
Cohen, Albert, 81, 118
Cohen, Lawrence, 26, 67, 138, 139
Coleman, James, 79
Commission on Law Enforcement and the Administration of Justice, 10, 16, 158, 164
Communities. See Neighborhoods
Cooley, Charles, 61
Crime, 2–3, 17
    carrot and stick approaches to, 158–159
    effects on family structure, 88
    explanations for. See Crime, explanations for
    historical trends, 28
    international comparison, 28–32, 189–190
    and morality, 60, 80, 94–95
    public perceptions of, 25–27, 33
    reporting of, 16, 19, 26, 37–38, 169
    suggestions for reducing, 178–188
    suitable targets, 67–68
    timing of trends, 5–6, 27, 89
    See also Offender characteristics; and specific crimes
"Crime amidst plenty" paradox, 122
Crime control, 9–10, 178–188. See also Criminal justice system; Education; Social control; Welfare
Crime, explanations for, 5, 32–33, 56–69, 105
    biological explanations, 32–33, 57–58
    characteristics needing explanation, 54, 56, 68–69, 121, 153
    control theories, 66–67
    cultural deviance theories, 65–66
    defiance theory, 170, 180
    labeling theories, 61–63, 105
    migration effects, 130–132

motivations of offenders, 7, 60, 75–76, 80, 87(figure), 93–95, 111
power-control theory, 73
psychological explanations, 32–33, 57–58
rational choice explanations, 58–61
situational theories, 67–68
strain theories, 63–65, 81–82, 92–93, 117–118
symbolic interaction theory, 63
Criminal justice system, 4–5, 9–10, 164–171
"back-end" vs. "front-end" approaches, 153, 164–167, 171
and family, 150
future of, 185
mechanisms of crime regulation, 153–155, 164–167, 171
and race, 153
as response to loss of legitimacy in political institutions, 152
spending trends, 85–86, 87(figure), 153, 164–171, 175
See also Police; Prison
Criminologists, political attitudes of, 104–106, 112
Cultural deviance theories, 65–66
Czechoslovakia, 30(table)

Daly, Martin, 58
DARE. See Drug Resistance Education Program
Data collection, 12–14
biases in, 15, 18–19
"event counts" measurement technique, 108–109, 109(figure)
International Crime Survey (ICS), 30
longitudinal vs. cross-sectional studies, 188
National Crime Victimization Survey, 15–17
self-report data, 12, 14–15, 18–19, 168
supply effect, 36, 40, 43
types compared, 17–19
Uniform Crime Reports, 13–14
victimization data, 12–13, 18–19
World Health Organization, 29

Death penalty, 164–165, 167
Defiance theory, 170, 180
DeFronzo, James, 59
Denmark, 29(table)
Desegregation, 179–180
Deterrence, 59, 94, 154, 164, 169–170
Deviance theories, 65–66
Devine, Joel, 120, 157
Differential association theory, 105
Discrimination, 49, 62, 97–98, 176
Divorce, 140, 142, 143, 147
Domestic disputes, 41
Drass, Kriss, 120, 123–124, 128
Drug Resistance Education Program (DARE), 150
Durkheim, Emile, 63, 65, 93

Eckberg, Douglas, 28
Eckert, Craig, 98
Economic indicators, 87(figure)
absolute vs. relative measures, 119–120, 174
for African Americans, 82–83, 116–117, 128–130, 156
and age, 82
income inequality, 8, 79, 82, 86, 87(figure), 116, 119–122, 126–130, 174, 177, 181
inflation, 8, 79, 82, 86, 87(figure), 119–121, 125(figure), 126–128, 174, 177
median income, 122, 123(figure), 126, 128, 129(figure)
poverty, 8, 116, 119, 174
timing of trends, 121–128
unemployment, 8, 119, 123, 174
Economic institutions, 7, 78–83, 114–134, 176–178
declining legitimacy of, 79, 81, 178
education-wages relationship, 127
and family, 149–150, 177–178, 183
labor market changes, 84–85, 126–127, 135
and political institutions, 177
postwar trends, 115–116
strain of unattainable monetary goals, 63–64, 81–82, 117–118

suggestions for increasing
legitimacy, 181–182
welfare as response to loss of
legitimacy, 152
Edin, Kathryn, 187
Education, 9–10, 64, 86, 155–157
delinquency-education relationship,
156
educational "inflation," 156
future of, 185–186
guardianship, 156
increased enrollment, 145–146, 159
preschool programs, 184, 186
quality of, 162
and race, 153, 161(figure), 161–162
as response to loss of family
legitimacy, 150, 152, 186
socialization of juveniles, 155–156
timing of spending trends,
87(figure), 153, 159–162
and wages, 127
Eisenhower, Dwight D., 97
Elliott, Delbert, 18, 38, 170
England, 29(table), 30(table), 190
Ethnicity
Asian arrest rates, 48, 50(table)
Hispanic arrest rates, 48
immigrants, 4, 118–119
minority crime rates in other
countries, 189–190
Native American arrest rates,
50(table)
See also African Americans;
Caucasians; Race
Etzioni, Amitai, 60
Evans, M. D. R., 182

Family, 7–9, 78–79, 83–85, 87(figure),
140–146, 174–175
attachment to, 66, 137
and criminal justice system, 150
economic influences, 8–9, 84–85, 135,
144–146, 149–150, 177–178, 183
education as response to loss of
family legitimacy, 150, 152, 186
effects of crime on, 88

ideological challenges to
"traditional" family, 83–84,
141 143, 149, 178
legitimacy of, 67, 79, 83–85, 137–140,
146–149, 178
measures of disruption, 140
mechanisms of crime regulation, 7,
76, 83, 85, 136–138, 140, 142
nonfamily households, 135–136, 139,
142–143
and political institutions, 149–150,
178
and race, 136
single-parent households, 85, 140,
144, 147–148, 148(figure), 150, 177
stabilization of structures (late
1990s), 151
suggestions for increasing
legitimacy, 182–184
unfriendly taxes, 188
and welfare, 150
Farrington, David, 140
Felson, Marcus, 26, 67, 138, 139
Feminism, 83–84, 149
Finland, 29(table)
France, 29(table), 30(table), 189
Freeman, Richard, 166, 168
Fukuyama, Francis, 77, 142, 177
Furstenberg, Frank, 139, 179–180

Gang Resistance Education and
Training (GREAT), 150
Garrison Heights (Philadelphia), 139,
179
Gender, 39–42
and behavioral choices, 73–74, 176
and crime reporting, 37–38
economic relations between men
and women, 135
family structure, 182
and labeling theories, 62
and parental control, 73–74
population statistics, 36, 53(table),
54
possible convergence of male and
female crime rates, 40–41
See also Men; Women

Germany, 29(table), 189, 190
Glaser, Daniel, 3
Glueck, Sheldon and Eleanor, 137
Goldin, Claudia, 121–122
Goldscheider, Frances, 135, 143
Goldsmith, William, 127
Gottfredson, Michael, 33, 40, 42, 94
Granovetter, Mark, 73, 77
Grasmick, Harold, 60
GREAT. See Gang Resistance
    Education and Training
Green, Donald, 60
Guardianship, 68, 75–77, 80, 83, 85,
    87(figure)
  by families, 83, 85, 136, 138
  by schools, 156
Gurr, Ted, 28, 96

Hagan, John, 73, 104
Handy, Charles, 181
Harris, Anthony, 170
Hauge, Ragnar, 15
Head Start program, 186
Hindelang, Michael, 18, 38, 53–54
Hirschi, Travis, 15, 33, 40, 42, 66, 94,
    137
Hispanic Americans, 48
Hobsbawm, Eric, 3
Hofferth, Sandra, 143–144
Homicide. See Murder
Houston Parent-Child Development
    Center, 184

Immigrants, 4, 118–119
Income inequality, 8, 86, 87(figure),
    119–120, 128–130, 174
  public acceptance of, 181, 182
  and race, 128–130, 130(figure)
  suburban vs. inner city, 132
  timing of trends, 116, 121–127,
    124(figure), 177
Income, median, 122, 123(figure), 126,
    128, 129(figure)
Inflation, 8, 79, 82, 86, 87(figure),
    119–121, 124–128, 125(figure), 174,
    177
Inner cities. See Neighborhoods

International crime trends, 28–32,
    189–190
Italy, 29(table), 30(table), 76
Jackson, Pamela Irving, 189
Japan, 29(table), 71–72, 116, 190
Jencks, Christopher, 187, 191
Jenkins, J. Craig, 98
Johnson, George, 127
Johnson, Lyndon, 10, 16, 125, 126, 158
Juveniles
  attachment to families, 66, 137
  born to unmarried women, 147–148
  and criminal justice system, 150
  and economic stress, 81–82
  parental control, 136–138, 140
  self-esteem of, 81, 118
  See also Age; Education; Family

Kasarda, John, 156
Katz, Jack, 95
Kelley, Jonathan, 182
Kelly, Raymond, 171
Kennedy, John F., 112, 118
King, Martin Luther, Jr., 99
Kinsey, Alfred, 14
Korean War, 125

Labeling theories, 61–63, 105
LaFree, Gary, 120, 123–124, 128
Lance, Bert, 100
Langan, Patrick, 167
Larceny, 20, 24–27, 40
Laub, John, 137
Legitimacy, institutional, 72–75
  of economic institutions, 63–64, 79,
    81–82, 117–118, 178
  and effectiveness of corrections,
    169–170
  of family, 67, 79, 83–85, 137–140,
    146–149, 178
  measures of, 92, 96–97, 106,
    107(figure), 174
  origins of, 75
  of political institutions, 79–81,
    98–100, 177–178
  responses to losses, 85–87,
    87(figure), 152–172

suggestions for increasing, 178–188
transmission of, 75, 136
Lemann, Nicholas, 131
Levy, Frank, 126, 131, 177
Lieberson, Stanley, 188
Lieske, Joel, 96
Litigation, 98, 106, 107(figure)
Loeber, Rolf, 140
Lombroso, Cesare, 57
Long, Sharon, 116
Luckmann, Thomas, 71, 191

Margo, Robert, 121–122
Marvell, Thomas, 43, 168
Marx, Karl, 94, 119, 176
Massey, Douglas, 132
McKay, Henry, 105, 118
Mead, George Herbert, 61
Men
    and changes in "traditional" family,
        141–143, 149
    gender identity, 149
    incarceration rates, 166
    income inequality, 124
    shift to nonagricultural labor, 145
    See also Gender
Merton, Robert, 63–65, 81, 93, 108,
    117–119
Migration, 130–132
Military operations, 91–92
Miller, Abraham, 108
Miller, Warren, 100–101
Millet, Kate, 141–142
Moody, Carlisle, 43, 168
Morality
    moral justifications for crimes, 80,
        94–95
    moral validity of social rules, 75–76
    and rational choice theories, 60
Motivations of offenders, 7, 60, 75–76,
    80, 87(figure), 93–95, 111
Motor vehicle theft, 24–27, 31, 40,
    45–46, 50(table)
Moynihan, Daniel Patrick, 67
Murder, 22(figure), 41, 95
    and age, 43, 45–46
    and gender, 40

incarceration rates, 168
and inflation, 120
international comparison, 29(table)
juvenile arrest rates, 45(figure), 46
prewar statistics, 28
and race, 4, 47, 50(table)
and time spent living away from
    family, 139
and welfare, 157
Murray, Charles, 162–164

National Crime Survey (NCS), 16–17
National Crime Victimization Survey
    (NCVS), 15–17, 26, 37, 52–53
National Criminal Justice Information
    and Statistics Service, 16
Native Americans, 50(table)
NCS. See National Crime Survey
NCVS. See National Crime
    Victimization Survey
Neighborhoods
    community-oriented policing, 171
    effect of civil rights movement,
        179–180
    effects of population turnover and
        heterogeneity, 118–119
    Garrison Heights (Philadelphia), 139
    migration effects, 130–132
Netherlands, 29(table), 30(table)
New York City, 171
New Zealand, 29(table), 30(table)
Nicaragua, 100
Nieburg, H. L., 95
Nixon, Richard, 100
Northern Ireland, 30(table)
Norway, 29(table)
Nye, F. Ivan, 14–15

Oberschall, Anthony, 93
O'Brien, Robert, 26
Offender characteristics, 35–55
    age, 42–46
    gender, 39–42
    race, 47–55
Ohlin, Lloyd, 64, 65, 81, 118
Oil crisis, 126

Omnibus Crime Control and Safe
Streets Act, 164
Osgood, D. Wayne, 58

Parsons, Talcott, 72–73
Perry Preschool, 184
Piliavin, Irving, 138
Poland, 30(table)
Police
citizen-police relations, 155
community-oriented policing, 171
crime prevention by, 164
discrimination by, 49
effectiveness of, 26, 31
in New York City, 171
spending for, 158, 165
Political activism, 80, 87(figure), 92–93,
95–96, 108–112. See also Civil
rights movement
Political institutions, 7, 78–81,
87(figure), 91–113
and civil rights movement, 97–98
criminal justice as response to loss
of legitimacy, 152
declining legitimacy of, 79–81,
98–100, 177–178
and economic institutions, 177
effects of rising crime rates, 88
and family, 149–150, 178
measures of legitimacy, 92, 96–97,
106, 107(figure), 174
political scandals, 81, 99–100
public perceptions of, 101–104,
102(figure), 103(figure)
and race, 102(figure), 103(figure),
180–181
suggestions for increasing
legitimacy, 179–181
and Vietnam War, 98–99
See also Civil justice system;
Criminal justice system
Political scandals, 99–100
Poverty, 8, 85, 116, 119, 158, 174
Power-control theory of delinquency,
73
Predictability, 71–72, 74–75
Prison, 158, 164–167, 166(figure), 185

and African Americans, 167–168
and age, 166
effectiveness of, 155, 168–170
riots, 95
Protection from criminal acts of others.
See Guardianship
Psychological explanations for crime,
32–33, 57–58
Public attitudes toward government,
100–104, 102(figure), 103(figure)
Public perceptions of crime, 25–27, 33
Putnam, Robert, 76

Race, 47–55
age and gender of offenders,
53(table), 54
crime reporting, 37–38
discrimination, 49, 62, 97–98, 176
female-headed households, 147,
148(figure)
income inequality, 130(figure)
median family income, 128–129
riots, 96, 110
robbery rates, 51(figure)
self-esteem, 170
and UCR arrest data, 37
See also specific ethnicities
Rape, 4, 17, 19, 22–23, 45–46, 50(table),
139
Rational choice explanations of crime,
58–61
Reagan, Ronald, 100, 165
Research methodologies. See Data
collection
Rehabilitation, 154
Reich, Robert, 127
Resource mobilization theory, 80, 93,
94–95
Riots, 92, 95, 96, 98, 108, 110–112
Robbery, 17–19, 22, 23(figure)
and age, 43–46, 44(figure)
and divorce, 144(figure)
and gender, 40, 41(figure)
incarceration rates, 166(figure), 168
and income inequality, 124(figure)
and inflation, 120, 125(figure)
international comparison, 31

and litigation rates, 107(figure)
and median income, 123(figure)
offender characteristics, 53(table)
and political activism, 109(figure)
and preschool enrollment,
160(figure)
and race, 4, 50(table), 51(figure)
and time spent living away from
family, 139
and welfare, 157, 163(figure)
Rosenfeld, Richard, 176
"Routing activities" theory, 67
Rude, George, 93, 110
Ruggles, Steven, 147
Russian Federation, 29(table)

"Safety valve" model of collective
action, 93, 110
Sampson, Robert, 137, 140
Sassen, Saskia, 190–191
Scandals, political, 81, 99–100
Schlosser, Eric, 190
Scotland, 29(table), 30(table)
Self-esteem, 81, 118, 170
Self-report data, 12, 14–15, 18–19, 38
Shaw, Clifford, 105, 118
Sherman, Lawrence, 170, 180
Short, James, 14–15
Simpson, O. J., 180
Single-parent households, 85, 140, 143,
144, 147–148, 148(figure), 150, 177
Situational theories, 67–68
Skogan, Wesley, 37
Social capital, 72, 179
Social control, mechanisms of, 75–78,
80, 87(figure). *See also* Criminal
justice system; Economic
institutions; Education; Family;
Political institutions; Welfare
Social control theories, 66–67
Social disorganization theories, 63–65,
92–93, 105, 118. *See also* Strain
theories
Social institutions, 6–9, 70–90, 86,
87(figure), 89
predictability, 71–72, 74–75
speed of change, 72–73

weakness of African American ties
to, 9, 74, 146–149
See also Economic institutions;
Family; Political institutions
Socialization
and criminal justice system, 155
and education, 155–156
in families, 76, 83, 85, 136, 142
Social movements. *See* Civil rights
movement; Political activism
Solomon, Frederic, 93
Spain, 30(table)
Sparks, Richard, 15
Stack, Carol, 139
Steffensmeier, Darrell, 40
Strain theories, 63–65, 81–82, 92–93,
117–118
Suitable targets, 67–68
Supply effect, 36, 40, 43
Sutherland, Edwin, 65, 105
Sweden, 29(table), 30(table), 190
Switzerland, 29(table), 30(table)
Symbolic interaction theory, 63
Syracuse University Family
Development Research Project,
184

TANF. *See* Temporary Assistance for
Needy Families
Temporary Assistance for Needy
Families (TANF), 187
Theft, 17, 45–46, 50(table)
See also Motor vehicle theft
Thomas, W. I., 61
Tilly, Charles, 96
Tittle, Charles, 60
Tonry, Michael, 189
Tyler, Tom, 170, 180

UCR. *See* Uniform Crime Reports
Unemployment, 8, 119, 123, 174
Uniform Crime Reports (UCR), 13–14,
20(figure), 21–23
compared to NCVS data, 26
compared to self-report data, 38
lack of data on nonwhite, non-
African American arrests, 48

types of data, 36–37
validity of, 13–14, 17–19, 37–38, 49

Victimization data, 12–13, 15–17,
    18–19, 37
Vietnam War, 74, 81, 98–99, 126
Vold, George, 120
Voting rates, 107

Waite, Linda, 135, 143
Wales, 29(table), 30(table)
Watergate, 99–100
Weber, Max, 75
Welfare, 9–10, 59–60, 157
    effect on crime rates, 157
    and family, 150
    future of, 186–187
    international comparison, 88, 190
    and race, 153, 164
    as response to loss of legitimacy in
        economic institutions, 152
    spending trends, 86, 87(figure), 153,
        162–164, 163(figure), 175
    and women, 164
Werthman, Carl, 138
West Germany, 30(table)
Whitewater, 100

WHO. *See* World Health Organization
Wilson, James Q., 105, 116, 122
Wilson, Margo, 58
Wilson, William Julius, 4, 131–132, 156,
    162
Witte, Anne, 116
Wolf, Preben, 15
Women
    behavioral choices of, 73–74, 176
    economic roles, 135
    female-headed households, 140, 143,
        147–148, 148(figure), 177
    isolation of housewives, 141
    in the labor force, 84–85, 145–146,
        183
    parental control of, 73–74
    and poverty, 85
    and welfare, 164
    See also Gender
World Health Organization (WHO), 29
World War II, 97
Wrong, Dennis, 73

Yale Child Welfare Project, 184
Yoshikawa, Hiro, 184

Zedlewski, Edward, 168